Rediscover Your Heart

Rediscover Your Heart

Seven Keys to Personal and Planetary Transformation

Fred Matser

FINDHORN PRESS

First published in 2008 by Findhorn Press
ISBN 978-1-84409-122-5

Jacket design by Damian Keenan
Text design by The Bridgewater Book Company
Dust jacket photograph of Fred Matser by Elizabeth Handy, reproduced with kind permission of the photographer and which first appeared in the book, *The New Philanthropists* by Charles and Elizabeth Handy (Heinemann 2006 and now in paperback).
Photo of Deepak Chopra by Jeremiah Sullivan
Printed and bound in the USA
1 2 3 4 5 6 7 8 9 10 11 12 13 12 11 10 09 08

Published by
Findhorn Press
305a The Park, Findhorn
Forres IV36 3TE
Scotland, UK
Telephone +44-(0)1309-690582
Fax +44-(0)1309-690036
info@findhornpress.com
www.findhornpress.com

Dedication

I dedicate this book to all people who are willing to experience life in its fullness and who are willing to take risks and go beyond their comfort zones to serve humanity and our beautiful planet with a caring and sharing attitude.

I also dedicate this book to my wonderful parents, children and wife, all of whom I love dearly and for whom I also wrote this.

CONTENTS

Acknowledgements

Way back in 1994, Caroline Myss suggested that I write a book about what she called, "The transformation of a businessman into a pioneer in the field of spirit". Due to a combination of laziness and being too busy, I did nothing until I talked about it with my very good friend, Jacqueline Young.

I had done some writing before but never a whole book about my life experiences and ideas. I wanted to write in English because of the potential to reach more people, compared to my native, Dutch-language market. I needed help and Jackie, a British author, skilful and great to work with, was just the right person.

I am grateful to Jackie for all the time, love and care that she has put into this book. I also want to thank my secretary, Michele, my former P.A., Clementine, Rola and John Nelson for their participation. I also owe special thanks to Simenon for his skilful and thoughtful work in the latter stages of the development of the book.

Toward the back of the book you will find uplifting contributions from some of my friends and acquaintances: to all of you who have contributed, I thank you very much!

I feel honored that Mikhail Gorbachev and Deepak Chopra were willing to write the Foreword and Afterword for the book; I also thank Jane Goodall for her kind words for the book jacket. My heartfelt gratitude to you all! I really cherish your friendship.

When I first met my publisher, Thierry Bogliolo, at the Book Fair in Frankfurt, I immediately had a good feeling about him. I thank him for having the courage, with Findhorn Press, to travel with me on this journey.

I am also grateful to all my spiritual teachers for their inspiration and support. I wish to especially thank the late Professor van Praag and Glynda Yoder for their important teachings. In my previous business career I also had the support of many dedicated people of whom I would like to mention the late Mr. Blase, the late Mr. Koyck and my friends Hans Rood and Ids van der Zijpp. I also wish to express my gratitude to my former secretary Tineke, to Bert Jan and to Egon for their support in many ways.

Sincere thanks too to all the co-readers: Chris, David, Diane, Dolf, Helene, Jerry, Patrick, Peter and Saskia.

Last, but not least, I would like to wholeheartedly thank my wife, Chris for her continuous loving support and understanding on all levels.

Photo © White House Photo, Courtesy Reagan Library, PD

Foreword

I have known Fred Matser for many years now. I first met him during my visit to the United States in May 1992. Among the thousands of people I have met during my trips abroad he stands out as a remarkable person, a true humanitarian, a man of deeds rather than words.

I have no doubt Fred could have maintained a successful career in business, continuing his family's tradition, but he chose a different path. His heart and mind reach out to disadvantaged people, particularly children, in various parts of the world. He wants to help, and he looks for ways of helping that, rather than making people dependent on more aid, empower them and provide them with the tools to be in control of their lives. I have always thought that this is the best way of fighting poverty and underdevelopment.

When Russia was going through a time of hardship after the breakup of the Soviet Union, Fred was truly a friend in need. His generous donation helped the Gorbachev Foundation to restart and complete a project that saved the lives of hundreds of children with leukemia. He also helped my late wife Raisa to launch The Raisa Gorbachev's Club, an initiative that is still ongoing, bringing together Russian women in a search for solutions to the social problems of Russian society.

Fred's concern for the environment is genuine, forward-looking and practical. He was of great help in establishing Green Cross International, which I founded to promote awareness of environmental problems and spur people to act in the face of the global environmental crisis—the greatest challenge to mankind's future. Fred's suggestions were instrumental in launching the Legacy Project, aimed at addressing the environmental consequences of the arms race, and in drafting the Earth Charter—a set of 'commandments' for a harmonious relationship between Man and Nature.

For me, Fred represents the emerging global civil society—the widening transnational network of people who want to see globalization with a human face. I believe that the role of such people and their organizations is extremely important and is bound to grow. In fact, I would say that both Fred and I are doing our best to make it happen.

It is necessary because the challenges of the twenty first century are many and they are daunting. To some they seem insurmountable, a cause for despair and even panic. But that is not how it should be. Remember how our common efforts during the 1980s helped stop the nuclear arms race and end the Cold War. When it seemed to many that the momentum of confrontational politics was unstoppable, that mankind was rapidly moving toward the edge of a precipice, we did not panic. We acted—by protesting in the streets, by developing people-to-people contacts, by negotiating agreements. That is why walls fell, armies disengaged, and missiles were scrapped.

Politicians have not made good use of the opportunities opened by the end of the Cold War. Enormous amounts of money are still being wasted on weapons production and trade and industrialized nations are not doing nearly enough to help the poor and the disadvantaged and to save the environment. Politics is lagging behind the rapidly evolving global processes. Without the prodding from civil society, from activists and advocates for the poor and for the environment, politicians would continue to drag their feet while the world's problems multiply—while the climate warms, while pollution increases, while the poor go hungry.

We need many more people like Fred Matser if we are to learn to live sustainably and humanely in our global world. We need millions and millions of men and women with the vision, integrity and ability to act that can make a difference for hundreds of millions. One person setting an example can help and inspire many others. This is what Fred has been doing. He is a real leader.

Mikhail Gorbachev
Former President of the USSR
Founder and President, the Gorbachev Foundation
Chairman of the Board, Green Cross International
Nobel Peace Prize Laureate
Moscow, January 2008

About Fred

There are many global citizens in the world but Fred Matser is a Universal Citizen. With Fred every man, every woman, every child has universal equal rank regardless of how the world perceives them. The famous and the unknown are treated with the same warmth, friendliness, and respect. This is the source of his charismatic approach to all things. He expresses his genuine Heart in the form of networking for good, creating caring projects for the most vulnerable, and spreading good cheer and oneness with "twinkling eyes". Those of us who know Fred know the universal respect he gives and the universal response he receives. In *Rediscover Your Heart*, the reader is privilege to information and personal history that Fred rarely discusses in person. He is truly the forerunner Citizen for a transformed world.

Glynda Yoder, *friend since 1986*

One of the Billions—An Invitation

Dear Reader,

Like you, I am just one of the billions of people and life forms on this planet. At the same time, I feel a real respons-Ability to cooperate with my fellow human beings to inspire and support a global transformation into a more caring and sharing society.

In my own life, I have traveled a path from modest beginnings through several surprising turns of events to positions of responsibility and leadership. I ran a real-estate development company at a relatively young age and had some amazing paranormal experiences that changed my view of reality. During that time, I became aware of suffering in the world on many levels. I gradually became more interested in initiating and funding creative approaches toward healthcare, the environment and peace building. On the way I have met many remarkable healers, humanitarians, public figures and other extraordinary individuals. The overriding themes of my work have been inspiration and empowerment through personal and planetary change.

Like many people, I have experienced personal tragedy and suffering. At the same time I have shared in abundant love and joy and have witnessed first hand how hope, inspiration and love can transform people's lives. I've also enjoyed watching the unfolding of various initiatives, including the Twinkling Eyes Club that I founded, spreading "miles of smiles" around the globe. Through all this I learned to become more compassionate and I am still learning.

Part I of the book tells my life story and shares some of the things I have learned, experienced and been inspired by on the way. At the end of each chapter you will find a Reflections section where I consider some of the lessons that I have learnt on my journey. I also give the Keys for personal and planetary transformation that these lessons inspired me to formulate. You may like to use these, or the affirmations that accompany them, to reflect on your own life. In Part II, I share some of the guiding principles that I believe could transform the way that we live our lives on this planet. There is also a glossary at the end that covers some of the more technical terms. In Part III, I have included contributions from a host of wonderful people I have been privileged to meet in my life, from small children to influential leaders, as they share their visions and dreams for the future.

I hope that what I have shared in this book will inspire you in your own journey to rediscover your heart.

I invite you to turn the page and travel the journey with me.

Fred Matser,
The Netherlands, 2008

Rediscover Your Heart

PART I

"Love Is In the Air—
Bring It Down To Earth"

Nina Matser

CHAPTER I
The Shadow of War—the Birth of Peace

It was a dark, spring evening during the Second World War in the Netherlands when my parents heard a loud knock on the front door. A chill of fear went through them as they looked at each other, for we were living under German occupation. Since my father worked secretly as part of the Dutch underground, he quietly sprinted upstairs to the safe hideout under the floorboards. Meanwhile, my heavily pregnant mother went to answer the door fearing that a Dutch collaborator might have betrayed my father.

My mother steadied herself before opening the door, worried that the German soldiers would barge in to search their home. She thought of her three-year-old son, Bobbie, who had a serious heart problem, and her two-year-old daughter, Marjoke, sleeping upstairs.

Opening the door my mother was relieved to see the friendly Dutch police inspector Schön. He whispered "I've come to tell you good news. The American and Canadian soldiers are on their way. We're going to be liberated!" I can only imagine the relief that went through my mother. As she rushed upstairs to share this glorious news with my father, she felt the first strong contractions that signaled my imminent birth.

I was born shortly afterwards, in the spring of 1945, in my parent's bedroom in our modest brick house in the small Dutch town of Hilversum. My parents had planned to name me Paul, but as that was the name of a Dutchman who had been a collaborator, they didn't feel it to be appropriate. Instead they agreed to name me Fred. Though it would have been more typical in Holland to have been named Frederik, for some reason they just liked this name. I have been called simply Fred all my life. Decades later someone pointed out that in Swedish my name actually meant 'peace'. This seemed interesting as I was born on the cusp of war and peace.

Eleven months after my birth, tragedy struck. My brother, Bob, who was only four years old, died from an infection linked to his heart problems. Since I was still only an infant, I have no recollection of this.

I can only imagine the utter heartbreak that my parents experienced. It was not common in those days of rebuilding after the war to dwell on painful events. Neither was it common to inform children about death. Post-war life needed to go on. Bob's death was not openly discussed in our family and rarely mentioned.

My parents' grief must have been compounded over the years by the knowledge that penicillin would probably have saved Bob's life, but at that time it was not available to them. I imagine they felt that by suppressing their pain and hardships they could spare their surviving children their silent suffering. This was a common way for war survivors to get on with rebuilding their lives. My parents had struggled to keep their young family together. They were like many in Europe whose primary needs were food, housing and survival. Looking back at my early years, it helps me to now understand why I have had challenges in expressing "difficult" emotions.

A couple of years later, in 1948, my younger brother was born and my parents decided to give him the name of Paul. They still liked that name, and by then their memories of the war were beginning to fade a little. In 1952 my younger sister, Anke, followed and so our family at that time consisted of six people. Yet this was only to last during the 1950s and 60s, for further tragedy lay ahead.

My father and mother in the late 1950s

Family Life

Our family life was comfortable and happy but also quite strict and frugal. My mother ran the household very economically and we had few extravagances. We were only allowed margarine and jam spread very thinly on our bread and given just a few thin slices of cheese each at mealtimes. A cooked egg was a once-a-week luxury on Sundays. Baths were also only a weekly luxury and were shared. The rest of the week we had to wash in cold water from a sink in the attic! At the time we children didn't like these shortcomings and used to complain. Now however I feel they were a good foundation for life as it has made me truly appreciate luxuries like good food, hot water and showers!

Bath night for all the children was on Saturdays before dinner. My two sisters would share the bath water first and then it would be Paul's and my turn. I used to thoroughly enjoy our baths together. We would spend ages playing with little ducks and boats and other toys and look forward to our hot dinner and the family games that would follow. Saturday nights were a kind of party night. We would have great fun playing lots of games like Monopoly or Scrabble together with my parents. These simple Saturday get-togethers are some of the happiest memories of my childhood.

My mother was always at home and was really caring. She always did her best for the family, feeding and clothing us as well as she could and instilling us with good manners. Looking back I realize she must have been suffering a lot inwardly during this time, from the pain of losing Bob, yet she did not allow her grief to get in the way of giving us the best childhood she could.

In contrast to my mother, my father was away from home much of the time and was always busy working. He was a real entrepreneur. After some formal training he went on to work in a real estate agency and then started his own business buying land and developing projects as well as doing sales and leasing. During the post-war period there was a huge need for housing. The government created many incentives to stimulate the economy, including tax incentives and subsidies for the building of social housing projects. My father, who had little money of his own, made full use of these incentives to build up his business, later called Johan Matser Corp. He was one of the very first, if not the first, major independent project developers in the Netherlands. He was a man of vision and intelligence who used his courage and creativity to build a substantial real estate development company.

It was always expected that Paul and I would join my father's business. Paul and I were very different people, and we did not have much in common other than our shared love of Dinky Toys and cars! Gradually we went our separate ways. As I set my sights on other things, the expectation changed to Paul being the one who would follow in my father's footsteps. However, fate was to play a hand and surprisingly change this expectation.

Lessons from my Father

As my father's business began to thrive our family financial situation improved and we were very fortunate to be able to travel abroad. My parents took my elder sister, Marjoke, and me on a trip to Belgium and Germany when I was about ten years old. Later on we also went on family holidays by car to places like France, Austria, Switzerland and Italy. It was quite unusual for Dutch families to travel abroad on holiday at that time.

I remember being the first child in my primary class to go outside of the Netherlands. I found these trips incredibly exciting with all the new sights and experiences. My siblings and I fought a lot over who would sit by the car window in order to get the best view! I vividly remember the revelation of seeing great mountains, with their lakes and snow-capped peaks, for the first time. I had never seen mountains before, since my home country is almost entirely flat. I think these trips opened up my eyes to a wider world.

My father's office was initially located behind the garage at the back of our home. As the business grew, he kept adding rooms until finally there was a five-room office in our back garden. This meant that our home life was not very private since anyone visiting the office had to pass through the little alleyway between the garage and our house.

In those days it was normal to work six days a week, so, even on Saturdays, there would be a constant stream of people passing by and popping in at our home. My mother was always making coffee. Perhaps these experiences helped me to get along easily with all types of people.

My father had a strong sense of responsibility for his employees. For example, he loved to share and would give spontaneous bonuses when he had a successful business venture. Frequently he invited others to share in potentially lucrative business deals. On the occasion of my parents' 25th wedding anniversary, my father did something unknown in those days: he created a premium-free pension fund for all his employees.

Though this fund took a huge chunk of his capital, he was pleased to be able to do it. It was important for my father to create the best conditions for his workforce. He took a sincere interest in their welfare, visiting them at home or in hospital if they were sick. He also made a point of employing physically disabled people and giving them equal opportunities. All of these initiatives were quite rare at the time, and illustrate his innovative and philanthropic approach that also inspired me in my own business life. On very hot days, he was even known to close the office and take all his employees swimming in the nearby lake! He also had a good sense of humor and loved to play practical jokes. I remember one time in particular when I accompanied him to a meeting with the Mayor of Hilversum. At a certain time the mayor had to leave the room for a moment and to my amazement my father produced a fake dog poop from his pocket. Winking at me, he mischievously placed it on the pristine carpet and waited for the mayor to return. Once the mayor was re-seated my father glanced over in the direction of the dog "mess" and the mayor followed his gaze. On seeing the mess, he jumped up with a horrified expression and ran out of the room calling for a cleaner. Meanwhile my father picked up the fake poop and concealed it in his pocket. When the mayor returned with a cleaner and pointed to where the mess had been on the carpet there was nothing to be seen. He looked around in confusion while the cleaner just stared at him as if he were crazy. My father just smiled and said nothing but caught my eye and we both enjoyed the private joke.

School Days

My elementary school was a ten-minute walk from our home. I went there for six years. My main memory is of being forced to write with my right hand even though I was naturally left-handed. Though I think I was an able student I was not keen on doing my homework! At that time I was easily distracted and my main passion was sports. I especially loved field hockey and would go to the hockey club at every opportunity.

As a result my schoolwork suffered and I ended up having to repeat two grades in high school in order to catch up. Eventually I became more serious about my studies. I had a friend in the same class—two years older than me—who made the same decision. We studied hard together and finally I completed school successfully with quite good grades just after I turned nineteen. My intention was to study psychology or sociology at university. I was also interested in geography and economics because I had very good teachers in both subjects. The two of them inspired me and I wanted to learn more. However, things were to turn out completely differently for me.

An Unexpected Invitation

During my teenage years, my father's health started to deteriorate. He was diagnosed first with diabetes in the late 1950s and then later with Parkinson's disease (rigid type). As his condition worsened, it became hard for him to keep his balance and he had increasing difficulty speaking. Saliva would dribble from his mouth, and he often had to hold his handkerchief over it. This was not easy for him, especially in his position as the head of quite a large company. Yet despite these difficulties he carried on working. By this time his company also had several subsidiaries and at any given time, depending on the workload, was employing from 120 to 200 people.

Every night after dinner my father would go for a walk. He was very conscientious about taking this exercise because of his diabetes. One of us children always had to go with him, and it was a choice between the walk and the washing up. The washing up was preferable because it took less time! So as a result my father often had to select one of us to accompany him on his walk.

On one occasion in the spring of 1964, my father picked me to walk with him. At that time I was in the process of trying to make up my mind which subject to study at university after passing my final exams at secondary school. I was expecting him to ask me about this during the walk. However, while we were walking down a lane lined with old trees, my father turned to me and, right out of the blue, asked me to join him in the family business.

I was shocked by this invitation. It was a complete turn around for my father. Throughout my school years, his one focus had been on my getting good exam results so that I could further my studies at the university. Yet now he was saying, "Come into my company instead of going on to higher studies and be my successor! I cannot wait for Paul because of my deteriorating health." Paul still had another two years to go at school, and I realized that my father must have been aware of how fast his health was deteriorating and that he might not be able to continue his work as he had hoped.

Two years previously, my father's company had moved to new premises: a big villa in a nearby neighborhood. I realized that if I was going to work with him, I would be around him all the time: I would see him in the office and I would also see him at home as I was still living there at that time. It would also mean giving up my own dreams of studying and being with my friends at the university and living away from home at students digs. I was very confused and did not know how to respond to my father's request. I said that I needed to think about it for a few days before giving him an answer. What should I do? I simply did not know.

After a couple of days, I made the decision to agree to my father's request. Given his failing health, I did not feel that I could say no. Yet at the same time I was reluctant to give up my own life plans. I agreed to join the business for a period of one year on the condition that, at the end of this time, I would be free to reassess my choice. This decision of course also had implications for my brother, Paul. He did not appear unduly concerned as he didn't seem to have a particular interest in the business at that time, nor even later as it turned out. So, after graduating from high school, I joined my father's business at the age of nineteen.

Growing Responsibility

My father's idea was that I should get experience in each of the different departments for several months—in marketing, sales, development, financial administration, design, construction etc.—so that I could get a good overall picture of the business. I started out being a receptionist. To my utter surprise, after only one week, my father gave me a desk around the corner from his in the boardroom. He said that from now on I was going to be his assistant and he wanted me to participate in all the meetings. To my further surprise, without consulting me, he began introducing me as his successor. This statement was contrary to our agreement, which was that I had the freedom to make other choices at the end of the year. On the one hand I naturally felt pride that he was appointing me as such but on the other I felt trapped.

I found the board meetings dull and uninteresting and longed for 5:30 P.M., when I would leave immediately to join my friends who were enjoying the student life in Utrecht. We had many good times drinking beer, partying and having fun. Often during my first professional year, I wouldn't get to bed until early morning but would then have to get up a few hours later to make it to the office by 8:30 A.M. It was quite a wild life. My friends were amazed that I could party and get up early for work while they were still asleep and actually so was I! I continued to be involved in sports. In 1966, while working at my father's business, I trained intensively for the National Dutch Ski Championships. In the end I was unable to take part because, disappointingly, I broke my thumb in a ski fall two weeks before the championship. But that same year I became involved as a board member for the Dutch National Ski Association.

My deadline of a year at the company came and went. I continued to work with my father, uncertain of the future. Twice afterwards I asked my brother if he would take my place in the company. If he accepted I could begin my

Ready for my ski test

academic study. Both times he declined. The first time was right after he left school and the second was when he dropped out of university after a year of studying law. It became very difficult to withdraw.

After serious consideration I decided to stay on with the company. I made the commitment to become more serious. I took weekly evening classes in Amsterdam to become a certified real estate agent, as I thought this would be a useful study related to the business. After two years I successfully passed the exams.

In getting to know the business, one of the things that helped me most was that I was not ashamed to ask lots of questions. In those days this approach was quite unusual as business structures were much more hierarchical than now. It was expected that one would unquestioningly follow the advice or suggestions of more senior staff. In asking all my questions, I came to realize that many people, even those much older and more experienced than me, often did not have answers to my questions or didn't really know what they were talking about. This gave me the confidence to learn and develop my own ideas and own ways of doing things as I realized there were not fixed answers or methods.

Gradually I began to like the work more and enjoyed the challenge. At the age of twenty three, I was Secretary to the Board; at twenty five I was a member of the Executive Committee, and at twenty seven I was made CEO. It was pretty unusual to be given this level of responsibility at such a young age, but my father's illness necessitated it.

I am grateful to all of my colleagues and employees for having accepted and supported me in these positions. Looking back I can also see that I had taken different positions of responsibility from a young age: for example in school and in the sports community, and perhaps fell naturally into that kind of role. Later, while working at my father's company, I also became involved in various national and international organizations related to real estate and held some leadership positions.[1] I have always been keen to share ideas and learn from others. At the time I felt proud at having been elected to these various positions and I enjoyed much of the work that was involved because I felt I could really make a difference. However, looking back now, I feel more honored and grateful than proud at having been given the opportunity to perform these roles. I realize that they gave me a wide range of experience both in, and outside of, the field of real estate and also taught me so much about leadership and co-operation. This helped me a lot in developing my roles in the family business over the years. In my early 1930s I was asked to become a board member of a much bigger company. I declined the offer as it would have meant leaving my father's company. The offer meant a lot to me as I felt that I was not just being seen as the son of my father, or someone who had moved up in the business just by default. I felt I was being recognized from an outside source for my own talents and abilities.

While working at Johan Matser Ltd., I enjoyed the creative challenge of project development. I liked to figure out how to create space, by making buildings attractive, functional and able to generate their own income. This

1 I was a founding board member of the L'Association des Promoteurs Européens des Centres Commerciaux (APECCO), an association of European shopping center developers, and of NEPROM (Vereniging van Nederlandse Projektontwikkeling Maatschappijen—the Association of Dutch Project Development Companies *www.neprom.nl*), which was recognised by the Dutch government as a representative organization for the industry.

lead me to develop a new project that my father had started, to rejuvenate the center of our hometown of Hilversum. Seeking to make best use of the available space, I developed a plan for a multifunctional center with facilities not only for shopping but also for a health club. The new construction was designed to blend in with the existing buildings around it. In a similar way, our company developed a football stadium that doubled up as space for offices underneath the stands. Parking space also doubled up—for office workers during the week and football supporters at weekends. Trying to use space in innovative ways was one way I sought to express my creativity and also perhaps showed a part of me that wanted to go beyond conventional thinking.[2]

I Want to Quit!

I ended up doing this work full time from 1964 through to 1982. Looking back, I can see that my work in the real estate development business was quite rewarding. However, I also remember a lot of difficult times as well, especially in the early years up to 1972, when I worked alongside my father. The difficulties came largely from my dual roles, as son and company worker, linked to my father's health, which worsened during this time. On the one hand, I was my father's junior colleague on the board. On the other, I was often his caregiver and interpreter in meetings. As my father's speech deteriorated, I was one of the few who could understand him.

I would be the one to convey his opinions and wishes during negotiations and meetings. During these times I had my own, often different or even opposing, views and opinions that I also wanted to express. So once I had made my father's position clear, I would then often be speaking again, expressing my own views. This was quite awkward and we had many difficult situations because of it.

It must have also been very frustrating for my father not to be able to express himself clearly and sometimes he resorted to other means. I remember one time when we were in a meeting and my father didn't agree with what was being said by the other participants. Because he could not clearly articulate his verbal disagreement, he got up and shuffled to the room next door and returned with a pair of mini boxing gloves and a stick that he kept in a special cupboard full of jokey artefacts. He put the gloves on the end of the stick and, to the great surprise of those present, started prodding the others with it to show he was prepared to fight over the issue! As well as acting as an interpreter, my physical

2 For further details of these projects, see Appendix A on pages 143–146.

care of my father at work included getting his handkerchief and mopping up the saliva from his lips or helping him eat food at lunchtime. While I gladly helped him of course, it was still not an easy situation for either of us to combine these roles. In the office my father and I sat at facing desks in the same room. Quite often we would have differences of opinion about business issues and I found these conflicts both difficult and draining. I realized that my father had a wealth of experience and insight and respected his views, but I also felt it was important to be true to my own convictions. Since I was not as good at compromising as my father, our disagreements were often quite strong.

At times it all got too much and I just wanted to quit. On one occasion after a big disagreement, I was so furious that I packed my bag and decided to leave. I was too embarrassed to walk out in front of the receptionist because of my emotional state and so I simply climbed out of the ground floor window, jumped over the fence and went home! However, even then, I could not escape since I was still living with my parents and had to face my father when he came home. I felt completely trapped because, on the one hand, I had nowhere else to go and on the other, I did not feel that I could let my father and the other office workers down by leaving.

At the age of twenty three I decided, while I was working, to follow courses in business administration at the University of Amsterdam in my free time. This satisfied some of my desire to understand economics and business at a deeper level. All in all, my time of working with my father was a mixed experience. I disliked the long meetings and the conflicts, but very much enjoyed the creative side of things and all the people contact. I learned a lot!

Dealing with Dishonesty

Our company had a good reputation for its integrity and our often innovative approaches. Pioneers in energy efficiency, we were one of the first developers in the early seventies to build houses with a very high level of thermal insulation. We also won several awards in the field of design. While working in this field, I met many wonderful, good and honest people, but I also witnessed first hand the less attractive sides of the business and those who chose to take a dishonest path. The real estate industry in the Netherlands did not have a very good reputation at the time, and there were many stories of corruption and bribery. In my working life in the industry, I was exposed to this shady side several times and have always found it disturbing. One example of this was in the late 1970s, when I invited a contractor to visit my home to give an estimate for an extension to my house.

I had known this man for many years as he had done work for our company on several occasions. He had a solid reputation. I trusted him and knew his work was good and his prices fair, which was why I chose to invite him to give me an estimate. At the time he was negotiating a big contract to build houses with the technical department of our company.

To my surprise, when he came to give the estimate, he implied that if he was to get the contract for the housing project he could "lose" the total cost for my own home extension within it. In other words, if he got the job with the company, I would get my home extension for free. I was appalled, especially as we had known each other for a long time and I thought he knew that I ran an honest business, and that each time, he had been chosen to work for our company simply on merit. I told him directly that I would not be involved in such a deal.

Such offers or "opportunities" can come up repeatedly in business life and many people may find them tempting. However, right from the outset of my career, I made a decision that I would not accept them. That was because I chose, and choose now, to work with integrity, openness and honesty. I knew that this would have business consequences, and as a result of this stance our company certainly missed a number of both major and lesser business opportunities. I firmly believed that in place of these corrupt deals other genuine opportunities would come our way—which in fact they did. I feel it is simpler to just be honest and able to sleep with a clear conscience at night.

I expected the same stance from our employees and told them that if they were ever offered bribes they must inform me. One day one of them told me he had been offered a cut-price kitchen from one of our sub-contractors. I then asked around and discovered that several of our employees in charge of giving out contracts already had such discounted kitchens installed! I did not sack them over this lapse, but made very sure that the practice was stopped and should not be repeated.

When I think about corruption, I feel lucky that I never found myself in such challenging circumstances that I might have felt compelled to accept such offers. On the one hand, I do not feel that such behavior is in my nature—it really goes against the grain of my personal belief system. But, on the other hand, if my situation was different and I, or one of my children, were in dire straits, how can I know how I would act or react? I don't think anyone can ever say they will never behave in a particular way unless they are put to the test.

My Brother

My younger brother Paul loved music, especially Latin American, and was keen on sound systems such as hi-fi. As my father's health deteriorated, he felt that he wanted to help Paul settle in some sort of business as he had by then stopped studying at university. Knowing of Paul's love for music, my father had the idea of purchasing a music and electrical goods store for Paul to run.

The store sold radios, records, televisions, and some household appliances such as washing machines and fridges. On top of the store was an apartment for Paul to live in. Paul took on the job, but without huge enthusiasm. He was only in his very early twenties and was responsible for managing the large store with about twenty employees. The business was not doing very well and was losing money. It seemed like it was too much for Paul, although he appeared not to be unhappy.

On August 4, 1970 we received some dreadful news—Paul's co-worker called me in the morning, saying Paul hadn't turned up for work. He and a colleague had gone to Paul's apartment and, not getting a reply, they had gone in to look for him. They were shocked to find Paul dead. This news was unbelievable to our family. I had spoken to Paul on the phone the evening before and he had seemed fine. It was so hard to understand what had happened. Yet the shock was about to become even worse as it soon became apparent that Paul had taken his own life. Nothing had prepared our family for this, as we had no idea that he was even contemplating such action and could not understand why he had done it.

In those days, suicide was not discussed, so the family, including me at the time, chose to hide the true details of Paul's death from most people. The story we told was that he had died because of a heart problem, just like the earlier death of my brother Bob. Paul's suicide was rarely discussed openly from then on, either in the family or outside of it, as it was difficult to talk about it. To this day we do not know why Paul took his own life. Gradually I felt that it was not right to hide the truth anymore, and so over the years I have selectively shared what happened with a few trusted friends. Even now, this remains a sensitive subject for me and very difficult to talk about.

At the time I was desperate to understand what had happened and to know why Paul had done it. I really tried to discover the reason, talking to people who had known him at the time, and trying to understand what he had been thinking and feeling—for he had left no note or explanation. I continued this for some time, but I never found any real answers.

However in March 2003, when I was in Spain with a group of friends, we were put in touch with a well-known Peruvian medium living there. When we met with her, she went into a trance and channeled[3] messages for everyone in the group. When it came to my turn she said, "Your brother is coming through. He is saying that he loves you very much and is in a good place now. He is saying that it was difficult for him at first but now everything is fine." I was surprised since I had never met this woman before and she had no knowledge about me or my life. Her words seemed to carry a very personal message for me.

How does one explain such a phenomenon? In some cases it can be easy to fake such messages by getting prior knowledge about a person and then pretending to obtain messages from the "other side". However, in this case I had traveled from a different country, I had never met the medium before and I had not shared the story of my brother with any other members of the group. Yet, she was able to deliver a personal, accurate and particularly relevant message to me. In any case, it was wonderful to receive such an affirmative message, and it gave me more peace of mind about my brother Paul. Yet his suicide is still a source of great sorrow to me.

Learning about Love

During my teenage years and early twenties, I had several girlfriends. I went through the experiences that most teenagers do—adjusting to my hormonal changes, overcoming shyness, falling in and out of love. Sometimes I found it disturbing to my rational mind, but it opened another side of life to me. It was an exploration for me in every sense of the word! One day in 1972 when I was in Amsterdam for the day, I bumped into a friend, Ineke van den Oever, whom I had not seen for many years. Immediately I thought "Wow, what an attractive, original young lady! How could I have forgotten about her?" We went for a coffee and tried to arrange to meet again but several times had to cancel. After a few months we finally did have dinner together and immediately became very close. In fact, we stayed together from that day on! After some time I proposed and, in 1973 we got married and went on to have three much-loved children: Nina (born 1974), Saskia (born 1976) and Lyke (born 1980).

3 "Channeling" in this context is defined as the reception of information by paranormal means. Mediums are said to be able to receive information via ESP (extra-sensory perception). This may be: auditory, where the medium hears voices internally giving them information; visual, where they "see" images in their mind's eye; or kinaesthetic, where they experience a sensation, e.g. a smell or a sense of touch or temperature change. Channeling is said to involve direct contact with another entity, sometimes described as an angel, a being from another planet or a disembodied spirit of some kind that communicates directly with the person or actually "takes over" the person temporarily. In the latter case, the person generally goes into trance beforehand and remembers little or nothing of what has been communicated during the channeling.

In the beginning we had a good marriage and our future seemed bright. At the same time, I felt quite a lot of stress from the burden of my responsibilities at work and at home. I used to work very hard and long hours. I went jogging long distances six days a week. Looking back, I think that, during these years, my light smoking, drinking and running, though not carried to excess, were my ways of releasing tension. I developed these habits in the last years of my father's life as his condition deteriorated. However, over time, I became more interested in health and fitness.

My Father

By 1977 my father's condition had deteriorated so much that my mother, even with a team of visiting nurses, could no longer care for him at home. We made the difficult decision to admit him to a hospital for round-the-clock care. It was just two kilometers from our home and the family was able to visit regularly.

I visited my father frequently but on the evening of May 6, 1977 something special happened that left a deep impression that remains with me to this day. We were alone in the room, and I was sitting at my father's bedside with my arm touching his, when he suddenly looked into my eyes and weakly, but purposefully, squeezed my arm while maintaining eye contact. In that moment, as our eyes met, I felt a deep connection between us, a kind of exchange of energy. I felt that my father was making a gesture toward me.

It was as if he wanted to share his being and heartfelt values with me. Our communication felt like one of those primitive rites of passage where the older, wise man passes on the mantle to his son. I felt that there was a kind of understanding between us and that he was saying that everything was OK and that he loved me. It was a very precious moment that is hard to put into words, but I remember leaving the hospital feeling deeply touched.

The hospital called our home early the next morning to say that my father had passed away at around 7:00 A.M. This dramatic news made me think about the previous evening even more. Had my father sensed he was about to die? Had he made that gesture knowing that it would be our final communication? Perhaps that is why that moment has made such a lasting impression on me?

Thinking about my father, one of the overriding memories of those who knew him would probably be his kindness. He had real compassion for anyone who was sick, and I can recall many stories of his acts of kindness for sick people, both in his company and neighborhood and farther afield. If he learned of a particular need, he would try to respond to it. For example, he provided funding for the treatment of eye problems in Africa and also helped provide clean water in Bihar, India after reading about a terrible drought there in 1970. My father provided the Caterpillar to drill wells in Bihar, and he arranged for its shipment to India.

A Dutch magazine ran a big article on this project but my father insisted that his name was not disclosed and it only included a photo that showed a back view of him. He did not want any fuss and preferred that his donations were not acknowledged publicly. Several years ago I heard that, after thirty years, that drill is still active. It goes from place to place and has provided thousands of people with access to water.

After his death, we wanted to honor my father and his compassionate nature as a family. We remembered him being particularly struck by a television program about lepers. We decided to donate money to a leprosy project in Colombia that was in desperate need after their fund money had been embezzled. We provided funds for a new building where the leprosy victims could be treated.

This building was named The Johan Hospital, after my father. But this was not the only legacy of my father. There was much I found inspirational in his behavior and attitude to life. As well as his good humor and compassion, my father also bore the discomfort and frustration of his failing health with great dignity. He never complained either about his diabetes or Parkinson's disease, which increasingly limited his scope for action. He never looked for sympathy or played the victim. I also learned from his attitude about his work. Although he was a successful businessman, he was not attached to money. He enjoyed the process and loved to play the game, but was not interested in accumulating vast wealth.

His passing away also made me reflect on deeper issues—what happens after life, what or who God is, and all the other questions that I normally did not spend much time considering. I had been to Sunday school but more as a duty than out of any genuine interest. I had no sense what God really meant to me in my daily life. Yet these early reflections on the occasion of my father's death were to sow the seeds for a whole new chapter in my life that was to come.

Stepping Down

I was thirty-two when my father died. His death reminded me of the promise that I had made to myself when I finally committed to staying in the family business at the age of twenty. At that time I had resolved that once I reached my thirties I would take a break and go and metaphorically "sit on the top of a mountain", symbolic to me of quietness and distance, and contemplate my future. I planned to review my life and give myself the chance to decide whether I wanted to continue in the business or do something different.

What became clear was that I no longer wanted to continue as CEO of Johan Matser Ltd. Two years after my father's death, in 1979, I started to look seriously for a successor. I thought that I had found the right candidate, but unfortunately, after two years, he left. I resumed the position again knowing that my life needed to head in another direction. In 1982 I found a suitable CEO, which allowed me to take more of a back seat. However, at the Board level I still retained ultimate responsibility for the company.

By this time I had spent eighteen years of my life working for the company; I had joined at age nineteen, been made CEO aged twenty-seven. At the age of thirty-seven I was finally able to step down. New horizons beckoned and some seeds of interest for my new life had already been sown.

Reflections

At the end of each chapter in this part of the book, I have included a short section with reflections on the lessons I have learnt from particular life experiences. These experiences led me to create seven Keys that I believe can be helpful in rediscovering our hearts. The Keys are important to my life and philosophy and I hope that they may also be useful to you, dear reader. Both the Keys, and the affirmations that accompany them, can be used to explore and reflect on your own life experiences, if you wish. I hope they may also be useful as tools for personal and global transformation.

Trusting in the Guiding Hand of the Divine

Reflecting back on this part of my life, of family, business and responsibilities, I came to see that many times, things did not go the way that I had planned or expected. Yet I sensed that there was always a meaning or "purpose" in the way that things turned out.

It seemed to me as if there was an unseen, "guiding" hand that was creating opportunities for learning and personal and spiritual growth that would later create shifts in the course of my life. So, although my plans for participating further in sport or going to university were frustrated, I realize that taking the position as my father's successor also taught me a lot. I was able to develop business skills and to learn to deal with the material world while also recognizing the value of hard work, philanthropy and compassion, as demonstrated by my father. I can see how strongly the ideas of social responsibility and wholesome family values were part of my early conditioning.

Yet I was also increasingly challenged to look into my own heart and listen to it. I realize now that this paved the way for the spiritual experiences that were to come later and my desire to implement spiritual principles in a practical way.

At this stage in my life I had no clear idea of "God", "soul" or "spirit", but I already felt a sense of the "Divine" that was in essence completely free of religion, dogma or names. I have never become a member of any religious group, although I later met many wonderful and inspiring spiritual teachers. In my currrent understanding, God encompasses all creation in all its dimensions, including ourselves. I believe we can each experience some of God's creation through our five senses; for example, inhaling a sweet rose, seeing the smile of a new born baby or listening to music. We can also experience God in the more subtle dimensions if we are truly open to them. Having this sense of the Divine inspired me to go on a journey of personal discovery of my own heart and to seek answers for the deeper questions in life such as:

- *Why are we here?*
- *What have we come here to experience?*
- *What is the purpose of our existence?*
- *What can we do about our world?*
- *And what does this mean for you and me personally?*

This journey has been, and is, a gradual process where I fall flat on my face many times a day, pick myself up, and remind myself that everything has a purpose. I am aware that with my free will I can make choices and decisions in my daily life, yet I have also learned to trust and surrender to the idea of there being a "higher purpose" behind everything that comes our way.

This led me to formulate my first key principle:

KEY 1: ***We can trust in the guiding hand of the Divine.***

AFFIRMATION: ***I trust that everything has a Divine purpose from which it is possible to learn and grow.***

CHAPTER 2
A Mind Bending Experience

In 1980 I attended the Young Presidents' Organization (YPO annual conference) in Madrid, with my wife, Ineke. The YPO, an organization of young business leaders, arranges high-powered events in different countries each year. Usually the program included well-known speakers, and that year Uri Geller, the controversial psychic, was due to address the conference. At that time I was still quite conventional and only had a small interest in the paranormal, but the program sounded intriguing.

We were invited to bring broken watches and clocks with us to the session with Uri Geller, and several of my colleagues had decided to do so. On the Monday afternoon gathering, 1,300 people from all over the world sat together for the session with him. At a certain point during his presentation, he asked people who had watches and clocks that didn't work to bring them up to the stage and place them on a chair. So many people approached the stage that many had to be turned away. Geller surveyed the pile of broken timepieces and then invited the whole audience to say loudly three times, "We want these clocks to work, work, work". The owners were then invited back on stage to collect their watches and clocks and, to my great surprise, two-thirds reported that they were now working!

Geller then said to the audience, "I had to disappoint some of you because there was not enough space on the chair for all of your watches and clocks, but please check these items in your pockets and see if they are now working." To my further surprise, more people then reported that their timepieces were now functioning, too. I was particularly flabbergasted by this whole display because two friends sitting next to me had broken timepieces that had been on the stage and that were now working. I had checked these items before my friends took them on stage and could find no way to get them working. I felt stunned as I was a person who liked to think things could be explained rationally, and yet here I was being confronted with a reality that appeared inexplicable!

Later on I witnessed Geller demonstrating spoon-bending and the levitation of a heavy person on stage. I am, of course, aware that such phenomena can simply be tricks or illusions, but a further amazing thing happened, which unexpectedly convinced me of the authenticity of these phenomena. The following day, during the lunch break, a group of us were talking about what we had witnessed with Geller when, to my utter surprise, someone challenged me to see if I could get members of our group together to see if we could perform this demonstration of levitation ourselves. I have no idea why the person picked me, but I decided to try it. A heavy person volunteered and I tried to repeat Geller's procedure, as we had witnessed it, in order to levitate him.

We began by sitting the man on a chair. I then stood by his left shoulder and invited three other people to stand with me around him; one was behind his right shoulder and the other two next to each of his knees. I then asked each person to place two fingers under part of the man's body—I and one other person placed our fingers under his armpits and the other two placed their fingers under his bent knees. We then tried to lift the man off the chair but could not move him at all as he was too heavy. I then repeated the procedure that I had seen Uri Geller use the day before. I placed my right hand over the top of the man's head and invited each of the other participants, clockwise, to place their right hands over mine without actually touching. Then we did the same with our left hands. All the participants' hands were now over each other. I then invited everyone to remove their hands one by one in a counter-clockwise fashion. We then tried to lift the man again, and to our amazement we found that we could lift him to the height of our shoulders with ease! I had been open-minded about doing the levitation but had had no expectation whatsoever of it working. I was amazed that it worked and having experienced it myself, I was convinced the phenomenon was real, although I still had no rational explanation.

That evening we were in a restaurant for dinner, when someone who had been present during the lunch break spontaneously asked me to try and repeat the levitation. This time we were in the presence of the Archbishop of Madrid and a different group of us tried to accomplish it. Again, the levitation worked, to everyone's surprise. I, too—again—felt amazed and yet I was also aware that the procedure somehow felt easy.

The Tesla Transmitter

Another speaker at the conference, Dr. Andrija Puharich, a scientist and paranormal investigator, lent further credibility to these events. Puharich was convinced of Geller's powers and had previously arranged for Geller to be investigated at Stanford Research Institute (SRI) in the US[4]. He also wrote a sympathetic biography of Geller. At the conference, Puharich described the rigorous scientific tests conducted on Geller and some of his own experiences of Geller's "powers." I found his presentation convincing. I was, however, quite surprised by another part of his presentation where he talked about the work

4 This research was written up in the journal, *Nature*, October 18, 1974, Vol. 251, page 559.

of Nikola Tesla[5]. Puharich had been researching one of Tesla's devices, the Tesla Transmitter. This was a magnetic-wave generator and Puharich had been startled to find that altering the frequencies emitted by the generator could make people quite agitated and ill. He was convinced that the Soviets had developed one of these transmitters near Vladivostok in the eastern part of the former USSR, and that they were testing it as a weapon. He was therefore making it his mission to inform the public at large about this perceived danger.

As an example of this, Puharich told of a time when a large group of people in Vancouver reportedly all suddenly experienced headaches and felt compelled to leave their workplaces. No explanation had ever been found for this strange phenomenon. Puharich had discovered from radio amateurs in the area that their reception had been disturbed at exactly the same time. Since the Tesla Transmitter used the same type of radio wavelength, Puharich had concluded that this was evidence that the Soviets were testing the device and that it had caused the disturbance. However, no proof exists that this was the case.

It must be remembered that this was at a time when the Cold War[6] between the US and the Soviet Union was at its height, and many Westerners regarded the Soviets as very secretive and a great threat. Various accounts exist of both the Soviets and the CIA investigating ways of using paranormal and other such phenomena as weapons against each other. In fact, Uri Geller himself has subsequently publicly claimed that the CIA tested his powers to see how he could be useful to them. Obviously, this was not particularly comfortable information, but what I took from Dr. Puharich's talk was the evidence from his scientific investigation of Geller. It seemed to me a good idea that research scientists were making serious efforts to investigate such phenomena.

A further strange thing happened when we returned to the Netherlands after the conference. My wife, Ineke, and I came home from an evening with friends. I put my house key into the keyhole of our front door and it would not open. I couldn't even get it in the keyhole! This was the same key that I had had in my pocket during the conference, and when I took it out of the keyhole I found that this solid key was clearly bent. Ineke suggested that I must have bent it by forcing it in the lock, but I told her this was impossible as it would have required a great deal of force and yet there were no signs of force being used on the key itself. In the end we had to use a different key in order to enter the house. This had had never happened before and I have no rational explanation for this.

---

5 Nikola Tesla (1856–1943) was an inventor, engineer and physicist widely regarded as a genius and the father of 20th century technology.

6 The "Cold War" was so called because it involved no actual armed combat, or "hot war" but was the escalating of hostilities and the nuclear arms race between the US and the USSR. It started in 1947, following the end of the Second World War, and ended with the dissolution of the USSR in December 1991.

Shifts in Perception

These events, together with other experiences that I had at the conference, triggered a real shift in my perceptions of life, myself and the world around me. I was a man who had previously thought he could explain everything using his rational mind, but now I was being confronted with a reality that was inexplicable and intangible. I could find no reference point in my existing mental framework to place these experiences. I still have no full explanation for them. I have since witnessed many other similar phenomena, often together with others, which are also inexplicable and yet apparently real.

I know that there are skilled conjurors who can perform similar feats, and that certain demonstrations of so-called paranormal phenomena can be faked. I am also aware that Geller himself is controversial and has been accused by some of trickery. Yet, looking back I regard that conference as one of the turning points in my life. From the day of the conference onward, my world view started to change. However, my wife did not share my growing interest in such phenomena and this caused a rift between us.

New experiences followed. At the same conference in Madrid, I met Greta Woodrew, a known and respected speaker in our YPO conference circles. In her talks, Greta made predictions about upcoming changes for our planet, including earthquakes in California, and these were taken seriously by conference members. Some of them even decided to move in the light of what she had said. At that time I also took some of her predictions quite seriously. I was concerned about the safety of our family, as the Netherlands was regarded to be at risk of flooding. After lengthy discussions with Ineke, we decided to explore the possibility of moving to Australia. In 1982 we went with our family to have a closer look. Our trip to Australia was a great experience and we enjoyed the country very much, but we felt too far away from our roots.

Everything Falls into Place

On our flight back to the Netherlands, we flew over Switzerland, as we had a stopover in Zurich. As I looked down from the plane over the spectacular, snowy mountain panorama, I felt a strong feeling of affection for the country, remembering all the happy times I'd had there. Memories resurfaced about wonderful winter holidays and an old wish to maybe live there one day. At the same moment I remembered a dream from my youth that one day I would love to volunteer with the Red Cross. I recalled that the World Headquarters of the Red Cross and Red Crescent Societies organization was in Geneva, Switzerland.

As these thoughts were going round in my mind, I had an extraordinary sensation of everything coming together and suddenly making sense. For no apparent reason, and without any conscious planning, I suddenly knew intuitively that we were going to live in Switzerland and I was going to volunteer for the Red Cross! When I stepped down from the position of CEO, it had created a space in my life for something new to come in. Now it had appeared, apparently out of the blue.

Obviously, I still needed to discuss this in detail with Ineke and to consider with her the implications for the family as a whole. Yet in that instant everything seemed to fall into place. I could see in retrospect that going to Australia and talking about the possibility of living there had helped to mentally prepare our family to move elsewhere. For a European, Switzerland also seemed to be a relatively "safe" and appropriate place for my family to be, in that it was high up in the Alps, compared to the low-lying Netherlands, yet much less remote and foreign than Australia. It was also only a little more than an hour's flight away from our home country, making commuting much more possible.

It was one thing for these thoughts and feelings to come together in a moment of apparent clarity, but it was quite another for this to actually become a reality. I wondered how I could get in touch with the Red Cross and what sort of work I could offer to do. In fact, I didn't need to worry, as everything just slotted in, almost effortlessly. Many people have experienced how, when something "feels" right, everything just seems to flow in a miraculous way. Well, that is exactly what happened to me at this time, as everything was resolved with extraordinary speed, and in remarkable ways, after my return to the Netherlands.The first thing I had to do was make contact with the Red Cross to see if there was a useful way in which I could volunteer my services. I got an introduction to the Secretary-General, Hans Hoegh, and within a week I met him in Geneva. Hans told me that the Red Cross wanted to start a worldwide program to combat child death and sickness due to dehydration caused by diarrhea. At that time, almost five million children under the age of five were dying from this every year. Yet most of these deaths could be prevented by the simple administration of oral re-hydration therapy (ORT)[7]. This is a cheap, easy and highly effective intervention that requires only salts and glucose in a particular ratio dissolved

---

7 The first successful clinical trials of ORT were conducted by the Cholera Research Laboratory in Dhaka, India in 1968 and this therapy has been described as "potentially the most important medical discovery of the 20th century" (The Lancet, 1978). It involves administration of a balanced solution of sodium chloride, sodium bicarbonate, potassium chloride and glucose in powder form and dissolved in water. A home-made alternative is 1 liter of water mixed with 8 teaspoons of sugar and 1 tablespoon of table salt with half a banana or ½ cup of orange juice for added potassium. For more information on ORT, see *www.rehydrate.org*.

in preferably clean water, and then given to the infant by spoon or baby bottle. Anyone can administer the therapy and no hospitalization is required. Hans wanted to launch this program at the General Assembly of the Red Cross and Red Crescent Societies in 1983, where Jim Grant, the Secretary General of UNICEF, was drawing attention to this issue in his keynote speech. He asked me if I would head up the program and make it happen. I spent a week considering all the ramifications of this offer, and discussing it with my wife, and then decided to accept. I agreed to volunteer the majority of my working time toward the program, while still maintaining my supervisory commitment to the family business in the Netherlands. I would report directly to the Secretary General's office, but I would do my own fund-raising for the program outside of the organization and would take full responsibility for it. I chose this route because I did not want the program to become bogged down in the bureaucracy of a large organization. This was also Hans' view. In October 1983 the program was duly launched and I was appointed its Executive Chairman. Within a very short space of time, everything had been arranged and I now knew what I was to be doing.

Representing San Marino

I immediately started work by putting a team together to implement the program. However, I needed a permit to live with my young family in Switzerland, which was difficult to get. I had called a friend, an advisor in the Netherlands, to ask how I might obtain a Swiss residency permit and he had promised to look into it. He later called me back with some extraordinary news; he had learned that the special representative for the republic of San Marino to the United Nations in Geneva was looking for a deputy and that I might be able to apply for the position!

San Marino is a very small country (25,000 inhabitants) completely surrounded by Italy, close to Rimini on the Adriatic Coast. At this time their appointed representative needed a deputy who would be competent for the job, but who did not necessarily have to come from the country itself. Such a post would give me the right to live in Switzerland, which would mean that I could do my volunteer work with the Red Cross and live in Geneva with my family. This opportunity seemed an amazing coincidence. It would also offer a unique opportunity to get to know the people and the country of San Marino. I therefore applied for the position and fortunately was chosen. The position involved sometimes representing the people of San Marino at the United Nations, which enabled me to gain experience of how the UN operated—something that was to prove very useful in my later work with international organizations. The appointment meant that I was able to obtain a residency permit and in August 1984, when my children were aged ten, eight and four, my family moved to Geneva.

We rented a house in the suburbs and often went skiing together at weekends in the winter and hiking in the mountains in the summer. My children attended an international school, which stimulated their wider view of the world, although most of the students there were from quite privileged families.

Nina, Saskia, Fred, Lyke, Ineke, when we lived in Switzerland

In many ways, we had a wonderful time living there, but in other ways it was not easy for my family, especially my wife. She would be left alone to cope on the four days each month that I had to return to the Netherlands to supervise my real estate business. The first time that this happened was only a few days after we had moved to Geneva, which was particularly difficult for my wife. I remember very well how it was raining on the day that she took me to the airport and I saw her crying as I left. I felt very bad about this and was also aware that my daughters missed their Dutch friends too, especially in the early days. I felt responsible if they were unhappy since it was me who had uprooted them to Geneva, so that I could fulfill my dream of volunteering with the Red Cross. So the transition was not an entirely easy one for my family, and in hindsight, I think that I was not sensitive enough to their feelings. However, I also felt that working for the Red Cross was something that I really had to do and I genuinely wanted my family, whom I loved deeply, to be close by. I felt very fortunate that they supported me in my choice, even though they had no special interest in the work that I was doing. I also thought that an internationally-oriented education for my children would always be an asset in their lives.

Transcendental Experience

I had been warned by a specialist in the Netherlands that my blood sugar levels were a little abnormal so, while living in Switzerland, I decided to try to take some preventative measures against developing diabetes. A trusted friend recommended an American therapist who specialized in dealing with health problems using natural methods.

The therapist advised me that it would be best to follow a program of detoxing. This included massage, bathing, drinking lots of water, and eating a vegetarian diet. During one of my sessions of therapeutic massage I became aware of the song that was playing in the background—"We Are the World". As I listened, I experienced a heightened awareness of the meaning of the words, as they seemed to enter my whole being. It was as if I was meant to hear the song in a new way. I wasn't trying to make something happen, yet during my treatment I had a state of being that I had not experienced before.

I felt light, calm and comfortable experiencing this great feeling and I allowed it in. I wondered if this was a kind of expanded state of consciousness. In this state I then had a strong feeling that a friend had suffered a skiing accident on the slopes nearby, breaking her collarbone. I then had an image of my injured friend arriving at the very place where I was, asking for medical help. I took a deep breath, as the thought seemed a little strange.

After my treatment was over, I went to open the door to leave, and there was my friend, standing in front of me. She explained that she had fallen while skiing and hurt her shoulder or collarbone, just as I had seen it. Her appearance felt so natural at that moment that I wasn't even surprised. Later I learned that this kind of experience is called precognition.

Some months later I had another healing session with this therapist. I was relaxing in a chair and had closed my eyes. At that moment, completely unexpectedly, I was again given an extraordinary experience. At first I felt a deep sense of peace and this was followed by an overwhelming feeling of pure bliss that seemed to have no beginning or end and was timeless. I felt that I was actually a part of an Infinite Oneness beyond time and space. I had multi-dimensional, multi-directional experiences of colors that, in a very basic way, could be compared to a kaleidoscope. Within this experience I felt totally and unconditionally loved for the first time in my life at that profound level. During this experience, wherever I allowed my attention to go, I was immediately there. It could be in front of me, within me, behind me, beyond me, all at the same time. Each time, I was there instantaneously. My skin no longer felt like a border between my surroundings and myself, as I became one with all that was around me. In a way it felt like my "self" was imploding and exploding within a bath of tranquility and yet the "me" was not there at all. The whole experience seemed to go on and on as if transcending eons of time, though looking at my watch afterwards I realized it had lasted only a few seconds. I knew that this had been a life-changing experience. I felt that, through the experience of this Unconditional Love, bliss and eternity, I had actually experienced the presence of the Divine.

Although this experience was quite extraordinary, it was also very real—in fact it felt more "real" than any normal life experience—and at all times I had total clarity. I was also fully aware of my surroundings before, during and after this experience. I had also been fully relaxed throughout and had felt no fear during this awe-inspiring experience, but had simply let go and surrendered to it. From talking to others, I have learned that many people have had these moments. For me, they are important experiences, as they can teach us that beyond the world of our five senses lies an Infinite reality that encompasses all dimensions.

Distant Healing

Following this experience, my horizons began to open wider. I met some truly remarkable individuals who inspired me in my new quest for greater understanding. Amongst these were some extraordinary and gifted healers whose abilities confound modern medical explanation. One was the very modest and unassuming Dutch lady, Nannie Veerman, daughter of the famous healer and paranormal psychometrist, Gerard Croiset[8]. In 1988 I was present when she demonstrated the healing work that she did every Saturday with five people with significant physical challenges. These people were all able to make only very limited, rigid and uncontrolled movements due to their disabilities, but once a

8 Gerard Croiset (1905–1980) was able to tell information about the life history of a person by holding an object that belonged to them, a gift known as psychometry. He became famous for his co-operation with Dutch police in helping to solve cases using this gift. His work was researched by the famous Dutch parapsychologist, Professor Ten Haeff.

week, in this healing session, they achieved complete relaxation. Nannie talked to them lovingly and sweetly in a quiet voice for a few moments and then stood back and started to move her hands. To my amazement, the bodies of all the people whom she was healing gradually stopped going into spasm and their limbs started to move smoothly and freely under the influence of her healing power. It was remarkable to see this with my own eyes. What was even more amazing was that she then left the room and was able to repeat the same phenomena through the wall from the next room! This effect lasted around half an hour while she continued to send her healing energy. Sadly, after she stopped the healing and withdrew her focus, the people's spasms gradually started to return.

Witnessing this incredible and moving healing effect made me question the relationship between physical healing and love. How was this effect possible? Was there some healing force that Nannie, with her loving heart and consciousness, could access and somehow pass on to these people? Or did her energy and love somehow enable them to access this healing force themselves via her consciousness? Or was it both? For me, this consciousness is the embodiment of Unconditional Love.

Nannie always modestly claimed that the energy of the people in the room helped her to heal her patients. You could certainly feel an atmosphere of love in the room, and all the people who she worked with were more relaxed and happy afterwards. Nannie has co-operated several times with scientists investigating her abilities. She was once filmed by a Japanese TV company that showed clear effects of her distance healing in the Netherlands on some people in Japan. As with so many healers, her abilities defied rational explanation and remain controversial. Yet I was deeply touched by her quiet, humble and loving approach and the astonishing results she seemed able to produce.

Some people attribute all healing to the "placebo effect"—in other words, her treatment had no actual effect, but her patients believed it was doing them good and so felt better. This raises the question, what really is placebo? If the mind can decide that a particular substance or treatment method is going to work and consequently it has a beneficial effect, then the mind becomes the healer. E. Fuller Torrey's well-known book, *Mind Game: Witchdoctors & Psychiatrists*, suggests that, while psychiatry may work with white Westerners, the application of voodoo may work much better in Africa with African people, so healing may be culture-specific and relate to people's expectation and belief systems. As Westerners, we may believe in pills and pharmaceuticals, whereas indigenous peoples may believe in totems and chants and different forms of healing. Belief systems may also change over time: Europeans believed in the efficacy of herbs for many hundreds of years and are now starting to rediscover their ancient interest.

Toward the end of my thirties, in the late 1980s, I decided to really study the phenomenon of the placebo effect in more depth. It was difficult at first having not studied academically for so long, but I soon found that I really enjoyed delving into the complex matters surrounding this issue. I read contributions from a variety of authors and all had different interpretations of placebo. I came to realize that the phenomenon of placebo illuminates the power of the mind. It can be harnessed as a powerful healing force if people replace their beliefs in the stress, anxiety, and fear that surround illness with a strong belief in inner peace, recovery and the healing power of love.

Thus at a deeper level, I believe our concept of placebo basically reflects how we experience the world around us. If we are willing to go beyond our ordinary self-limiting beliefs and expand our consciousness, we can open ourselves to the Infinite and to infinite possibilities. With an open heart and a clear mind, we can become a channel for God's love in action.

Experiencing the Infinite

All this was made very clear to me one Sunday in the late 1980s when I went to a concert in Amsterdam. Before the music began, I was sitting, idly thinking about how the next day was going to be a Monday, with that "Monday morning feeling" that we so often get, knowing that we have a week of work ahead.

How much nicer Friday nights are, with the prospect of a whole weekend ahead! As I gazed around the concert hall, I wondered how many other people might be having the same thoughts and feelings. The orchestra started playing and I began listening to the music but was still a bit distracted by my thoughts. However, as I listened I gradually relaxed and became calmer and then, suddenly and without warning, I had the most incredible experience.

All thoughts disappeared and in that moment I found myself totally at one with the music. It was as if the music entered into me and I actually became the music. It was a quite extraordinary, all-consuming sensation that is hard to put into words, but it felt like an experience without beginning or end. On the one hand, part of my consciousness was fully aware of being in the concert hall and yet another aspect of my consciousness was completely "somewhere else" experiencing the Infinite—timeless, formless Divine Consciousness, the great, creative source of the universe, itself.

The experience seemed to go on and on and on, although in our normal time frame it perhaps only lasted a few seconds. Then suddenly a thought crept into my mind, "Why me?" and in that moment it instantly became Sunday afternoon again and I was back in the hall just listening to the music.

It was as if a great, radiant light had been switched off the moment I began to question the experience. This reminded me of the well-known Dutch saying, "Doubt is the devil's pillow", which means that doubts can destroy Divine and magical moments. In that moment of altered consciousness in the concert hall, I experienced this profound feeling of Unconditional Love, and have experienced it at other times since, like many others. Following these experiences, I went through through considerable changes as a person. During these years the differences between my wife and I became more obvious. We began to feel we were no longer so well matched and started to develop in different directions.

Reflections
Opening the Mind to the Infinite

Reflecting on these experiences I see this was a time when my life began to open up in all sorts of unexpected ways and I began to realize that my conventional belief system did not hold all the answers. My experience in the concert hall led to a pivotal shift in my consciousness, opening me to a world beyond the five senses and the intellect. In that moment I felt no limitations and the sense of expanding beyond my human "self" had been both effortless and timeless. This stimulated my curiosity about spirituality and healing and led me into a new world.

The experiences that followed also helped me to realize the importance of learning discernment and its value in making wiser choices. I did not "seek out" these experiences—this initial one occurred spontaneously when I was in a relaxed state and was perhaps triggered by the music. Yet I have found since that many people have such experiences and I do believe that they are accessible to anyone. I have also found that it becomes gradually easier to "tune into" such experiences so that they may be experienced more readily. However, I also feel that it is important to approach them in a spirit of openness, humility and respect rather than with an egotistical attitude. For me, such experiences give us an opportunity to directly experience what I call, "the Infinite"—and this experience can be life transforming.

This led me to my second Key:

KEY 2: *We can free our minds to explore new horizons.*

AFFIRMATION: *I can go beyond my conventional belief systems and open up to infinite possibilities.*

CHAPTER 3
Embracing Humanity

As my consciousness expanded to embrace the Infinite, so too my heart opened to embrace a new sense of humanity. Through my work with the Red Cross and other humanitarian organizations, I would find my heart tested over and over again. Gradually my sense of what our heart really is and how it can best serve humanity began to deepen. It was a process that took time and involved much trial and error. I had to go on my own inner journey and rediscover my heart.

Working with the Red Cross

During my work for the Red Cross, I visited many countries, especially in Africa and South America. I had never been to any of these places before and felt very privileged to be introduced to the different peoples of the world and to learn more about their way of life. Nowadays people travel more widely and television and the Internet have brought these cultures right into Western homes, but at that time, this was not the case and I was excited by the novel sights, sounds and experiences that I encountered.

For example, I vividly remember my first visit to Egypt where we stayed in a very basic, rather dirty hotel and I was surprised to be woken at four in the morning by loud prayers from the nearby mosque. This was my first time in a Muslim country, and I had never heard such prayers at full volume before. The sight of prayer mats and prayer corners in every public place also amazed me. I have an especially strong visual image of the huge, central station in Cairo where we went that morning to catch a train out to Alexandria where we were to be working. The high ceilings of the station let through great shafts of sunlight, which were full of particles of dirt and dust. One of these illuminated a corner of the station where a large number of men were on their knees making their morning prostrations and prayers. It was an incredible and memorable sight, and so different to the Western train stations to which I was accustomed.

Another thing that made a deep impression on me during these visits was the assault on the senses, of real poverty. Like most people, I had read about poverty in newspapers and seen images of it in photos and on television, but this is sanitized and removed from one personally. I had also, of course, seen poverty in the West and vividly remembered my experiences of intense poverty while visiting Surinam in 1968, but nothing prepared me for this type of deprivation. It is not only the sight of it, with appalling living conditions, lack of proper food and clothing, but also the smell that assaults your senses. There is the inescapable smell of rot, decay, and filth, which stays with you.

At first my experience of these sights and smells was so overpowering and unpleasant that my instinct was to want to escape from it. Yet I could not. I was acutely aware that, although I myself could soon go back to my normal, comfortable existence in the West, these people had no such choice to escape from poverty. What changed everything for me was having direct contact with the people and looking into each other's eyes. As our eyes met, I would feel myself reflected back and felt inextricably connected to the other person and their suffering. In a way, I no longer felt any separation between us but felt linked by our common humanity. This strengthened my sense of wanting to be with these people and to support them in meeting their needs. These impressions from over twenty years ago have remained with me and were the start of my realization that we are all one family of human beings.

Danger

On some of these visits, we encountered quite threatening situations. For example, in one African country, we were warned by colleagues not to make any public criticism of the ruling President, as secret police and spies were placed everywhere and there was a risk of being taken off and killed. In a South American country, I also stayed in a hotel room where, I found out later, a government minister had been murdered just a few days earlier!

We also had quite a number of hair-raising and dramatic moments when traveling. On one occasion in Columbia, we had to fly from Bogota to Almeira in a small prop plane. The outbound early morning flight went without incident, and we had dramatic views below of Bogota high up on a plateau. However, on the return journey we encountered some extremely bad weather and a lightning storm.

The plane was going up and down, and I was worried about hitting the plateau on which Bogota stood, as visibility was so poor—the flight attendant told us how two planes had already been lost that year, from crashing into it. To make matters worse, two chickens, which had been on the lap of a lady passenger, became so frightened that they were squawking and flying about the plane, adding to my sense of unease. Eventually, to our great relief, the plane managed to land safely, but we were the very last plane to do so that evening as Bogota airport was then closed because the weather was so bad.

I have had three or four scary and rather dangerous situations like this on planes during my life. In each case, I've noticed that my first reaction is the natural one of tension, anxiety and fright. But at a certain point, I've realized I can't do anything about the situation and am simply in God's hands. At that point I have just let go and put my full trust in God, and my fear dissolves.

Smiling Faces in Surinam

I think that part of the inspiration for my work with the Red Cross may have been my early experiences of visiting Surinam in South America with my father. He took my mother and me on a visit there in 1968. This was the first time that I had been outside Europe, and the trip was a complete eye-opener for me. Surinam was at that time still a Dutch colony (it gained independence in 1975), and my father decided to visit after hearing that there was a great need for social housing and good opportunities for development projects. He put together a proposal for 2,500 new, low-cost homes to be built in the capital of Paramaribo, and I accompanied him on the trip in my capacity as secretary to the board of the company. However, my main memory is of the deep impressions that the people and the country made on me.

I was amazed at the mix of people living there, which included Creoles (African origin), Chinese and Hindustanis (from India) alongside the local people, each with their own culture, traditions, food, etc. I had never seen such a melting pot of peoples and I really liked it. I loved all the liveliness, music, singing and colorful markets and also the cheerful, open-heartedness of the people who were always smiling.

From the Western perspective, their happiness was somewhat perplexing, since they lived in very poor conditions. Their homes were often shabby and none had the luxury of air-conditioning against the intense heat, which you found in some of the houses in the more affluent areas. Streets and buildings were in bad repair, with poor sanitation. Yet the people's levels of stress seemed remarkably low compared to the average Westerner. Everywhere there were little children playing in the mud and dirt on the roads and putting their dirty hands in their mouths. I thought of all the hand washing back at home and wondered what germs and diseases they might be contracting, and yet I was most impressed by their bright eyes and beaming smiles.

This showed me clearly that it is not just material possessions that bring happiness and that you cannot simply judge what may be good for a particular group of people by Western standards. For example, these people may have had a poorer standard of living, but they seemed much happier and less stressed than the average Westerner. So who is really to judge which population is the better off? This was something I thought about often during my years with the Red Cross and later when I was touched by the simple joy and happiness of local people even in the face of quite adverse conditions.

In Surinam itself, this was a time of innocence in a developing country that has since been overshadowed by the drug trade. Everywhere we went we encountered warm-hearted, welcoming people and we developed close friendships with several local people that lasted for many years.

I have seen poverty many times since, particularly in Peru in 2005, and elsewhere, yet the enduring image has often been of people's wonderful smiling faces. The people may be very poor yet they are often also very clean and radiant in a way that you don't often see in Western countries. This is not to ignore the very real problems they have, such as disease and high infant mortality. But it is not the whole picture, and the bare statistics can often hide the simple quality of life that can elude us in the West.

"Child Alive" Saves Lives

During the 1980s, while working as a volunteer for the Red Cross, I visited various African and South American countries to discuss and arrange the implementation of the oral re-hydration programs. In many places there were no official records of births and deaths and mortality rates, so we made the decision to focus on actual implementation of the Oral Re-hydration Therapy (ORT) "Child Alive" program and to monitor progress and overall impact as a secondary goal wherever possible. With limited funding, our primary focus had to be on saving lives.

We knew that setting up a monitoring system could swallow up large amounts of funding costs and yet the figures could still be unreliable. We wanted to focus on really helping to empower the people who had a desperate health care need. So, wherever possible we registered and recorded statistics, but our main priority was the implementation of the therapy. In the three years that I had the privilege of coordinating the program, we got it operational in more than 18 countries. The program also promoted breast-feeding and birth spacing—encouraging longer intervals between pregnancies, which research shows leads to healthier children.

Since that time the program has expanded to many more countries worldwide, and it is estimated that millions of children's lives have been saved by ORT. In 1983, five million children under the age of five died due to dehydration, and nowadays this number has halved. At the UNICEF 40th

Anniversary Celebration in 1986, our "Child Alive" team was given the Maurice Pate Memorial Award for the successful implementation of the ORT program[9]. This was an enormous honor but most important of all, of course, was the fact that this program has saved countless young lives.

Our "Child Alive" team at the Red Cross

A New Beginning

After three years of running the program and two years of living in Geneva, my family and I decided in 1986 that it was time to return to the Netherlands[10]. The Child Alive program was now well established and I felt my work with the Red Cross was done. I also felt that, at this stage, our company back in the Netherlands needed greater input from me than I had been able to provide. In addition, my work with the Red Cross had stimulated my interest in health care. I had seen from Child Alive how simple remedies could have a huge effect on people's health. The ORT program also showed how health issues were interconnected—dehydration, for example, affects the immune system.

9 See report in the UN Chronicle, Aug 1986.
10 The decision to return to the Netherlands meant that I also had to step down from my position as the representative for San Marino. I had really valued the experiences that I had had in holding this post and felt most grateful to the people of San Marino, whom I had represented, for their support and trust.

Those moments when I was opened to the Infinite gave me a sense of wholeness, which I felt could be applied to health, too. I was greatly helped in my exploration of new approaches to health and life in general by an inspiring professor of parapsychology at Utrecht University, Henri Van Praag. The stimulating talks I had with him confirmed the validity of my experiences of wholeness. He encouraged me to develop my ideas about health and give them concrete shape. From this emerged a growing sense of the value of integrated health care, bringing together the different disciplines of orthodox, complementary and paranormal approaches to medicine.

1989: The New Stream Health Center

The first fruits of my increasing interest in health led me to explore the idea of setting up an integrated health center in my home country in 1986. At the time, our real estate company had a building available, a former modern art museum that was 9,000 square feet and also had a good parking facility. I set up a working group with various health professionals and we brainstormed ideas for transforming it into an integrated health care facility. The concept of integrated medicine barely existed in the Netherlands at that time and when this Center opened in 1989, it became the first major integrated health center in the country.

A start-up team of medical and complementary medical specialists and people with other administrative and business skills was created to establish and run the new center. Wilbert Linnemans and Albert Barelds, with their backgrounds in research and social health care respectively, were the center's managers. Daan van Balen, a psychotherapist specializing in facilitating groups, Jacqueline Young, a British health practitioner who had already been involved in setting up integrated health centers in the UK, and Iet Dalewijk, an occupational therapist, were also part of the team.

As part of the brainstorming process, we also considered and visited other integrated centers that were newly established in Europe. This included a visit to London in the UK where we visited Dr Patrick Pietroni's pioneering Marylebone Health Center, which was sited in the crypt of a church and combined orthodox medicine with various complementary therapies, including acupuncture, homeopathy, osteopathy and counseling. We also visited the renowned Hale Clinic, which housed over sixty orthodox and complementary practitioners, and where one of the team, Jacqueline Young, was practising at the time. In the end we came up with a multi-level concept incorporating:

- *Orthodox, complementary and paranormal practitioners working side by side*
- *an educational facility for health and self-development training*
- *a research facility to investigate integrated medicine.*

We set about creating the space and systems and recruiting the right people, to make this vision a reality. Professor van Praag introduced me to a network of people who could help. The renowned organic architect, Ton Alberts, agreed to redesign the building's interior in his unique style. He used all natural materials and incorporated wonderful flowing lines avoiding right angles and sharp corners, creating a very therapeutic and healing inner environment.

We also used paint and furnishings of soft pastel pinks and blues and great care was taken to make the building "healthy". For example, at considerable extra expense, all electrical fields, from light switches etc., were insulated so that staff and patients would be unaffected by them. We even had a Faraday cage, which shields all electro-magnetic waves, built into the walls of one room[11]. I used to go and sit there sometimes, as I felt a wonderful sense of peace and calm, not being subject to any kind of electrical interference.

A team of practitioners, including orthodox medical doctors, complementary medicine practitioners (such as acupuncturists and manual therapists), psychotherapists and also a paranormal healer were assembled. The upper floor of the building was designated as the clinical facility with the treatment rooms, meditation rooms and the research room. The lower floor, designated as the education center, had a lecture space for up to 120 people, plus five rooms for smaller seminars and meetings.

A further key concept was developing a holistic approach to health care that involved co-operation between practitioners from different disciplines and with the patients themselves. We took great care to select highly qualified, experienced and reputable practitioners who were really interested in exploring new ways of working together and of empowering patients to make their own healthy choices. Our aim was to go beyond the "them" and "us" situation that was developing between orthodox and complementary medical health professionals at that time.

We wanted to open up the area to dialogue, investigation and research and to explore the best ways of facilitating co-operation and to determine the most appropriate types of health care for different conditions. Accordingly, the center was named "The New Stream" to represent these pioneering concepts and

11 This was also quite pioneering, as electrical sensitivity was virtually unknown at this time but has since become more recognized as a source of illness in certain sensitive individuals.

inspired by the stream that flowed nearby. I agreed to finance the building's initial set-up and running costs, with the aim being that the center would be self-financing within five years. We established a charitable foundation for this purpose, as the intention was not to profit from the enterprise but rather to contribute to the promotion of new models of health care. The center attained a measure of success, carrying out 5–6,000 treatments per year, hosting a range of innovative educational events, stimulating some research and perhaps inspiring others to develop their own new ways of working. However, there were also various problems and I feel many important lessons were learned from its creation, including the following:

1. We did not have enough support for the idea from the general public. In a sense, the center was ahead of its time, and we experienced quite a lot of mistrust and even some downright opposition. I particularly remember that we invited all the local family physicians to our opening and yet only one, out of more than thirty invited, came to find out more about what we were attempting. It seems they were stuck in their own belief systems and not willing to be open-minded about a different approach.
2. At that time, most treatments in our center were not covered by health insurance. This meant that the majority of treatments had to be funded privately by our clients, which was not a popular concept in the Netherlands at that time. Even with the subsidy we provided, many people said they liked the idea of the therapies but could not afford to have them.
3. Team building amongst the practitioners didn't work as well as we had hoped. Although we tried various group activities, regular team meetings and consultations and so on, time schedules, different interests, and perhaps conflicting egos, sometimes got in the way of real integration.
4. Not everyone really shared the vision of the center in practice. Some were content to just "do their own thing" or were more interested in furthering their own individual aims.
5. I was involved in various other initiatives at the time and so could not focus as much attention as I would have liked on The New Stream, although I trusted the management team to take responsibility for maintaining the project.
6. Providing extensive support funding may not have encouraged those in charge to take enough responsibility for the financial running and sustainability of the project. In fact, The New Stream did not succeed

> in becoming self-financing and was supported by my Foundation until 1998. Since then it has continued to operate but on a smaller scale. The clinic space is now leased independently to a commercial health organization while the education center is leased separately to a media company.

I learned a lot from this experience. The New Stream project was aimed at empowering people, and it led me to set up initiatives based on this principle, such as the Start Fund projects[12]. For these, our Foundation provides the initial sum to start enterprises—"seed-funding"—but the remainder has to be obtained or generated by the project initiators themselves, and they have to have their own committed team of people who are dedicated to seeing the project through.

The experience also made me learn about patience, and I realized that I must have the wisdom to sometimes give time to philanthropic initiatives, and take more care in applying the same standards that I would in my normal real-estate and project development business. For example: doing extensive information gathering; absorbing the information before making a decision rather than being too spontaneous; having proper job descriptions, goal statements and agreements, etc.

On reflection I realized that, although I had always followed these in my regular business, I had, mistakenly, let some of them fall by the wayside with The New Stream, thinking they were unnecessary. Though I asked the management team to put these practices into effect, I didn't check that they had done so. I was perhaps too trusting. All the people involved were very nice and skilled in their own way but also lacked certain business skills that I feel I could have contributed.

Overall, I believe The New Stream did succeed in contributing to the development of integrated medicine in the Netherlands. It also helped many people therapeutically and educationally and may have been an inspiration or catalyst for some other health ventures. However, I also feel that in some ways it was ahead of its time and that if some of the lessons described above had been learned and tackled effectively, it might have been a greater success and had the opportunity to continue in its original form to this day.

12 see page 70.

Romanian Orphans

Toward the end of 1989, after the fall of the Ceau¸sescu regime[13], I started to hear the horrendous news stories that began to appear about conditions in Romania and, in particular, the sickness and suffering of orphaned and abandoned children there. I learned that despite food shortages and poor conditions, Ceauşescu had been determined to increase the population of the country.

He had apparently pressured women into becoming pregnant, using various inducements and punishments to try and ensure that each woman produced up to four children[14]. As a result of this policy, tens of thousands of children were dumped in state institutions because their families could not, or would not, care for them. Others were handicapped or actually orphans.

To make matters worse, thousands were infected with the AIDS virus. It is said that this came about because of repeated blood transfusions with reused, infected needles and contaminated blood that was used to "build up" the children. It has even been alleged that children may have been deliberately infected as part of a gruesome government experiment[15].

I spoke to one of the New Stream managers, Albert Barelds, who was also a trained social worker, about how these children might best be supported. It was very difficult to get accurate information about the extent of the problem, since Romanian government agencies were in disarray following the revolution, I therefore asked Albert to visit Romania to get first-hand information and to investigate how it might be possible to contribute toward improving conditions. Albert flew to Bucharest in March 1990 and visited a major hospital there. He was very shocked by what he found, and I am grateful to him for writing the following account of his visit for this book:

"I will never forget the hospitals in central Bucharest with small babies and toddlers lying in dirty, metal cribs with no loving care or attention and absolutely no stimulation around them. No toys, no color—only dirty white walls in dark wards. Very few nursing and medical staff were available, and they were either afraid to touch the children or disinterested, as many were orphans

---

13 After a popular revolution, Ceauşescu and his wife were forced to flee and were later captured and executed on December 25, 1989.

14 These included higher taxes for childless couples, banning of divorce and sex education and financial incentives for having more children. As a result, the Romanian population almost doubled in the 1980s.

15 This story was carried in the Romanian daily newspaper, *Evenimentul Zilei* "The Day's Event" after the alleged discovery that all children tested were found to be infected with an identical AIDS virus strain, an event that is apparently exceptionally unlikely, as many different strains exist. It has been alleged that a foreign pharmaceutical company paid for the children to be experimented on in order to investigate the AIDS virus, and that the government may have believed that, since the children were all orphaned or abandoned, there would be no comeback. This claim has not been substantiated but many believe this to be the appalling truth.

and/or from a gypsy background and therefore discriminated against. When I visited a few of the orphanages around Bucharest, I realized that the situation was so much worse than we had envisaged.

"Hundreds of children, from babies to early teens, were kept in poor buildings with hardly any trained staff to monitor them, let alone care for them. I cried when I saw the conditions that these children had to live under: no care plans, no schooling, no sport, no mental or emotional stimulation, no support and hardly any food, while control was achieved through physical punishment and enforced isolation. When in poor health, the children were given blood transfusions rather than a proper diet and medication! Needles were used over and over again, obviously increasing the rate of infection. During my few days in Bucharest I was also told by senior health department staff that the situation I had observed was serious, but nothing compared to what was happening in many orphanages in rural Romania. I realized that the future for these children was very, very bleak".

It was decided that we could best help by focusing aid at a specific institution, preferably outside of Bucharest, since most of the foreign aid was initially being concentrated there. Albert therefore made a second visit to Romania in June 1990, and this time visited country orphanages and regional hospitals in Galati and Constanza. In Galati, he found even more harrowing conditions:

"The scenes I saw were horrific and should not have been possible as they were so inhumane. Groups of children without any clothing were left to sit in their own excrement in dark rooms with no ventilation. Physically and mentally disabled children were kept in metal cribs, and had become injured and disfigured through their longstanding confinement.

"Children were kept in an outside area not fit for a dog, and the only attention I saw any of the children get was punishment. The smells in some of the rooms made me physically sick and made me want to turn around and run away. Yet of course I could not. I had made up my mind, in the first of the many orphanages that I visited, that the very least I could do for the children was to share a few moments with them and let them know that someone cared. These visits left mental scars that were very hard to live with for many months after my return."

Following Albert's report from this visit, it was decided that we would focus our aid on the Galati Hospital since it was of a size appropriate to what we might be able to deal with from the Netherlands. We connected with a few dedicated and enthusiastic construction workers from Amsterdam who were willing to go to Romania during their summer holidays in order to build toilets and washing facilities, install heating and so on. We were also able to provide toys, clothes, food and other provisions. This raised the spirits of the children and staff enormously, and the child mortality dropped dramatically from around twenty per year to less than six per year. We continued to provide support until it was possible for maintenance of the institution to be taken over by a Dutch Christian organization.

Today the situation in Romania is much better, since various aid organizations have improved conditions in many orphanages and other institutions. There is also now increased access to retroviral drugs for children infected with AIDS and some decrease in the total number of children in these institutions. However, the need for aid and support is still very great, as tens of thousands of children remain abandoned in such institutions with very little hope for the future. I have since personally witnessed similar conditions in other countries, notably the Ukraine, where the Fred Foundation has been extensively involved in a number of projects[16] for several years now.

Reflections
Embracing Humanity

In various experiences I have found that I needed to go beyond my own belief systems while at the same time remaining true to myself and trusting my heart. I realized that it is important to use not only my mind and intellect but also my heart and intuition.

Looking into the eyes of fellow human beings, I feel connected and am reminded that we are all part of one human family. Approaching the suffering of others with compassion and open-heartedness has shown me the common humanity that links us all. I have also learned how sometimes the simplest of interventions such as clean water, hand washing or even just a smile can have a really profound effect.

In working with the Red Cross I thought a lot about the relationship between the so-called developed and under-developed worlds and came to think of our society as en-veloped, that is, restricted by over-complicated systems and structures that weaken rather than empower us. I also became more aware of the importance of approaching others in their context with respect for their own culture and social systems, rather than rushing in and imposing Western values and belief systems or exporting our own stress.

16 See Part III, Contributions 4, 6, 16, 20 and 32.

This also made me think about the difference between emotions and feelings—a concept that I explore in more detail in Part II. It seemed to me that the people I met in the developing world's rural areas were often more able to "go with the flow" in their lives and were more in touch with their feelings. I began to explore the idea that reconnecting with our deeper feelings may be a key step in rediscovering our hearts, connecting with the Infinite and becoming able to enter more deeply into the service of humanity.

This led me to my third Key:

KEY 3: *We can rediscover our hearts and serve humanity.*

AFFIRMATION: *By expanding my consciousness I can integrate my mind and heart and serve humanity compassionately.*

CHAPTER 4
Freeing Myself from Fear: Work in Progress

Hand in hand with my journey in "rediscovering my heart", I also went through a series of experiences, which helped me towards a deeper understanding of the importance of empowerment. In autumn 1985, while still living in Geneva, I first heard audiotapes by Jerry Jampolsky, an American psychiatrist who developed a psycho-social-spiritual approach to health known as Attitudinal Healing. The central theme of the tapes was taken from his first book, *Love is Letting Go of Fear*.

What I understood from Jerry was that our innate nature is loving, but its flow can be blocked off by fear. Listening to the tapes, I was able to understand this concept at a deep level for the first time, which brought about a dramatic breakthrough in my thinking. I began to realize how much, even unconsciously, many of my attitudes and actions were guided by internal fears.

This made me reflect particularly on people's attitudes, including my own, to all the predictions of impending doom and imminent cataclysms that were rife in the 1980s. I have already mentioned the prediction I was given at the YPO conference about a cataclysm that was due to occur in 1984 but which, thankfully, failed to materialize. Yet this was only one of several that I and others encountered, and I realized how these predictions had created a climate of anxiety, without the underlying fears being really addressed. One situation I encountered demonstrated this powerfully.

The psychic American woman and her husband whom I had met at the conference had decided to act on the "messages" she had received predicting an imminent world cataclysm. Like many others who had heard these "messages", they decided to move to a so-called "safe" mountain area in the US and to build a house, including two small apartments and a healing facility. I had come to know both her and her husband quite well by this time, and she invited me, and a business friend of mine, to join in the venture. We agreed to substantially finance part of the project and in return we were each to be assigned a small flat that was part of the property. This would be available for use by our families but could be used by this lady and her family at other times.

In due course the property was completed and one evening my friend and I, and our then wives, were invited to visit the complex for the first time and to have dinner together. In the course of the evening, to my shock, the psychic proceeded to have a major argument with her husband. The disagreement continued for some time in front of everyone and we all were pretty disturbed by it. All of a sudden, in the midst of all the discord, I had a powerful moment of clarity. I suddenly saw the psychic and her husband in a different light from the "spiritual" people that I had perceived them to be, and instead realized that they appeared to be full of fear. I also realized that I was actually supporting that fear by being involved in the project. At the same moment I realized how much of my action in supporting the venture had been precipitated by my own fear about the future and the need to protect my family if a cataclysm did occur. Then I remembered Jerry Jampolsky's words, "Love is letting go of fear", and reflected how, even though I thought I had embraced this concept, I had actually still been acting out of my own fear.

In that moment I resolved to let my fear go and I knew I wanted no part of the venture anymore. Shortly afterward, my wife and I left, and I've had no contact with the woman and her family ever since. In the material sense, this was quite an experience for me, since I had made a financial investment in the property. However, I viewed this as a great lesson from God and simply walked away from it.

Reflecting back now on this event and the "messages", which were so prevalent at that time, but which failed to materialize as predicted, I realize that I did allow myself to be influenced by them to some extent. I can see that they created some fear and anxiety in me, and that I partly allowed myself to believe that those people somehow had greater access to information than I did. This was in part because some of them really were psychically gifted. It did not, however, make them infallible on all issues. Nor did it prevent some of them from manipulating their knowledge to their own personal advantage.

I now realize that this was misguided and that it is much more important to trust firmly in your own inner guidance and to focus on loving rather than on fear. We can choose to let go of fear and instead put our trust in our Creator. Certainly in my own case, the awesome personal spiritual experiences that I have been fortunate to experience in my life, have all occurred at times when I have been able to let go of fear, relax and completely surrender and trust in my connection with the Infinite. Of course, it is also possible that perhaps some of the cataclysmic "messages" were genuine and that maybe the disasters alluded to were averted by people's conscious prayers, or by other means, as has indeed been claimed by some. It is impossible to know for sure.

With Diane Cirincione and Jerry Jampolsky in the early 1990s

Meeting Jerry and Diane

While I was volunteering with the Red Cross in 1986, I went to a conference in Colorado organized by the late singer/songwriter John Denver, and Thomas Crum[17] called "Choices for the Future". Jerry Jampolsky and his partner Diane Cirincione[18] were due to be speakers. Having been impressed by their audiotapes, I was hoping I would have a chance to meet them. In the event, I actually missed their talk through a mishap and was disappointed to only very briefly have the chance to say "hello" to Jerry at the end of the event. However, coincidentally, on my return flight I found myself standing behind Diane at the airport check-in. We got talking and decided to sit together on the flight, where we talked at length. Through Diane I was introduced to Jerry soon after, and finding how

17 Tom Crum is a speaker and workshop leader specialising in conflict resolution and stress management and the author of the book, *The Magic of Conflict*.

18 Dr. Cirincione is a clinical psychologist and international lecturer. She has co-authored a number of books with Dr. Jampolsky as well as being an author in her own right.

much we all had in common, we have all become lifelong friends. My close connection with Jerry and Diane also later led me to establish an Attitudinal Healing Center[19] in the Netherlands for, having seen the wonderful benefits of this kind of work, I wanted it to be available to people in my own country, too.

Empowerment in Health

Through Jerry Jampolsky I was introduced to a remarkable woman, Caroline Myss. Caroline is a pioneer in the field of medical intuition—the ability to intuitively profile a patient's physical/psychological/emotional and family history, using (in her case) only the name and age of a patient and their permission. In this way, underlying conditions may be brought to light and healed. Years of research in medical intuition led Caroline to explore more deeply the dynamics of healing, which resulted in her study of why people do not heal. In investigating the underlying reasons why people sabotage their healing processes, Caroline identified a syndrome she calls "woundology", characterized by a person's reliance on the power of illness for manipulation of his or her world, as opposed to attaining an independent, empowered state of health. She gave me some useful insights into my own life process and it was her encouragement that led me to write this book. She visited the Netherlands on a lecture tour with Dr. Norman Shealey, an American doctor specializing in integrated medicine who used her diagnostic skills with his patients. I became friends with her and we later re-met several times, including at Findhorn[20] in Scotland, where we were both speaking at a conference.

Peace Child

One of the most inspiring examples of empowerment I encountered was with children working on the Peace Child initiative. Peace Child grew out of the music and lyrics of *Alpha Omega*, written by David Gordon[21], and *The Peace Book*, written by Bernard Benson—a children's book about how children helped to bring peace to the world. Gordon became interested in using his music to promote peace and in incorporating Benson's text. He recruited theatre director David Woollcombe, who, with his wife Rosey Simonds, produced a

19 Dr. Jerry Jampolsky founded the International Center for Attitudinal Healing now located in Sausalito, California in 1975. Today there are now over 130 Independent Centers for Attitudinal Healing in 29 countries on five continents, offering free support services to families who are suffering from the effects of chronic or catastrophic illness, loss and grief.
20 *www.findhorn.org.*
21 Best known for launching the career of his brother Steve, as the 1960s pop star Cat Stevens (now Yusuf Islam).

performance based on their synthesis of the two works, known as "Peace Child". David and Rosey went on to establish Peace Child as an organization that aimed to facilitate conflict resolution in different countries through working with children and young people on performances of the musical. In each country, the children rewrite the musical according to their own experiences of violence and conflict, and performances have taken place in many countries, including the former Soviet Union, Central America, Cyprus, the former Yugoslavia, India, Israel and Northern Ireland.

I first met David around 1985 and became involved in supporting the Peace Child initiative. David and Rosey are two wonderful, warm-hearted and genuine people who have worked selflessly to put children first. They believe in the natural intelligence of children and always asked their opinions in developing the Peace Child initiative. In 1986 it brought the first Soviet children to the US on a youth exchange program in a joint Soviet-American production of the Peace Child musical, which toured through twelve cities. In 1987 my family and I joined the Peace Child group, on its return visit to the Soviet Union. At this time there was still a Cold War between the Soviet Union and the US, and the Berlin Wall still stood as a stark reminder of the separation of our different parts of the world.

We traveled with the children who performed the musical in various parts of the Soviet Union. On this trip, we had the opportunity to meet and talk with many Soviet children and their parents and caregivers, and I found these meetings really inspiring. Grim faces on the cold street gave way to warm welcomes in homes. I felt that the musical really played a part in finding a sense of common humanity between us and in bridging the culture gap.

The process of children coming together, which I found very moving, was in sharp contrast with the world of adult conflict we saw on TV. I later learned that when the then President of the Soviet Union, Mikhail Gorbachev, and US President, Ronald Reagan, met for their historic peace talks in Iceland, they were shown the video of the Peace Child musical performed by Soviet and American children.

Soviet-American Citizens' Summit 1988

Because of my involvement with Peace Child and our visit to the USSR, David Woollcombe kindly invited me, in 1988, to the first Soviet-American Citizens' Summit in the US. I went there with my wife Ineke, and together with David and his wife Rosey, we were one of the very few non-US or Soviet participants. At this summit, businessmen and women, writers, musician, artists and military people were all brought together. It was amazing to talk with and listen to all these people, since Westerners had rarely had this kind of contact before. The way Soviet citizens from all walks of life were willing to make contact with us and exchange ideas, despite the background of the Cold War, was very encouraging. President Gorbachev himself was not present, but the delegates included his foreign policy advisor, Rustem Kairov.

Aid to Moscow and Yeltsin's Take Over

This stimulated my interest in helping the Soviet Union. A few years later, Jim Garrison[22], a long-time bridge-builder between the US and the Soviet Union, told me that the conditions in Moscow hospitals were quite poor, so I decided to become involved with bringing aid to them.

Jim, a very energetic and spiritual man, was planning to fly medical supplies to the Soviet Union and invited me to participate. A huge Russian Antonov plane, the largest type of aircraft in the world, was hired from the Soviet Union for this purpose. It left San Francisco for Moscow in December 1991 with all the supplies plus a delegation of twenty, including Jerry Jampolsky. I boarded the plane in Copenhagen, where it stopped for refueling, and I can remember its vast size and all of us seated in the hold amongst the aid parcels (for there were no comfortable seats as in a passenger airline!). On arrival, it took seventy trucks to unload all the aid packages!

Once in Moscow, we had various meetings with people to discuss how we could most usefully offer aid. These included three meetings with the then Minister of Foreign Affairs, Eduard Schevernadze[23]. At a certain point we were also invited to the Kremlin to meet with one of President Gorbachev's chief advisors at the time, Mr. Alexander Jacovlev. The atmosphere was quite tense, and you could feel that the Soviet Empire was beginning to crumble. At the

22 President of the Gorbachev Foundation US, and President and Chairman of the State of the World Forum *www.worldforum.org* and the new Wisdom University. I was introduced to him by Jerry Jampolsky.

23 Schevernadze was Foreign Minister under Gorbachev at this time and later joined Yeltsin after his take over in 1991. He eventually became the President of Georgia.

Schevernadze accepting my colorful tie

same time it was so impressive to be standing in the heart of the Kremlin, which I had previously only seen on TV. The USSR at that time was a super power with by far the biggest land surface in the world. I also remember this visit as one of the most dramatic and impressive times in my life, for it turned out that we were in Moscow at the time of Yeltsin's final maneuvering to take over, just days before Gorbachev's resignation and the end of the Soviet Empire[24].

We were actually due for our final meeting with Schevernadze at the very moment that this actually occurred. We had first met him in his ministry soon after our arrival and, since he was wearing a rather somber tie that day I had, as a spontaneous gesture before leaving, presented him with the colorful tie that I was wearing, which he had good-humoredly accepted. On the fourth day of our visit, he was due to receive us in another building but arrived thirty minutes late, in quite a flustered state. He told us that he had been unable to get into his office, as Yeltsin's men had taken over!

24 A coup by disaffected politburo members opposed to the pace of President Mikhail Gorbachev's reforms took place from 19 to 21 August 1991. It failed and Gorbachev was subsequently reinstated but support had already shifted to Boris Yeltsin, who assumed power following the dissolution of the USSR and Gorbachev's resignation in December 1991.

He stayed for our farewell reception and then left to find out what was happening. It was only in retrospect that we realized at what a momentous point in history we had been in the Soviet Union—the very point of the collapse of the Soviet Empire, which, until then, had always been seen as the greatest threat to Western security. As we watched events unfold over the next few days, we started to think about all the implications of this dramatic change of power. I, like many others, felt real concern about what would happen to all of Russia's nuclear scientists and researchers.

If they lost their jobs through the end of the Cold War, their expertise might go to other countries seen as unfriendly to the West, such as Libya, which was regarded as quite a threat at that time. I wondered if the West might pre-empt this by providing funding and initiatives enabling such specialists to utilize their knowledge on peaceful projects such as power generation. Some months later, I met Gorbachev soon after he had stepped down from his leadership post, and was able to discuss my concerns with him. In 2005, a high-ranking US civil servant told me that over the last decade several hundred million dollars of US government money had been allocated to facilitate the job transitions of these Soviet scientists from the nuclear war industry. It is reassuring to know that this issue was addressed as nuclear armament continues to be a significant global concern.

Meeting President Gorbachev

By this time, Gorbachev was no longer the President of the Soviet Union, but he was still much in demand on the world stage and was busy establishing his Gorbachev Foundation (The International Foundation for Socio-economic and Political Studies)[25] and the Green Cross International. I later had the opportunity to meet Gorbachev myself and felt honored to meet this impressive man. I was invited to meet Mr. Gorbachev at a breakfast meeting hosted by the former US Secretary of State, Henry Kissinger[26]. I was standing talking with Henry Kissinger near to the door when Mr. Gorbachev arrived. They greeted each other and Kissinger then introduced me to Mr. Gorbachev as "my Dutch friend". It seemed funny to be introduced by Kissinger as his "friend" even though I had only just met him! Afterwards, I joined a post-breakfast meeting between Mr. Gorbachev, his assistant/translator Pavel

25 See *www.gorbachevfoundation.org*. It is a non-governmental, non-profit think tank analyzing social, political and economic trends in Russia and the world while promoting democratic, moral and humanistic values.
26 Kissinger was Assistant to the President for National Security Affairs from 1969 to 1975, and Secretary of State from 1973 to 1977.

Mr. Gorbachev singing Russian songs at our home

Palachenko, Jim Garrison, and five US academics. The discussion centered on the offering of academic scholarships in America for Russian students. While this sounded worthwhile, it seemed to assume that an education abroad was a priority.

During the meeting I shared the view I had gained working for the Red Cross and Red Crescent Societies: that it was important to actually visit a country and listen to people's needs rather than just impose Western value systems on them. Gorbachev must have liked this comment for, at the end of the meeting, he said he would like to talk more about this with me. He invited me to arrange a time for us to discuss this further in Moscow. In 1992 I went to Moscow and met with Mr. Gorbachev again. It was interesting to see how Moscow had changed since my last visit, with the first Western-style hotels and office buildings springing up.

I felt honored to have this invitation and was looking forward to our conversations together. As part of this visit, I went to a children's unit in a local hospital and to other places supported by the Gorbachev Foundation. This particular hospital urgently needed a bone marrow transplant unit, which would have been the only one of its kind in Russia for children with leukemia, but State funding for the unit had been lost with the dissolution of the USSR. The project was at a standstill, as the newly established Russian government did not feel obliged to honor the funding commitments of the previous Soviet regime, and Gorbachev and his wife, Raisa, were working to try to get the project restarted.

Moved by the children's plight, I came up with a plan for matched funding that I proposed to Gorbachev later that day. It was agreed that we would both personally commit 25% of the funds to the project (Mr. Gorbachev donated his share from monies that he received from his US lecture tour and on this basis, we would ask the Russian Government to fund the remaining 50%). The government agreed to provide their share, and to guarantee the provision of on-going treatment and maintenance costs, and in this way we created what was perhaps the first public-private partnership in Russia.

After securing the funding, I was able to arrange for the original German contractor to honor the old contract without a price increase. Development got underway and the unit became a reality, and it has since been able to successfully treat many children afflicted with leukemia. A year later we helped set up residential units for parents of the sick children in a building close to the hospital. This was really needed, as many parents could not afford to keep traveling from their homes, often a journey of several days, and the children were deprived of family contact while they were ill.

Mr. Gorbachev made a deep impression on me; he made quick decisions involving a lot of his personal money and influence to help with this, and other, humanitarian causes. He and his late wife, Raisa, whom I met several times as well, both had an authentic, heartfelt interest in people, especially those in need. I really appreciated the trust he put in me to execute this plan.

I made several return trips to Moscow to discuss various projects with Mr. Gorbachev. In the Netherlands, I established a Dutch foundation to raise support and funding for other socio-medical projects in the former Soviet Union under the management of the Gorbachev Foundation. There is still a great need for this type of work in the former Soviet republic, as needs continue for medical care, housing and food supply.

State of the World Forum

Through Jim Garrison I became involved with the State of the World Forum. He flew over from the US to brainstorm together about his ideas for setting up a new world forum to debate important issues such as nuclear disarmament and to create vehicles for global change. He went on to set up the first State of the Word Forum event in1995[27], and these forums ran to the end of the decade, bringing together a network of leaders and other committed individuals and groups dedicated to global change.

In 1995 I attended the first State of the World Forum, which was a great initiative, inviting representatives from many fields in many countries to join together and debate planetary issues from different perspectives in a harmonious rather than confrontational way. There was a fantastic cross-fertilization of ideas at the Forum, and we all came away inspired and with many new ideas for change. It was a great initiative on Jim's part.

At the first Forum, I noticed that women and indigenous people were quite underrepresented and, having discussed this with Jim, I organized a preliminary meeting with ten or so people from around the world to discuss how this representation could be increased for the next Forum. These included: Phil Lane, a native American Indian from Canada; Domenica Ghidei, a Somalian refugee living in the Netherlands; Suthida (later Phil Lane's wife), from Thailand; a native American woman representative from the US government in charge of funding for education of indigenous people; Prince Alfred von Lichtenstein (whom I had met at a conference in the US) and his Chinese partner at that time, Ewai, who has since sadly passed away. This meeting helped to bring about a better representation for women and a more prominent role for indigenous people at the next State of the World Forum.

I particularly remember one of the delegates at a subsequent forum, Thich Naht Hanh[28], whose conduct at a lunch where he was the guest of honor was particularly impressive. While all the conference members sat at tables and were served a three-course meal, Thich Naht Hanh simply sat on the stage, slowly and quietly peeled an orange, ate it bit by bit and then left. I was stunned and ate very little, noting how clearly he had demonstrated that often "Actions speak louder than words". I was also keen to support there being all organic food and self-service at future conferences. I felt it important that we should consider where the food came from, how it was purchased and its environmental impact. I felt that if meetings like this Forum could encourage participants to think about food with greater consciousness, this would be more in line with the topics being discussed and would enable us to "practice what we preached".

---

27 *www.worldforum.org*. This is a non-profit organization bringing together a world network of leaders to discuss and act upon issues of global concern.

28 The Vietnamese Buddhist monk, peace and human rights activist, poet and author.

Food purchasing is actually for me an example of our culture's excesses, for we tend to constantly buy more without asking ourselves if we really need it. Studies have also suggested that in the West we throw away around 40% of the food that we buy, either as leftovers or as food past its sell-by date. By any standards, this is an appalling waste, especially considering the countless numbers of people in the world who go hungry every day.

The Start Fund

Following the State of the World Forum, I became involved in a new project that brought together many different strands of my experiences, along with my increasing understanding of the importance of empowerment. The trigger was the matched funding principle for the bone marrow transplant unit in Moscow that worked so well. It inspired me to establish a new fund in the Netherlands in 1996 under the auspices of the Fred Foundation, to provide empowerment through seed funding. It was originally called the CIE Fund—Care for the In-vironment (Health) and the Environment[29]—but for simplicity has since been renamed as the Start Fund, highlighting its provision of seed funding to kick-start projects.

The aim of the Fund was to stimulate self-reliance and to provide individuals or groups with financial support for inspiring projects in the fields of both health care (for which I coined the term "in-vironment") and/or the environment. The Fund awards start-up or "seed" money, typically between 20 to 50% of total project costs, on a sliding scale in relation to the total costs of the project, which must be below 100,000 euros. Applicants must raise the remaining project costs from other sources within nine months as part of the conditions of funding. I see the Start Fund's role as that of kindling fires, whereby we provide the seed funding to support people with inspiring ideas and the skills to implement them while they commit to obtaining the matched funding from elsewhere. This system has worked well and the Fund has now successfully supported over a hundred projects.

One example is Bahia Street. This is a non-profit organization based in Salvador, in the province of Bahia, Brazil. It is focused on breaking the cycle of poverty and violence by education in Bahia through:

- *providing a place of peace, where young women, youths and adolescents on low-incomes can deal with racial and gender violence and oppression*

---

29 For more details on the CIE fund, please see *www.fredfoundation.org*.

- *educational programs for impoverished girls to become educated and committed leaders within their communities*
- *social and emotional support for these girls and their families*
- *mobilizing the community (professionals and institutions etc.) to support educational and health activities*

Other projects include a women's development project in Russia, various projects in the Ukraine and a kindergarten in Rwanda, to name but a few. These projects are based on the principle of small-scale support—modest amounts of money used to good effect locally—showing how well this type of funding can work, even in the poorest areas. The CIE/Start Fund projects have been genuinely inspiring to witness and they support my dream of contributing towards an empowered society.

Reflections
Global Change and Empowerment

One of the principal things that I learnt through my experiences during this period was the role of fear in blocking empowerment. I realized that the people I had come into contact with who were dedicated to service and who inspired me, had the courage to go beyond fear and doubt. This enabled them to spark changes within themselves and also locally, nationally or even globally.

I realized that empowerment means taking responsibility for our own lives, rather than giving our power away to others. It also involves supporting others in making their own choices.

This led me to my fourth Key:

KEY 4: *We can empower ourselves.*

AFFIRMATION: *I choose to free myself from fear to allow changes within and without. In supporting myself and others in this process we can together develop a caring and sharing society.*

CHAPTER 5
Love of Nature

I developed a love of outdoors from a young age on forest walks with my grandfather. Early on some Sunday mornings, he would turn up at our front door on his morning walk and ask if I'd like to come with him. We would walk into the forest, mostly in companionable silence, just listening to the sounds of the birds. My awareness of the beauty and power of nature grew through my life and travels. I have always especially loved the Alps and feel so good in the snow and the crisp, clean environment there.

Another impressive experience I had in appreciating the beauty of our planet was when I first visited the US as a young man in 1971. I had never before encountered such vastness as I saw on the American plains and was also struck by the contrast with the high plateau (mesas) that rose suddenly from the landscape. The Grand Canyon and the Petrified Forest were particularly dramatic and so different to the Alps because of their enormous scale. The Alps felt cozy by comparison! I also particularly remember one day when we were walking on the planes of the Petrified Forest. On one side of me I could see clouds with a rainbow and rain showers creating "rain rays" while on the other side I saw sunbeams and sunrays in changing patterns as they touched different parts of the landscape.

In the late 1970s and early 1980s, I was jogging long distances regularly and spent a lot of time outdoors. Yet I was so preoccupied with the actual exercise that I didn't really notice the environment around me much, except to think, "When I retire I'd like to spend more time enjoying nature." In the early stages of our marriage, my wife and I used to go for a walk with the children each Sunday. I used to really enjoy these excursions into the countryside, but after a while my wife didn't like going so much anymore and as the children became older they, like most adolescents, preferred walking through shopping malls to walking in the fresh air!

Our culture tends to respect artificial things more than anything from nature. In general, people are more likely to be excited by the "miracle" of the latest hi-tech gadget than the miracle of a flower developing from a seed. I believe this is a result of cutting ourselves off from our inner nature. Aren't we numb to much of our feelings and don't we over-emphasize our mental capacity? Much later in my life, through my "paranormal" experiences, I feel that I was given an insight into nature at a deeper level. I saw that the reflection of the Infinite could be experienced in nature—in its diversity and beauty. We might see the Divine in a leaf or flower, for example. But it is with our consciousness that we can truly appreciate nature as "Divine energy" in action and experience a sense of wonderment. Our own perception of nature's beauty is an aspect of this divinity, too. Our feet and toes, which represent such a small part of our total body surface area, ensure our connection to the earth via gravity—another miracle of the Infinite: the miracle of balance[30]! The more I became aware of nature the more I felt one with her. Nature has no voice or vote and no official ambassadors and yet I have come to believe that it is our universal "mother" and of vital significance to us all.

As I came to appreciate more and more not only the beauty of nature but also its great importance to the planet and its future, I became increasingly involved in supporting and establishing environmental charitable projects. Some of these have been aimed at increasing environmental awareness; for example, the Foundation for Environmental Awareness, founded in 1989. It created and supported several projects, including an environmental musical, with teaching materials and audiotapes, which went to many schools in the Netherlands (see page 204). It aimed to increase environmental awareness and encourage recycling and other environmentally-friendly activities. Other projects/sponsorships have enabled children, young people and adults to actually experience nature—often for the first time.

An example of one of these sponsorship activities was Robert Swan's Inspire Antarctic Expeditions[31], which takes young people, teachers, businessmen and businesswomen on an amazing adventure into the Antarctic. They can experience the awesome magnificence of the iceberg landscape, learn about the fragile ecosystem of the area, and participate in environmental clean-up operations. His expeditions have so far removed over 1,000 tons of rusting metal debris and garbage from the area and more are planned. I got to know Robert and the Fred Foundation sponsored one of his expeditions.

I was also part of the start-up team for a group that organizes leadership training in wild and natural environments. The aim is to bring people in leadership positions from the business community into nature in order to reconnect them with their inner nature and the outer natural world so that they will consider it more in their policy-making and business decisions. An executive who went on one of these group wildlife experiences in South Africa came back

---

30 I once read a piece by an American journalist which suggested that the poorer your equilibrium, the worse your health may be and vice versa.

31 Robert Swan OBE, is the first man to walk to both the North and South poles. He has since dedicated his life to ensuring the preservation of Antarctica—the world's last great wilderness. He was a keynote speaker at the Rio de Janeiro Earth Summit. His ice-strengthened vessel, 2041, is named after the year in which the review of the Environmental Protocol of the Antarctic Treaty will begin. See *www.2041.com*.

and told me it had profoundly changed his life. His previous approach to work had been based more on competition. Now he made a shift in his working life, and common ground and nature became greater priorities in his decision making process.

Meeting Jane

I met Jane Goodall[32] in 1995 at the State of the World Forum in San Francisco, USA and was very impressed with her well-informed and sincere lecture. I really felt that she was someone who "walks her talk". We became close friends and in 1997 I went with a group of people from the State of the World Forum to visit her research facility in the Gombe National Park in Tanzania. It is here that Jane did most of her groundbreaking research on primates, and it has become the longest-lasting wildlife research project in the world, fifty years old in 2010. Jane is particularly known for naming the chimpanzees she studied. When she originally submitted details of her research to Professor Robert Hind at Cambridge University, he told her that each chimpanzee must be numbered. Jane, however, insisted on using the names and eventually he accepted this. This seemingly trivial point was pivotal in helping scientists to see that animals are not just "cases" but have identities and personalities, too. She did a lot of important work to demonstrate how individual each chimpanzee's personality is and to illustrate novel aspects of their behavior that had not previously been understood.

Fred the Chimpanzee

Jane gave me the honor of having a chimpanzee named after me in early 1997 but we had not seen him during our stay at Gombe. She told me that he had become ill and so I was prepared for this if I saw him. We were about to leave to go back to the town of Kigoma (a two-hour boat ride away) when someone came rushing down to our boat calling out, "I have seen Fred!" So we went back into the forest while everyone waited on the beach near the boat and I was lucky enough to see him. He was just a young chimpanzee and indeed looked in poor health. At one point our eyes actually met—it was a very special moment for me. More than one month later, back in the Netherlands, I became seriously ill with a high fever and was taken to hospital. Strangely, around the same time that I became ill, Fred the chimpanzee died. Jane later told me that she did not dare to tell me about Fred's fate until I recovered as

32 Founder of the Jane Goodall Institute (www.janegoodall.org) and a UN Messenger for Peace.

Fred the chimp with his mother (behind, partly obscured)

she believes in the meaning of coincidences and, knowing how sick I was, she did not want to influence my state of health at that time.

Once recovered, I helped found the Jane Goodall Institute in the Netherlands with its "Roots & Shoots" program. Jane is now over seventy years young and still very active and busy setting up Roots & Shoots groups all over the world. The aim of this innovative program is to inspire young people of all ages around the globe to take action in their communities to help people, animals and the environment we all share. Jane has a family home in the UK but returns to Tanzania at least twice a year. She travels around 300 days a year to talk about the Jane Goodall Institute projects, including Roots & Shoots, and how we all make a difference with our actions every day. She was also been appointed a UN Messenger for Peace by the former UN Secretary, Kofi Annan and re-appointed in 2007 by UN Secretary General Ban Ki-Moon.

Respect and Compassion for Life

Jane has done much to highlight the need to preserve animal habitats in the wild and to argue against abuse of animals in science, captivity, films, etc. and to work with local communities in conservation endeavors. I strongly believe that all animals should be treated with compassion and respect. Such an approach could transform our farming systems, improve the well-being of animals and benefit humans in the process.

For example, I once read a report by a farmer who said that when he played classical music to his cows, their milk yields went up and their rate of infections went down. I was also interested to read about some work done by Professor Popp, back in the 1980s, on light emissions known as photons. These photons can be measured and, as part of his work, he investigated the photon emissions from different foods, and apparently found that organic, free-range eggs had twice as many photon emissions as battery hens' eggs.

This suggests to me that the hens with better living conditions produced eggs with greater vitality and "life force". I have come to believe that food that has been given careful attention during preparation and which has been cooked with love, is probably much more nutritious than food that has been mass-produced without any love or awareness. If food is eaten with conscious gratitude for all the good it is doing us, the effect might be even greater. Perhaps one day it may be possible to validate and measure this effect and the "light energy" of food might even be included on labels!

We can also see this in an even wider context: that the principle of awareness, respect and love applies to all life, in whatever form it takes. For we are not apart from nature but are part of her; and we are governed by the same laws, living on the same planet as all the other expressions of life. It is this sense of wholeness that I felt so deeply in my paranormal experiences when I was opened to the Infinite. Yet I was to find myself tested to the limit on this very issue of wholeness from quite a different direction—within my own family.

My Family: Wholeness and Separation

I was present at the births of my three daughters and regard their births amongst the most important events in my life. My own father did not pay that much attention to his children as he was always working and I missed having many experiences with him. For this reason, and because I simply wanted to, I decided to spend as much time with my children as possible.

I have always really enjoyed time spent with my daughters: playing games with them and making up bedtime stories – we had great fun together. One series of stories that I invented for them was the adventures of some characters that I called Tom, Tim and Tanneke. They loved to hear stories of all the things these three got up to and we were very surprised when, years later, I happened to come across a children's book with these three names as the title!

Sadly, what once was a big dream of having a happy family became in the end the reality of a couple crumbling apart, with three innocent children who also had to deal with this very sad truth. Plans of how Ineke and I would grow together and support one another were not fulfilled. Communication became difficult. The love and beauty that we once shared had faded away and frustration and irritation came in its place. It was very painful to see how our children were affected by the dysfunctional relationship of their parents. Of course, I accept fully my part of the responsibility for the failing marriage.

We went through an excruciating time of separation and finally divorce. I choose not to go into more detail here as, in my view, it would not serve a purpose. The process itself has already been harmful enough for all involved. In December 1996, we reached a settlement. I could go on with my life and our children were freed from this painful period that was not caused by them. More than ten years later, their mother and I now have an amicable relationship and are able to function as parents to our three wonderful, adult daughters.

As a result of my experiences, I can empathize a lot with the pain that fathers and children go through in divorces and separations, and I am especially aware of how precious the time with your children becomes once you are no longer in the family home. I was also very aware of "stolen" or "lost" time—how time that the children are allocated to spend with you can "disappear" if they nip back home to get something they forgot and now want, and sometimes do not return for some time. I had the privilege of getting a place very near to our old family home and of being flexible with my time and able to fit it around the children's schedule, so this did not become a big issue.

However, I am very aware that many working fathers do not have this privilege and can feel very cheated when their few precious hours with their children slip away. I have always valued having "quality time" with each of my daughters and tried to make time for them, both together and individually.

Integrating Male and Female

I had long been aware that as a man I found it difficult to express my feelings. My life in business had strengthened my intellect and analytical ability. It developed my skills in coordinating and the side of me that was dynamic, active and good at putting ideas into practice. However useful these traditionally "male" qualities were, they were not fully in balance with the other side of me: the part that was more receptive, more in touch with my feelings, more involved in caring and sharing. I was aware how difficult it can be for men, including me, to embrace this "female" side. These "male" and "female" sides exist in both men and women and both are important.

Yet when I reflected on this in the late 1980s, it came to me very clearly that the chaos in the world was due to an imbalance of "male" power: too dominated by the intellect, too competitive, too aggressive. I felt it was important to somehow help to redress this balance, especially in men, starting with me.

To support this process, a friend of mine, Marieke de Vrij, helped me to establish a men's group in 2002. I had known Marieke since 1989 and knew her to be a gifted and inspired workshop leader. Funnily enough when I mentioned my idea for the group to her she said that she had been feeling for several months that she wanted to contribute to this idea, too. We started the group with around twenty men, from a variety of different ages and backgrounds.

The group now meets three times a year for a full day. In each session the men share stories and experiences and at the end receive guidance from Marieke. During the time that this group has been active, we have seen some remarkable changes in all of us, as attitudes change and we become more able to open our hearts and express our feelings.

Health Care Experienced Differently

Meanwhile, my gradual healing was reflected in other developments in my life, as I became involved in developing health care further in society at large. Building on my experience with the integrated health care center, New Stream, and my continuing conversations with Professor van Praag, I was thinking more and more about developing further integrated health care initiatives. I felt strongly that our current orientation for health care, being based on identifying the problem and then fixing it, was inadequate and that we needed to look more at the concept of wholeness in this as in other fields. I wanted to highlight the importance of the whole body and the whole person, instead of just focusing on the diseased part of the body or the illness.

After all, no doctor actually heals a cut in a person's finger—the healing power that comes through our body does it. I felt that health care needed to somehow incorporate the role of our innate wisdom and healing power. I was also stimulated by my encounter with Patch Adams[33], the medical doctor and clown who I had met at the Soviet American Citizens' Summit in 1988. He had been entertaining delegates in a full clown's costume on a giant unicycle! Patch has dedicated his life to bringing the "fun, friendship, joy and service" back into health care, and defines global "peace, justice and care" as his life's mission.

I liked the way Patch interacted with people and appreciated his sense of fun, which has brought so much healing to people's lives. He has done so much to revolutionize our approach to health. We spoke together at the conference and he gave me his book, *Gesundheit*! (Good health!). He told me about his Gesundheit! Institute Hospital Project in West Virginia, a proposed forty-bed rural community hospital, with a new model of health care based on compassion and friendship, with free treatment, which was aimed at changing society. I subsequently met him several times in the US and, impressed by his work and ideals, I invited him in 1991 to give some lectures in the Netherlands. This lead, some years later, to setting up a conference in The Hague called "Healthcare Experienced Differently" to explore new ways of approaching health care.

In January 1994, I arranged the conference with the help of some friends. Over two hundred doctors, nurses, caregivers, health charity representatives and political leaders attended. I invited Patch Adams and Freek de Jonge[34] to participate in the conference as well. The idea was for participants to sit together and look at health care afresh.

Increasingly I had become aware of the need to get beyond the cycle of "problem-solution" to a more holistic way of seeing ourselves and the world around us. This applies also to health care, where the conventional model is of a patient who has an illness (problem) that needs healing (solution). I make no judgment about this model, but I wanted to explore fresh approaches as well.

---

33 For more on this and Patch's work see *www.patchadams.org* and also Patch's contribution to this book on page 216
.**34** Freek is The Netherlands's leading cabaret performer and stand-up comic. He is also a novelist, singer and TV presenter. See *www.freekdejonge.nl*.

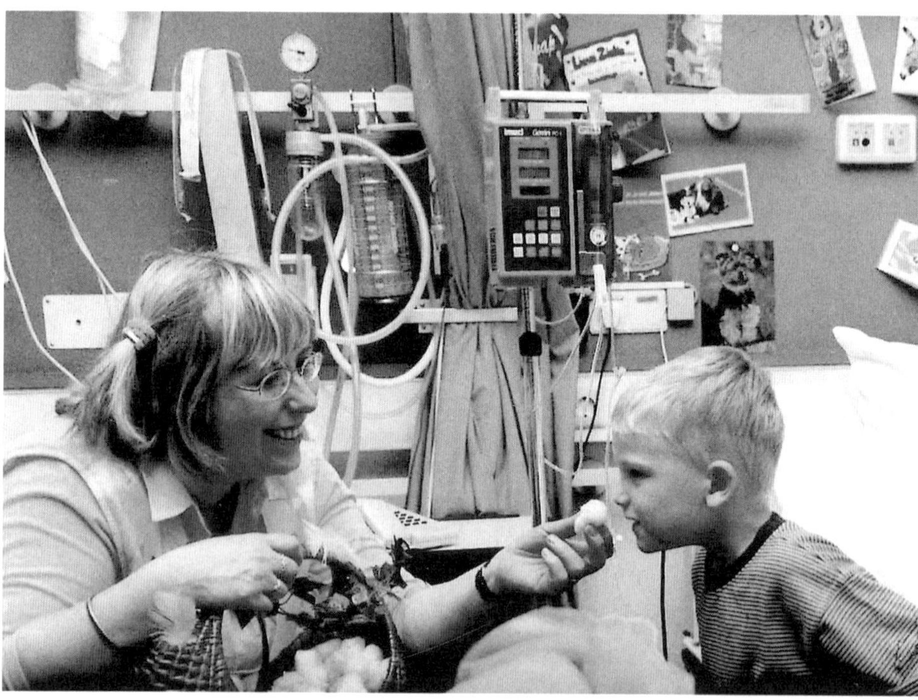

Members of "Experiencing Healthcare Differently" in action

My idea was based on the fact that a patient, even one who is seriously ill, is alive so they must be at least partly healthy. So we could seek to work to extend that healthy part so that, in the end, the illness vanishes.

One of the outcomes of the conference was the setting up of the foundation, Healthcare Experienced Differently, (now called The Healing Company[35]). The foundation was set up jointly with myself, Lydia Helwig-Nazarowa, Pieter Sluis and Sandra Kloezen.

It has now been operating in the Netherlands, in one form or another, for many years, involving nearly two hundred volunteers. Typically, at a hospital, health care facility, or nursing home, the volunteers go to the wards for one or two days and entertain with music, songs, storytelling, clowns and even give foot massages. Ordinary pillowcases are replaced with colored ones; all the hospital staff—cleaners, nurses, doctors, administrators—are invited to wear tags with only their first names; everyone is given little gifts, given massages, things to taste and smell and so on. In this way, everyone's sight, smell, taste, hearing and touch experiences are stimulated in new ways as part of their healing.

Just these simple little changes can have a profound effect. I remember once taking the elevator in a health care facility being visited by our group that day and sharing it with a medical professor who was wearing one of the first-name-only badges in place of his usual formal one. A young nurse got on at one of the floors and seeing his label greeted him beamingly with "Hi John!"—something she had never dared to do before. It was interesting to see how this broke down barriers between them.

Another moving example of Healthcare Experienced Differently in action was the experience of my old friend, Dorine Bijl, a singer and therapist, visiting an old people's home one day with the group. She noticed an old man sitting alone in a chair in a corner and wanted to go to him. One of the home's care workers tried to discourage her, saying it would be a waste of time, as the man had not responded to anything for years. Dorine went over anyway, sat next to the man, and started to sing an old song from around the time of his youth. To her surprise, she saw tears start to well up in the man's eyes, which made her realize that he had taken note of her song.

This simple action showed the care workers that this man was a human being with feelings and, although he did not react much in a normal everyday setting, he was aware and indeed able to respond to the right stimulus. This simple story illustrates the importance of different attitudes in healing.

---

35 See *www.hetbeter.nl.*

"I Have AIDS—Please Hug Me"

I experienced something similar in the Attitudinal Healing support groups set up by Jerry Jampolsky and Diane Cirincione at their International Center for Attitudinal Healing in Sausalito, California in the face of a new crisis in public health: AIDS. When people first started to become more aware of HIV/AIDS, around 1982, there was a lot of fear and anxiety, coupled with ignorance about the disease.

Diane and Jerry responded to this by establishing Attitudinal Healing groups for people diagnosed as HIV-positive. I was privileged to be allowed to sit in on one of these group meetings and was deeply moved by the members' accounts of their experiences. The group, made up of around twenty men, sat in a circle and shared their thoughts and feelings. I particularly remember a man talking about the heart-rending loss of his partner, previously a group member, and the realization that he himself would be dying soon. The loving acceptance within the group was very touching. At each meeting, they would be dealing with the difficult loss of members who had already died from AIDS as well as the addition of newly diagnosed members.

A poster that Jerry and Diane created in 1986 to address psycho-social needs and also educate about the disease particularly struck me. It had a simple drawing of a person and the slogan, "I have AIDS—Please Hug Me. I can't make you sick!" This seemed very potent to me, as all of these people were as much in need of love, hugs and physical contact as anyone, yet they were in some cases being shunned like lepers, with many people being unnecessarily fearful that they might catch the disease.

The WHO (World Health Organisation) in Geneva produced the poster in numerous languages and distributed it to about 140 countries. In 2008, for the 60th Anniversary of WHO, this poster was selected as the best educational tool used worldwide and was chosen to represent all of the AIDS work done by WHO during their year-long anniversary celebration, beginning at the United Nations Headquarters in New York City. My contact with the HIV+ Attitudinal Healing group left a deep impression on me. It seemed to me that this group exemplified Jerry's theme of "Love is Letting Go of Fear". Instead of being fearful of the disease, or of those who were HIV+, loving compassion allowed this irrational fear to dissolve. Studies have shown that fear can lead to physical changes in the body, including depressing immune function, so it would seem that fear can actually play a role in disease and dying. Yet, for me, if one had a hundred more years to live or just one more moment of life, the most important question would be the same: "How can I release my fear and find inner peace?"

I HAVE AIDS
Please hug me
J. Keeler
I can't make you sick
AIDS HOT LINE FOR KIDS
CENTER FOR ATTITUDINAL HEALING
19 MAIN ST., TIBURON, CA 94920, (415) 435-5022

Letter in Response to 9/11

At the same time I realized that fear is contagious, for it is easy to be affected by the fear of others. I have also seen this spread of fear take hold in situations such as the rough plane ride that I had while working with the Red Cross; each time, I have seen how love and trust in God can melt the fear away. I was also deeply moved by how, in the aftermath of the horrendous events of the 9/11 attack on the Twin Towers, so many of the phone messages home from people caught in the Towers or on the hijacked planes were powerful expressions of love. This event inspired me to write a piece that I posted on my website and which I reproduce in the box below. I am reprinting it here because I feel that the principles expressed still apply today.

To ALL women and men of this world.

We all live in this world side by side.

We all experience this world by letting our minds and feelings (through our hearts) be inspired. I am one of you and I am still perplexed by what occurred on September 11.

Pain and sadness flash through us all. Especially those that were closely involved with the disaster and its victims; they have been hurt deeply.

People are standing up—we call them leaders—who claim they shall retaliate for the injustice that has been committed and the deep pain that has resulted. If we aim for peace and harmony, is that then our direction? Of course we have to find those that are responsible. Of course we have to hold them responsible and bring them to justice.

Yet isn't it just as important to connect from love with one another to emotionally process the pain and find mutual support? Luckily we can do that with our families and our close friends. Could we maybe also extend our horizons and include in our respect people who think and feel differently to us because they are from different cultures or religions? And can we maybe also include them in our love? Do we always have to agree before we can share respect and love? It does not matter if we walk our path as a Muslim, Jew, Christian, Buddhist or Atheist; we all live together on this earth.

In accepting what has happened, we don't have to agree with it. Our differences could rather be an invitation to dialogue, from the mind and through the heart, so we meet with respect for our differences and in the spirit of inclusion—not exclusion. Let us, both men and women, create space so that we can accept the "female" quality of feeling as well as the "male" quality of thinking. Maybe we can teach ourselves to connect more with our feelings and then our actions will be different as they will come from the heart. In this way, maybe we can help prevent the products of our thinking—that is the result of our mental actions without heart—becoming unguided missiles that fly criss-cross over this world and hit without mercy.

Let us try to look at the things that we have in common rather than at the things that separate us and the implications of both commonality and separation.

Yes, we are different. Yet the fact that somebody is, or some people are, different does not mean we have to exclude them or change them according to our preferences.

Everybody has their own free will. Accordingly, everybody has his/her own responsibility for her/his choices. Whatever our "leaders" decide to do, nobody can take over, or take away from us, our responsibility to act, or not to act. I propose that we all consider the option to choose respect for ourselves, others and what inspires us—to remain in our own power, or to come to our own power. Let's anyway choose to remain calm as much as we can and keep our minds and our hearts, and the feelings that follow, clear and open so that inspiration can flow through us.

We can choose mutual support. We can choose to support ourselves and others, to see and process our fears. We can choose to love one another unconditionally and to not let ourselves be excited into emotions of vengeance in order to retaliate.

Our children and our grandchildren observe us. Often they are depending on us. Let us all live from respect for ourselves, for all others and for Existence, of which we all are an inseparable part, so that our children and grandchildren can experience us as an example.

According to my own truth, life is about all that has been given, and not just about the facts of life. Can we be grateful for what has been given? Can we forgive ourselves and others? I am one of us and I wanted to share this with you. I fall flat on my face too—many times a day. Just as many times I get up again, maybe just like you.

Fred Matser

With thanks to all those that have inspired me and all those that are still inspiring me.

September 22, 2001

Reflections Wholeness and Integration

The Sunday morning walks with my grandfather gave me a sense of the oneness and wholeness that can be experienced in the natural world. I became aware of how nature is both strong and vulnerable and all elements are part of the whole.

Reflecting on this I could see that it is so easy in our daily, urban lives to forget this wholeness or connectedness. Instead, the emphasis on separation leads us to see things in terms of "them" and "us".

I realized that terrible global events like 9/11 or intense personal difficulties can test our belief in these concepts of wholeness and connectedness to the limit. For me, my difficult divorce was an instance of this. Yet these experiences also seem to give us opportunities, challenging us to explore unity in all its aspects. For if we live in a world of separation then we may also miss possibilities for being part of our global family and global home.

This led me to my fifth Key:

KEY 5: ***We can live in the spirit of unity.***

AFFIRMATION: ***By learning to integrate different parts of my being and focusing on our common humanity I can work for the interests of all.***

CHAPTER 6
Spiritual Exploration

Together with all the projects and initiatives I was becoming involved in, new avenues continued to open in my spiritual development. It was as if I was being invited to expand my consciousness to explore different possibilities within the unfolding mystery of the Infinite. More changes came in my personal life and I met a wonderful person, Chris.

The first moment I met her at the home of Jerry and Diane I was struck by her. I looked into eyes that were crystal clear and I sensed the presence of a deep and gentle soul. In her modest, subtle and elegant way, I felt her profound love. Chris, who came from Hawaii, was to join me on my inner and outer journey, selflessly supporting me in all I did, sharing her wisdom, humour and abundant love.

Crop Circles

I have a long-standing interest in crop circles. These mysterious formations started to appear in cornfields in certain parts of the UK in the early 1980s and attracted large numbers of people and worldwide media interest. Although many have dismissed these as hoaxes, and certainly hoaxers have been at work in some cases, some serious researchers decided that this phenomenon was authentic and worthy of investigation.

I had seen various photographs of crop circle and was intrigued by their intricate and precise patterns and wanted to see and experience them in real life. So in 1998, Chris and I went to England, to join a group and see the crop circles for ourselves. We were fortunate that Colin Andrews[36], considered to be one of the foremost research authorities on crop circles, kindly organized the trip for us and acted as our guide. Colin believes that the circles have been created as signs and symbols to give us information about environmental and other earth changes and about what we are doing to our planet.

He told us that most of the circles appear in the UK, although there are a few in the US and that they are almost always in fields of corn. On that occasion we boarded an ultra light open-air aircraft and flew over various crop circles near Marlborough in Wiltshire. In this area alone, almost fifty crop circles appeared in 1998. We marveled at their beauty and structure as we viewed them from the air.

36 Colin Andrews, together with colleagues Pat Delgado, Busty Taylor and Dr. Terence Meaden, was one of the first people to investigate crop circles. For more information on his work, see *www.cropcircleinfo.com*.

One example was photographed by Lucy Pringle[37] and is reproduced, with her kind permission, below.

In 2004 we returned to the same area and happened to get talking with an elderly man in a shop in the village of Avebury, who also turned out to be quite an expert on crop circles. He very kindly took us in his car to visit one of the newest crop circles that had recently appeared in a nearby field.

On this occasion, as previously, we were able to actually walk into the field and enter the crop circle formation itself. Some people have reported different types of sensation when they enter the circles, from feelings of "energy" and elation to more ominous sensations of discomfort and menace. In my case, I can honestly say that I did not feel anything special or different. However, I did distinctly notice that there were hardly any broken stalks in the corn, where it had been flattened to make the design, which would be almost impossible if a human was deliberately crushing the corn to create such a pattern. Although I had heard about this phenomenon, it was still very surprising to witness and made me really think that there must be something behind it that we do not yet understand.

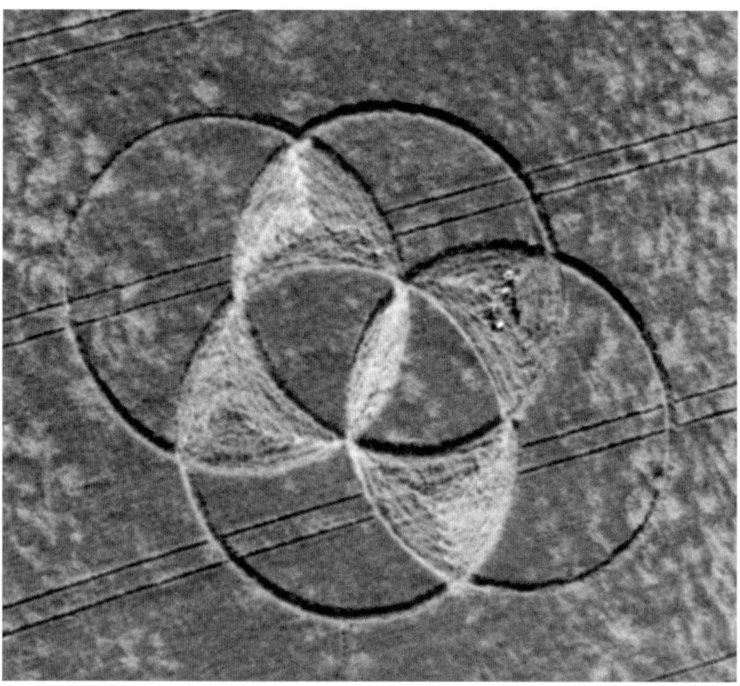

A Crop Circle. Photo © Lucy Pringle and reproduced with her kind permission

37 See *www.lucypringle.co.uk*.

When you study a lot of the images of these crop circles taken over time, it does seem as if there must be some kind of message, or even a language, that is being conveyed in them, as certain types of formation repeat over and over. Another possible explanation is that the crop circles do contain some kind of force that might have a specific purpose, such as healing. We still don't know the real meaning behind these crop circles, but it is certainly a fascinating phenomenon that will no doubt reveal more of itself over time as new crop circles continue to appear.

Synchronicity

Like most people, I have had many experiences of extraordinary synchronicity in my life. One of them occurred around 1997 when I was in Snowmass, a town up in the Rocky Mountains, in Denver, Colorado with my partner Chris. It was a weekday morning and we were in the car just driving around and looking for somewhere to stop and go for a walk. Suddenly, I spontaneously said, "Let's try to the right," and so we took a right turn and found somewhere to park.

We then went for our walk, listening to the sounds of our footsteps crunching in the snow, as the place was completely deserted and there was silence all around. After walking for a while we turned and started to go back towards our car. Some way along the path we saw a group of around seven people appear, walking towards us. They were clad in winter garb and woolly hats, so their faces could not clearly be made out. However, as they got nearer, to my great surprise I found that I suddenly recognized one of the voices! It seemed to be that of Vincent Harding, a priest friend of the late Martin Luther King whom I had met at a conference[38] back in 1990, together with Caroline Myss and Patch Adams. I had become involved in his organization which provides educational opportunities for young black people, but had not had any contact with him since. We soon recognized each other and were amazed that we had bumped into each other in such a remote place, selected purely on the basis of an instinct pulling me up a particular road.

I took this as yet another example of the connectivity of all things. I was also interested to have recognized him purely on the basis of his voice. Considering that I have met many thousands of people over the years, I was also intrigued that a single voice memory from several years before could be that strong and wondered if voice memories may be even more distinctive than facial ones.

---

38 The Council Grove Conference—an annual cutting-edge forum on science meets spirituality, founded by Dr. Elmer Green, the biofeedback expert.

This incident was one of a number of synchronicities that have occurred in my life. Let me share with you some more of these coincidences that seemed in some way remarkable to me. Some of them revolve around birds:

One Saturday, around ten years ago, the weather was lovely and I was sitting working at my kitchen table at home with the doors open to the garden, when a racing pigeon flew into the room and perched on the windowsill in front of me. This had never happened before, even though we often had the doors open in the kitchen. I shooed the pigeon outside and went back to sit at the table, but the pigeon flew back in and once again I had to encourage him to fly back outside.

The next day, on Sunday, it was another beautiful day and I was again sitting at the kitchen table with the doors open, this time reading my paper, when the same pigeon flew in again! On this day it came and perched right on the table in front of me, fixing me with its eyes. I watched it and let it remain there for a while and then again encouraged it to fly outside. Two days later, on the Tuesday, I received a letter announcing that an acquaintance of my father had just died. This man had always been really grateful to my father, who had saved him from bankruptcy by giving him some building work when it was most needed and, I remembered, his hobby had been to race pigeons.

The pigeon in the kitchen

Every year thereafter, he continued to show his appreciation by sending cards and dinner invitations to my family. Had the racing pigeon that had entered my kitchen in some way been a sign from him, indicating his gratitude once more before he passed on? I will never know, but the pigeon never came back after I had made that connection in my mind and no bird ever entered my house thereafter either.

Birds also featured in my learning experiences with Professor Van Praag. We used to sit talking in a little room at the top of his house, which had a window at one end. One day he said to me, "If you look at the window you will see some pigeons appear."

I looked over but couldn't see any birds, yet he told me he could feel that they were coming. Sure enough, within minutes, some pigeons actually appeared and came to sit right on the window ledge.

This made quite an impression on me because the timing was so amazing—there were no birds in sight and yet they then just suddenly appeared, as if out of nowhere, right when he said they would! I wondered if this had just happened by chance, or if it was a regular occurrence at a particular time of day that he knew about, or if he actually had some sort of extrasensory perception or psychic ability that I was not aware of. I never found out and he never explained it to me!

A final bird story is one that I always find both touching and amusing. I was at a lunch party sitting next to the father of a friend of mine and somehow the conversation turned to the subject of life after death. He told me that his wife of many years had recently died and said how much he would like to be in touch with her if there was indeed life after death. As we talked I told him some stories I knew of people who feel they have received messages from "the other side" and which they have taken to be evidence of life after death. This led us to talk about whether or not we believed in God and he told me the following story:

He had been sitting on his terrace at home one day following the death of his wife and wishing that he could believe in God. He decided to issue a challenge to God and formulated the thought in his mind: "If you do exist, then prove it by sending a bird down to sit in front of me within the next three minutes". In less than a minute a small bird flew down and perched right in front of him on the edge of the low terrace wall! I thought that he was going to tell me that this strengthened his belief in God, but no, he ended the story by saying, "But then I thought to myself—oh it's only a 'musje' (a wren, which is the most common garden bird in the Netherlands)." Because the bird was a common one he immediately dismissed the possibility that this could have occurred in response to his challenge to God and instead made it into an everyday experience. Of course it could indeed have just been due to chance, but on the other hand…

I also experienced some extraordinary synchronicity related to the "female principle" when I attended a conference at the spiritual community at Findhorn[39], in Scotland some years ago. It was the autumn of 1989 and I was invited by Jan Backelin to speak about our integrated health center (The New Stream) at a Findhorn conference on business and spirituality. I had the opportunity to meet Peter and Eileen Caddy there, two of the original founders, and felt that I really connected with Eileen, who was a very warm and friendly person. It was there that I met Caroline Myss, who gave a talk at the conference as well. During the same event at Findhorn, I took part in some workshops. One evening I was in a group of twenty-four people and, as part of a group exercise, we were asked to come forward and take a piece of paper out of a box. Each paper had the letter, A, B, C or D written on it and the idea was that the papers would randomly assign each of us to one of four groups to do some self development exercises. To my great surprise once all the papers had been taken, it turned out that we had three groups with five men and one woman and one group with one man and five women. I was the one man in the mainly female group.

The odds for this happening were quite remote. It occurred to me that this was a reflection of my family life, where I have been predominantly surrounded by females: my mother, three aunts at that time, two sisters, (my father, uncle on my mother's side and two brothers had all died), three daughters, my wife and step-daughter (Chris's son sadly died also).

As I reflected on this alignment, I came to the conclusion that a theme in my life is to contribute to the re-empowerment of the female principle, within myself as well as more generally in both men and women. I have seen so often that the problems that I have had in my own life and that we have in society are related to the devaluing of the female. For me, the female principle embodies attributes such as receptivity and openness, which may be present in both women and men.

---

39 The Findhorn Community was begun in 1962 by Peter and Eileen Caddy and Dorothy Maclean. It now operates as the Findhorn Foundation—a spiritual community, eco-village and international center for holistic education that aims to help unfold a new human consciousness and create a positive and sustainable future.
See *www.findhorn.org* for more information.

Initiation

Experiences of synchronicity sometimes take many years to manifest. An experience long forgotten can suddenly link directly into the present in an interesting way. One example of this for me concerned the authors, Elisabeth Haich and Selvarajan Yesudian. Elisabeth was a renowned Hungarian artist, born in Budapest in 1897, who developed a strong interest in esoteric knowledge and yoga and who wrote a best-selling book called *Initiation*. The book tells the story of a twentieth-century European who is initiated into the priesthood in ancient Egypt.

There has been considerable speculation as to how much of the book was autobiographical, fantasy or real memories of past lives, as claimed by the author. I came across the book myself in 1985 while I was living in Switzerland and working for the Red Cross. One evening, when I had almost finished reading it, I attended a dinner and happened to sit next to a lady who worked for the World Council of Churches in Geneva.

During our conversation, I happened to mention that I was reading Elisabeth Haich's book and, to my surprise, my dinner companion not only knew of the book but had also read it herself that same year. As we talked about it, I happened to say how much I would have liked to meet the author when to my amazement my companion said, "Oh, she is still alive—she lives in Zurich!" I could hardly believe that the author was living so nearby, especially since neither of us was native to Switzerland. My amazement was even greater when I learned from this lady that a co-author of several books with Elisabeth, the yoga teacher, Selvarajan Yesudian[40], was living in a village just four kilometers from where my family and I were living at the time in Geneva. I later discovered that Yesudian was still giving yoga classes in Geneva and I had the good fortune to attend some of them.

When I first spoke to him and our eyes met, something suddenly clicked in my mind and I remembered a yoga book that I had read when I was eighteen years old and practicing yoga in the Netherlands.

The book[41] had made a deep impression on me and I always remembered the face of the man on the cover and the intensity of his amazing eyes. I described the book to Yesudian and asked him if he could have been the man

---

40 Yesudian was the son of an Indian physician who went to Hungary in 1936 to study medicine. There he met Elisabeth Haich and they began to teach yoga courses together. They fled Hungary at the end of the Second World War and eventually settled in Switzerland where they established a series of very popular yoga schools. They co-authored some best-selling books on yoga and also wrote books individually. Elisabeth died in 1994 aged 97 and Yesudian followed her in 1998.

41 *Yoga and Health* by Selvarajan Yesudian and Elisabeth Haich (published 1953).

on the cover. To my astonishment he confirmed that it was indeed him! Through Yesudian I was given an opportunity to visit Elisabeth Haich at her home. She was already in her eighties and yet she proudly demonstrated to me that she could still do yoga poses and even put her leg up behind her neck! However she was not very forthcoming about the book—I got the impression that she was tired of having been asked about it so many times over the years—so I never did find out the truth about the book's source.

Still it was a privilege to meet both her and Yesudian in person and the amazing coincidences that had led to these meetings seemed to me an example of the powerful, unseen connections that can exist between people, somehow drawing them together over time and space. But perhaps the greatest contribution Elisabeth Haich and Selvarajan Yesudian made to my spiritual development was contained in the Introduction to her book, *Initiation*. Written by Selvarajan Yesudian, he relates a conversation he had with Elisabeth, then his spiritual teacher:

> *"I don't want you to simply follow me on the path I am following to reach the goal," she has told me. "Go your own way, on the path you select yourself, corresponding to your innermost inclinations. Don't accept any statement because I made it. Even if it is true a hundred times over, it is still not your truth, it is still not your experience, and it will not belong to you. Bring truth into being and then it will belong to you. Regard the lives of those who have achieved truth only as proof that the goal can be reached."*

When I have reflected deeply on different occurrences of synchronicity, which have occurred for myself and others, it seems that they have often revealed a deeper meaning. They may have yielded a spiritual lesson, or led to an experience or meeting that has created a shift in my thinking or action or have appeared to be a wonderful sign of our connection with the Infinite. Often they have focused my attention on phenomena that have not had a rational explanation and this has encouraged me to explore, to reawaken my inner senses and to reconnect with a deeper knowledge of my own spirituality.

On certain occasions these experiences may even become a type of "initiation" or "rite of passage". In all the ancient spiritual traditions, those seeking spiritual enlightenment were required to go through various initiations to test their stage of development and readiness for the next step. Sometimes these initiations (such as those described in Elisabeth Haich's book) involved facing a terrifying ordeal or a great temptation to see if this would deflect them from their chosen path. Only the most dedicated and pure in heart would pass the initiation and therefore be deemed worthy of embarking on the next stage of their spiritual development.

Nowadays some spiritual teachers have suggested that we may go through particular initiatory life experiences in place of some of the more formal initiations of the past. Some may be dramatic events that demand our awareness while others may pass by virtually unnoticed. Yet they are all significant in their own way and exist so that we may learn something that we need to know about ourselves—our strengths and weaknesses, our readiness to progress or to surrender—or about life, consciousness or the meaning of truth.

In my own case, one of these pivotal, initiatory experiences was the time when I unexpectedly came close to death.

Experiencing my own Mortality

The fever that I had caught during my Gombe trip with Jane Goodall in September 1997 continued to trouble me after my return to the Netherlands. My condition deteriorated to such an extent that I was admitted to hospital but there I was misdiagnosed and sent home. My condition worsened and soon I was so weak that I could not walk, or even stand, unaided and was confined to a wheelchair. For this reason, I was readmitted to hospital. This time I was correctly diagnosed with having a particularly virulent and serious strain of malaria—*malaria tropica*. In the days that followed, my openness and receptivity to the Infinite were tested to the limit as I came the closest I had ever come to dying. On the first day after my second admission I was so ill I felt as if all the life force was leaving my body.

I felt like a sack of potatoes and it was hard to take in everything that was happening around me. I was taken for an X-ray but was so weak I could not even stand up for it and had to be draped over the X-ray machine in order for the X-ray to be taken. I felt utterly drained and had no energy to fight for my life and not even any energy to feel afraid of dying. I felt completely helpless yet my consciousness was clear and I remember being able to pray and completely surrendering myself to God thinking, "Father, wherever you want me to be—on this side of life or on the other side—there I will be." After this prayer left my heart, a feeling of calm came over me and I felt full trust in God. To my surprise, I found myself not going to the other side and I'm deeply grateful for that.

Gradually the life force started to return to me but I continued to be very sick for some time and remained in the hospital. I remember one day lying in my hospital bed and, tired of looking at the ceiling, I turned my head to look out of the window. I was hoping to see a tree or something to remind me of the beauty outside. I began to notice a garbage man lifting up the trash cans and emptying them without effort. At that moment I would have jumped at the chance to trade places with him. Without energy to move, or think or communicate, I wished so earnestly that I could indeed change places with him. It made me realize how precious life was as I felt I would do anything, and any job, if only I could get my health back.

After some time, I was able to get about in a wheelchair and was about to be discharged to continue my recovery at home. Before leaving, I was sent for another X-ray and after it had been taken I saw the radiologist looking at it with a frown. I asked him what the matter was and what the X-ray showed, but he wouldn't tell me anything, saying I must wait to speak with the chief radiologist, as he was only a trainee.

My brain went into overdrive, as this was only a few days since my "conversation" with God, and I became convinced that I must have some serious condition like cancer. It was at this point that I was hit by a wave of fear. Twenty minutes later I was informed that the X-ray was clear—the radiologist had only been frowning because he was newly qualified and was concentrating hard to read the X-ray! But in that interim period of twenty minutes, I had spent much of my time contemplating having cancer and examining how I felt about dying. It is only in times of crisis that you take time to consider such issues and I found this a valuable experience. It was amazing to experience fear just a few days after being on the edge of life and death when I had experienced no fear at all.

Thankfully, after being diagnosed correctly, my recovery went well. Yet this remained an important experience for me. Not only was I naturally very grateful to have my health back, but it also made me realize that at any given moment you never know if you are going to live or die—that is truly in God's hands—and you don't know how you will respond until the moment actually comes. I felt grateful to have been given this glimpse, making me more aware of my own mortality and of the preciousness of the lifetime I had been given. This strengthened me in using my lifetime well.

During my hospital stay, I shared a room with another man. Occasionally I could hear him sigh from the pain during the long periods of time that the nurses worked on him. When the curtain that separated us was left open I could see his small frame wrapped in bandages like a mummy. He looked in his mid-thirties. Each day these bandages would be removed and then reapplied. He lived with pain, discomfort and suffering while being unable to move. During a friendly conversation, we shared our reasons for being hospitalized and he spoke with gentleness about his chronic debilitating skin ailment.

Because of his medical needs, he lived in a nursing home for the elderly to receive daily care. Then every two months he would return to the hospital for more intensive treatment. He never complained and the nurses told me he was always charming and friendly to those who had to change all his bandages daily. As he spoke I didn't sense anger, pity or bitterness and I wondered how he could be like this. Witnessing my neighbor's gentle acceptance of his condition made a deep impression on me and helped me on my own healing path. His gracious conduct, gentleness, and acceptance of his situation have always inspired me and stayed with me.

A Gentle Healing

After having malaria, I looked at life differently. Though physically weaker, I began to appreciate things with much more awareness. I was very happy to be alive and to share my life with my partner, Chris, and her loving ways. Her presence was, and is, always comforting.

My healing process took a further turn when we decided to live in the country. My daughters had all graduated from school and I knew I wanted to move away from the noise and bustle of the town to experience a more tranquil, slower, rural environment. On one of Chris's visits, we drove to the east of the country and together we discovered a beautiful farm for sale in Epse. By this time, my relationship with Chris was deepening, yet the commute from her beach home in Hawaii to Holland could not have been longer. One Sunday morning we were talking about our separate homes and lives with an old friend, Egon, when he paused and said, "But do you have room in your hearts for each other?"

Our friend, Jerry had also said something similar. We soon decided to let go of our fears and follow our hearts by living together. Chris made the loving decision to make the move to Epse with me in 1997. It felt so courageous of her to leave her home in Hawaii; and to come from a bright, sunny, colorful island to an often rainy Netherlands so that we could share our lives.

Through Chris, I came to know her daughter Mel, who later became my step-daughter. Mel is a beautiful, elegant young lady with a bright mind. Having three daughters myself, whom I have known all their lives, it was a new experience to come to know this lovely young woman who already had a whole life behind her. Naturally it took time for us to get to know each other. Over the

With my wife, Chris on a bicycle

years we have become accustomed to the different ways that we each look at the world. We have grown much closer and now share a great friendship and can also have fun together.

Not too long after my recovery from malaria we moved to the farm in Epse. As I drove 85km to my office in Hilversum twice a week, I began to notice that as I got closer to the city, my mind would start to speed up. Yet on my return trip, as I got closer to home, I would relax both mentally and physically. In general, living a more rural, slower-paced life, I felt more detached from my business and charity work and was more able to "let go" when I got home. Being in this peaceful part of the country, I felt connected with nature.

My neighbors were mostly farmers and were in tune with the more natural rhythm of the seasons and the land. We enjoyed the quiet life in Epse and we were lucky enough to have a cheerful man named Ferdi living on the property with us. He would help us tend to the cows, vegetable garden and other chores. We couldn't have managed without his help and friendship.

When family or friends came to visit, it was so nice that we had real quality time together, as they would tend to come for longer stays, rather than the quick visits that we so often have in towns and cities. This gave us time to really connect with one another.

In 2000, Chris and I got married. For the wedding we had a house full of family and friends. Some even came from as far away as Hawaii. We had everything planned for our celebration and ceremony nearby. On the morning of our wedding, we woke up around 5 A.M. and both felt awful, as if we were coming down with the flu, and wondered how we would get through the day. Suddenly Chris remembered a CD we had been sent as a wedding gift. The CD was created by a friend, and was meant to harmonize our energies with the sound of Tibetan singing bowls. We listened to it, and fell back asleep. We woke up exactly at 8 A.M., in time for the wedding, feeling completely refreshed, calm and ready for our special day.

Tonio—our Dog

As we lived on a farm, people would ask us what kind of animals we had. Sometimes Chris would reply, "Mice." We got three magnificent Scottish Highlander cows to help us manage the grass in the summer time. As they are hardy animals, they could stay outside all year and it was lovely to see them graze in the fields. Yet after getting to know Chris's daughter Mel's pug, we began to feel we would like to have a dog too. While dining out one evening in a nearby café, Chris spotted a tan and white dog sitting quietly under a table. She thought it was a mixed breed, but after speaking to the owners we found out that the dog was actually an old Dutch breed called a Kooiker. Chris said to me, "Wouldn't it be great to have one of those dogs one day?" Soon after this we heard of a local breeder who had a litter of seven puppies. All the puppies had been sold but the first born was now available again, as the lady who had bought him had changed her mind since she had to move to an apartment. We went to have a look at the puppies and we both noticed one particular dog and somehow felt that he was "our" dog. Later we found out that this dog was in fact the one that was now available!

We brought him home in a box and put him next to our bed that evening on my side of the bed. I awoke several times in the night and each time I put my hand in the box and he would lick my fingers. A few weeks later we received his official pedigree papers and were amazed to discover that he was born on March 15th—the same day as my birthday! We decided to name him Tonio, after a good friend Ton, who was a very sweet man who had passed away. Tonio has now been with us for many years and has become an integral part of the family. He is a very sweet dog. For me, having Tonio in our lives has been a great experience: he just loves unconditionally. He is a real friend. It is fantastic to experience how you can communicate with an animal being, without him being able to talk. I have

With my mother on the farm in Epse

become aware of his different moods. He seems to sense when we are unwell and comforts us. It is amazing to see when we walk into the village with him that he knows where he gets his little cookies or a little piece of sausage at the butcher.

After five years of living in Epse, I was finding it increasingly draining as I was now commuting to my office three times a week due to increased demands of work. The journey was also taking longer, as traffic increased. I also wanted to spend more time with my mother, who was now living alone following the sad passing of her partner of more than twenty years. For more than sixty years she has lived in our old family home, close to my office.

Also, my three daughters all now lived in Amsterdam and the distance from Epse made it more challenging for us to spend a lot of time together. The reality of living on the farm was time-consuming and Chris started to yearn for a simpler life. So for several practical reasons we made the decision to move closer to Amsterdam. Yet we made the choice to take the gifts of our peaceful country life with us onto our next home. Soon after our decision to head east we fell in love with a charming village on a river in between Amsterdam and Utrecht. In 2002 we moved into an historic house there on the riverside. Now it is a short walk over the drawbridge to shops in the village and my office and an easy drive to visit my mother and my daughters.

Psychic Surgery

In 2002, my wife and I had dinner with Prince Alfred von Liechtenstein in Amsterdam. During our conversation, he mentioned that he had arranged for the well-respected Filipino healer, Alex Orbito, to come to Vienna and that we might have an interest to come too. Chris said that she had met Alex years ago while living in Hawaii. Her teenage son Zack's brain tumor had reoccurred and there was little left medically that could be done to further help him. She had heard that Alex was a genuine and gifted psychic surgeon and, as she was without other options, she took Zack to see Alex. Chris admitted being skeptical about psychic surgery, but as a mother she felt that she needed to explore whatever might help. Alex treated Zack four times in two days. Each time he felt better after the healing and seemed to be getting stronger. Weeks later, he said that he wanted to ask the healer a question. Zack called Alex and asked, 'I forgot to ask you if you removed my cancer?' Alex responded, "When I do my healing work, I am an instrument of God. I can only remove negativity at the time; the rest is between you and God." These words from Alex helped her son live during the last year of his life.

Having heard this story, I was interested to meet Alex and see his psychic surgery, where the healer is said to enter the body with his bare hands, with my own eyes. As Alex Orbito was invited to the Academic Hospital in Vienna to give a demonstration to a group of medical professors, this seemed a good opportunity to be present in a scientific setting. After arriving at the hospital in Vienna, we sat around a large boardroom table with a group of about ten older medical professors and physicians. Prince Alfred had arranged this meeting to build a bridge beween the medical community and spiritual healing. We were all introduced to Alex, who seemed to be a very modest, gentle and soft-spoken man. Accompanying him was a kind and warm Dutch woman, Marika Verheijen, who helped organize his workshops and travels.

Prince Alfred told the group that after meeting Alex about twenty years ago, he had had many experiences of Alex's healing. Because of his personal experiences, he wanted to offer this healing to others. This would be a unique chance for the group to witness it for themselves. We were then shown a documentary film of Alex doing healing work. The quality of the filming was not very good and it was difficult to actually see what Alex was doing with his hands. The film was also quite lengthy and, as I glanced around the room, I noticed that several of the medical doctors were taking a nap. It seemed like they had lost interest.

After the film, Prince Alfred asked Alex if he was willing to demonstrate his work on a woman, who was herself a medical doctor from Vienna. The group seemed to become interested. Their female colleague had had a severe skiing accident some years ago and said that she had experienced Alex's healing work previously. Alex was willing to work on her but made it clear that he was not there to do a "demonstration" but to do a healing. He said, "My mission is not to convince, but to allow healing."

Alex went into the adjacent room with the patient to light a candle and pray for five minutes and then we were invited to join them. We gathered closely around the treatment table where the woman was lying calmly. She explained that she suffered pain from her accident. Working on her abdomen, Alex's thumb and two forefingers penetrated her skin. As Alex's fingers moved inside of her, liquid began to drip down her side while he seemed to extract something.

She appeared to be completely relaxed and free from any discomfort. He wiped her skin off with a tissue and the skin appeard to close up and was just a little pink where he had apparently gone in. It all happened so quickly it was difficult to absorb what I had just seen. Alex placed his hands on top of the woman's abdomen, bowed his head as if he had just finished saying a prayer, and said, "OK." With that we all went back into the other room, along with the woman who had been lying on the table, to have tea and sandwiches.

Seeing Alex's fingers apparently disappear into the woman's body right in front of my eyes was a huge shock and I felt quite dizzy. My mind was reeling from seeing what was logically impossible. It was one thing to see such a phenomenon on a video screen and accept it in principle. It was quite another to see it first hand. After a few minutes I recovered and Marika said that Alex would like to offer others there the chance to experience this for themselves. I was very surprised to see that almost all the doctors lined up to have their turn. As I watched each person coming out from having their session with Alex, they seemed to appear years younger and vibrant. It was hard to believe that this was the same indifferent group as at the beginning.

The following day we went to join Alex for further healings and one of the first people to be operated on this time was my wife, Chris. A small tumor had been found on an X–ray in her left breast and Alex now operated to remove it. He put his hand into the side of her breast, and as he removed it I actually saw a small, round lump of tissue, the size of a small marble, between his thumb and index finger. After his "surgery," Chris was left with a small, pink spot on her breast that disappeared after two days. A week later she was X–rayed by her doctor and the tumor was found to have gone.

I had two "operations" that day as well—one on the right side of my belly and one on my chest near my sternum. It was incredible because I actually heard a pop as Alex's hands seemed to enter my body! It was such a strange sensation to feel Alex's hands apparently inside my body, but the whole procedure was over very quickly before there was time to fully process it. The operations did not hurt at all and I felt that Alex did much more than just operate with his hands. Tremendous love radiated through his eyes and the whole experience gave me a very special feeling that is hard to describe.

That evening, instead of going to a party in Alex's honor, to which we had been invited, Chris and I stayed quietly in our hotel room, just allowing the feelings and sensations from the healing to work through our bodies. I felt deeply touched and grateful to have had this experience even though I could not fully explain or understand it. That day Alex operated on about eighty to one hundred people, and he did the same the next day. Throughout, he maintains a prayerful attitude and very quietly moves from one person to the next, speaking only very rarely. He always says his hands are simply guided by God and that he just tunes in and acts accordingly. The outcome of the healing is up to God's will and the individual themselves. He is just an instrument and makes no claims himself about his healing powers.

The next evening, Alex was scheduled to go on an Austrian TV talk show called *Vera*. It was named after the show's host, who happened to also be a medical doctor. Alex was reluctant, as he does not seek to promote himself in such a way and usually shuns the limelight, but in this case he agreed to it simply because Prince Alfred had requested it and made all the arrangements.

When Alex agreed to appear, he told Prince Alfred that he couldn't promise "any instant operation on demand for TV", since his healing work is very sensitive to the surrounding energies. Prince Alfred understood this very well but the TV crew had high expectations for a dramatic "show". However, they were also extremely skeptical; when I chatted with the hostess prior to the show and asked if she believed in psychic surgery, she replied emphatically that she did not.

There were various items on the program and the audience was full of bartenders, as the item preceding Alex was a competition to find the best mixer of cocktails! When it was Alex's turn to appear, Alfred briefly introduced him and his work and then a male volunteer with a certain diagnosis, selected by the program makers, lay down on the table for a healing. Alex placed his hands on the man and tried to concentrate despite all the noise and the distractions of the audience, performers and the bright lights of the studio, but nothing happened. We were all sitting in the front row and everyone waited in great anticipation, yet still nothing happened. After a few more minutes, Alex simply removed his hands, walked quietly over to the hostess, and said that he could not do the healing under such circumstances.

Everyone was shocked and there was a moment of chaos as the hostess did not know how to respond. The show soon ended and some of the audience started to leave. The producer was quite agitated and said to me that this was going to cause a lot of problems, since it had already been announced in the morning press that Alex's healing would be shown on the program the next day. (The show was being pre-recorded).

In the midst of all this, Alex caught my eye and I offered myself as a patient if he wanted to have another try in front of the cameras, but with less pressure now that most of the audience had left and the atmosphere was calmer. Alex agreed, the cameras were quickly re-installed around us and Alex operated on me; but this time, unusually, I found the surgery a bit painful and the post-surgical mark remained for six weeks, whereas in the other cases it would only be visible for about two days. I believe this may have been because the difficult conditions in the studio made it harder for him to connect with the field of healing consciousness he needs to do his work.

Later, an Austrian medical/pharmaceutical group tried to take Alex to court for carrying out non-medical practices, and he has also been similarly persecuted in other countries. Alex is always saddened when this has happened but he just quietly continues with what he sees as his mission. It is said that he has now given over a million healings all over the world, and there are countless stories of people that have been helped or cured by him. These have been written about in many books[42].

42 See his website: *www.pyramidofasia.org* for details of these.

The Visionaries' Circle

Shortly after the terrible events of 9/11 in New York in 2001, Deepak Chopra, the best-selling author, doctor and spiritual teacher, set about creating an Alliance for a New Humanity, which seeks to accelerate a global movement for a better world. It aims to help create global communities of personal and social transformation through connecting, communicating, inspiring and supporting. The Alliance organizes various events, and in August 2007 Deepak invited forty people from all over the world, to come together in Taos, New Mexico for a week, to share visions for a new humanity under the theme, "the Visionaries' Circle".

I had first met Deepak about ten years ago and then met him again in 2006 when our mutual friend Ray Chambers[43] invited me to join him for an Alliance meeting in Puerto Rico. On this occasion I had the chance to get to know Deepak much better and discovered what a wonderful, loving and spiritual person he is. We made a strong connection with one another and, following on from this, Deepak invited me to join the "Visionaries' Circle" group.

In Taos we had a week-long program of talks, meditations, and outdoor activities and there was much profound sharing, learning and exchange of visions. One activity, a ride in a hot-air balloon, had been planned for the middle of the week, but was postponed to Saturday morning because of weather conditions. This meant that some of the group had already departed and could not participate. The thirty or so of us who remained, got up at 5 A.M before sunrise, and went to a place on the plateau above the Rio Grande. There, we had a joint meditation as dawn began to break, just before the start of the balloon ride. As the sun rose, the balloons were prepared for flight, and within about twenty minutes our five balloons took off one by one and then slowly descended into the canyon of the Rio Grande.

It was an amazing experience to float down into the canyon, being carried by the wind with just the sound of the occasional blast of hot air released into the balloon by the pilot to control our height. Occasionally, we came a bit close to the rock on the side of the canyon, blown there by one of the natural air draughts. We really enjoyed the truly spectacular views as we followed the path of the river from above.

After about an hour, our pilot used the burners to release more hot air into the balloon, making it ascend out of the canyon and allowing it to drift a little toward a suitable landing site. Just as we were about to land, we noticed an

---

43 Ray Chambers is an American philanthropist, and the initiator of "Malaria no More USA". He was recently appointed as Special Envoy of the UN Secretary General for Malaria.

open ultra-light plane in the distance, flying towards us. As it came closer, we were able to make out the features of the pilot, who seemed to be really enjoying himself, flying in the early morning on this wonderful bright, nearly windless day. We waved at him and he smiled and waved back as he flew by us. Then we turned our attention to the imminent landing of our balloon. Once on the ground we all helped to deflate the balloon, loaded up the car and then set off to meet our companions from the other four balloons for a small breakfast. Then we all returned to the hotel to continue our meetings together.

We did some short meditations, with Deepak guiding us through some mantras, and then part of that morning's teachings was devoted to the subject of death and dying. I was very struck by how profoundly Deepak beautifully explained the continuity of consciousness through life and death. I was particularly struck by his explanation of the cycle of life and death in our cells. He pointed out that our bodies are composed of cells that each has a limited life cycle, lasting from a few minutes to seven years.

He explained that each cell has a built-in consciousness of its own life cycle, which encompasses the fact that its death contributes to the structure and function of the body as a whole, as old worn-out cells make way for new ones. This reminded me of the concept that we are symbolically "cells" in the body of the universe, each one of us making a contribution to the development of the whole. On this planet, when our time comes, we make way for a new generation. What we leave behind—through our relationships or our work, the way we interact with the planet—can benefit all humanity and beyond. The parent who takes care of their child, the worker who puts thought and care into their job, the gardener who tends and nurtures their patch of nature—all these are vital contributions. We continued to explore these topics as the day progressed and shared a lot of visions for contributing toward a better life for all on this planet. That evening it was arranged that we would have our farewell meal together down in the canyon at side of the Rio Grande River. This meal had been planned for Sunday evening, but was brought forward because some more of the group had to leave early on Sunday.

We were supposed to end our program at 6 P.M. but collectively decided to continue until 6:20 P.M. so that all could have the opportunity to finish sharing their visions. We then all took a bus from the hotel that was to drop us at a spot near the edge of the canyon from, where we could walk down to our dining site at the riverside in the canyon.

We began our walk across the plateau before descending into the canyon and after a few minutes again heard an ultra-light plane flying toward us. As it came more clearly into view, we remarked to each other how it looked like the same plane and the same person that we had seen flying in the morning. A couple of the group members took pictures of the plane, and I again noted the happy face of the pilot who was so obviously enjoying his flight. The plane flew on, and as we began our descent, the attention of the whole group was suddenly, dramatically focused on a rattlesnake that had appeared on the path in front of us. Conversation stopped and we all stood in silence watching it, not wanting to walk around or disturb it. It seemed extraordinary that we had been considering death that afternoon and now here it was, staring us in the face. Luckily the snake then slithered away into the bushes and we were able to continue our descent down the winding path into the gorge.

Less than a minute later, we rounded a bend and I glanced over to the other side of the canyon. Something caught my eye in the rocks and as I looked at it, I realized to my alarm that it was the wings of an ultra-light! They were stuck to the rock like the wings of a dead butterfly, and it immediately crossed my mind that this must be the plane that we had just seen fly by moments earlier.

I drew the attention of the group to what I could see and some of those in front said that they had heard a bang just before turning the corner. We all began to wonder if this could have been the impact of the ultra-light, smashed against the rock by a sudden air current although there was no wind. We could make out red-and-white markings and the group members who had taken pictures of the plane just moments earlier checked back in their viewfinders and confirmed that these were indeed the colors of the wings of that plane. The realization that a terrible accident must have taken place dawned on the group. Spontaneously, four of the youngest and most athletic men in our group, Erik-Jan, Patrick, Gabriel and Richard, began to clamber down into the canyon to get across the river and climb up to where the plane was stuck to the rock. Their descent was very precarious, as that part of the canyon was very steep and there might also have been other rattlesnakes nearby. But, without thoughts for their own safety, these four were determined to reach the pilot to see if they could help.

This descent was beyond most of the group members, including me, so the rest of us watched and waited, and held the pilot in our prayers and contacted the emergency services. It took the men around forty-five minutes or so to get to the plane. As the first one got there, I called across—for the ultra-light was about level with us but around half a kilometer away as the crow flies—"Is he still alive?" One of them, I think Erik-Jan, tried to call back but he was too far away. We then looked through our guide's binoculars and saw him wave his arms and gesture that the pilot was dead. This was not a surprise but it was still a terrible shock. Although we didn't know the pilot personally we nevertheless felt connected with him, having seen him twice.

It was getting dark and seeing that there was nothing that they could do for the pilot, the four crossed back over the river and began their journey back. Meanwhile, the rest of us prayed for the pilot's soul to have a safe journey back to its source, the Infinite. We were all, of course, very saddened by what had happened, and also concerned for the pilot's relatives who were yet to learn of this accident. One of our group members was particularly distressed, since she had only recently lost her brother in a helicopter accident.

Within the hour, the emergency services arrived, and the firemen lowered ropes to pull our group members back up the incline as it was so steep. We then all walked back to where the bus was waiting for us and as the dark of night quickly descended, the police took witness statements from the men who had gone to the scene of the accident. Once this was over, we boarded the bus and went to the bottom of the canyon. We were all deeply moved to have been present at this man's passing. We were also amazed at how being confronted by a deadly snake and then a witness to the tragic death of this pilot was linked directly to the topic of death that we had been discussing that very afternoon. The whole evening had been both shocking and profound, and we were all processing what had happened in our own way.

Finally arriving at the bottom of the canyon, we gathered together at a picnic site. Later that evening, Deepak addressed us: "You who are here have all decided to be here and to witness the consequences of this terrible accident. Some of our group decided not to be part of this, since they already left earlier. The events of this whole day are reflections of a higher plan. We would not have been part of this if it had not 'happened' that we changed our plans, brought our farewell meal forward to tonight, and closed our session at the later time of 6:20 P.M. It is clear that today each of us, being here, have had to face death and we all need to experience our own 'deaths' in a way, too. So I invite all of you to go inside and ask yourselves what you need to leave behind here in Taos." He then closed with a prayer for the pilot who had died and ended with the words, "May this man's soul fly into boundless freedom."

At the very moment that he spoke these words and all our thoughts were focused on the man who had died, there was a sudden, surprising rush of wind that seemed to come out of nowhere. This was particularly striking, since the whole evening had been practically wind-free. The rush of wind went through our group for around ten seconds and then all was still again. It was a deeply impressive moment, as we had no direct explanation for where the wind had come from and it was as if, by praying for the man, nature was providing the wind for his soul to fly to freedom.

After this, as we all took time to reflect on what we would leave behind in Taos, I realized that I wanted to make the utmost use out of my God-given life and to cut out all those activities that do not serve this purpose. We all continued to reflect and share and sometime later we re-boarded our bus and went back to the hotel.

The next morning as we prepared to leave, I mentioned to our guide, that, if it would be possible to contact the family of the pilot, I would like to pass on how happy this man had been right before his death. Some weeks later, via an email from Carolyn, Deepak's assistant, I received an emailed copy of the service leaflet from the pilot's funeral, which was held on September 1st, and I found out that he was Paul R. "Pete" Adams, October 12, 1935—August 25, 2007. The leaflet also contained a nice photo of his smiling face.

As I read the leaflet, I was touched to learn how much Pete was loved, cherished and admired by his family—his three sons, two daughter-in laws, niece, four granddaughters, a sister, brother and sister-in law—and his peers. I also learned that he had graduated from Princeton University in 1957 and that he had had various careers spanning the pharmaceutical industry, restaurant ownership and real estate. He was described as an "unconventional and renaissance man" who was "creative, intelligent, passionate about life, extraordinary and deeply spiritual". What was most extraordinary was to read the letter, which he had written earlier , to be read out at his funeral in the event of his death. His son, Mike, whom I later spoke to, most kindly agreed, also on behalf of his other two brothers, that I may reprint it here[44].

I was very moved by his words and struck by how closely the letter expressed, in essence, the themes that we had been discussing during our Visionaries' Circle in Taos, as well as the synchronicity of all the events that had occurred. Everyone who has read this letter since has also been deeply moved by it. It seemed as if this extraordinary and wonderful man had prepared a gift that not only touched his immediate family and friends but which was now "taking wings" and already touching others around the world. In mid-September I had the chance to speak directly on the phone with Mike, one of Pete's sons. I felt him to be a very warm, understanding person and we made a good connection. I shared with him how I had seen his father flying in both the morning and the evening on the day of his death, and how he had seemed to be so very happy and carefree, taking real pleasure in his flying. Mike in turn told me how much he and his brothers loved their father, how well he got on with his father, and how he feels his presence even now, stronger than ever.

---

44 I later learned from his son that Pete had written his letter in 2001, the year of the atrocities at the Twin Towers.

"The Letter"

This service is in my memory, but right now I am totally OK—I am in the bosom/arms of God and with all my family, friends and animals. I am totally at peace and far beyond any happiness we have ever known on earth. I will always be with you when you think of me or need me. Always.

AND mostly this service is for you, the survivors. To grieve, to cry; to be sad and to be happy; to laugh, to love; to open your hearts to one another, and reflect on the meaning of your lives. To put aside the differences and see the real beings among you. God is Love.

That true, unfettered, unconditional, non-judgmental love that is beyond all personality and form that we have all experienced at one time or another. If only for a fleeting moment or two. In that moment it doesn't matter if we are male or female, black or white, ugly or pretty, rich or poor, Anglo or Hispanic or Jew, young or old, "somebody" or "nobody."

In that moment, we know God.
We are Love.
We are God.

I love you all,
Peter

Another member of our group, Richard, who was one of the people who had gone down to the site of the plane crash, was also able to speak to another of Pete's sons, Pete Jr., and learned of a further extraordinary coincidence. He discovered that the pilot, Pete, had been at Princeton University not only in the same year as his own father but in the same class and that they had known each other! The whole experience also had a profound effect on Richard, since he had lost his own father seven years earlier, and the two men were able to share a lot together about their experiences of loss.

Another strange coincidence was revealed in an email from another group member, Erik-Jan, who was also one of the people who had been at the scene of the accident. He had talked at length with another of Pete's sons, Chris, who said he had gone down to the crash site with his brothers a few days after the accident to collect their father's belongings – such as his gloves. On the way down he said that he had suddenly and inexplicably experienced a strong fear of rattlesnakes even though he did not see any during his descent. Of course, he had no knowledge of the rattlesnake that had appeared to us right before his father's death. It was a strange link.

The same day that I read this e-mail from Erik-Jan, I went for a walk with Chris, near our home and I saw, for the first time in the Netherlands, a water snake, slithering through the grass into the water. Then the very next day Chris told me that our cleaning lady had found a small garden snake in the kitchen of our house! Again, this had never happened before.

All these sudden sightings of snakes made me think about their symbolism. I discovered that in some indigenous cultures they are regarded as a symbol of wisdom and as guardians between the physical and the spiritual worlds; also that their characteristics are thought to symbolize alertness, vigilance and courage. All of these things seemed to fit so well into the experiences that we had all just shared.

Reflections
The World of Spirit

The experiences described in this chapter have often seemed to defy logical explanation or demonstrate synchronicity. They have challenged me to determine their truth or their possible deeper meaning.

Being presented with phenomena like the crop circles and paranormal healing, I have had to open my mind and consider the evidence. This led to shifts in my perspective as I considered new possibilities.

My close encounter with death through malaria felt like a process of initiation. I was helpless but, drawing on my inner resources, and with the support of others, I came through the experience. My trust and faith in "God", or the Infinite, were reaffirmed and I saw my life through new eyes.

The experience of being present at the time of Pete Adam's passing seemed an extraordinary incidence of synchronicity that had a greater purpose. Receiving his wise words and having contact with his family afterwards were a profound privilege and blessing for all in our group. Perhaps we were all "meant" to be there at that time in order to learn from his life and words and to help spread them further.

I feel that having an open mind, a pure heart, and a willingness to explore these wonderful mysteries can enable us to explore the truth and meaning behind them.

This led me to my sixth Key:

KEY 6: *We can find our own path to Truth.*

AFFIRMATION: *May I have the courage to explore the mysteries of life and seek the truth without judgment.*

CHAPTER 7
How Can I Help?

Today the earth is going through many unique changes and we are faced with challenges both at a global and personal level. Yet we can all contribute to building a more caring and sharing society.

For this we do not need to be rich or famous. For the changes we make in our own lives, in ourselves, as well as the contribution we make to society, all make an impact on the world as a whole. We are one of billions and if each one of us does what she or he can, then our whole planet can move forward in its development towards a higher consciousness.

The first question we can ask ourselves is about help itself. In my life I have also become involved spontaneously with trying to "help" various people. Reflecting on these experiences, I started to question how one could be most effective in supporting people. Originally my question to myself would have been, "How could I best help this person?" But I now feel that the word "help" has become misused.

For example, when I was at the Red Cross my colleagues and I wanted to "help" others, yet I came to realize that actually we often exported our own stress and problems; that Western models of "help" were not always appropriate and that we needed to learn from those we were meant to be helping. I felt that we should really have been learning how to help ourselves as well in order to be effective in the "developing world". Instead of "helping", I have now come to think of things in terms of supporting the person, if they wish it, towards their own development, regardless of their abilities or disabilities, cultures and religions.

I have also learned that sometimes the best way to help is to actually step back and let people develop their own capabilities. As the saying goes, "Help yourself so that we can help you."

In this chapter, I have assembled five experiences and adventures that may inspire ideas for supporting our own development as well as that of our planet.

1. Sowing the Seeds of Unconditional Love

The Twinkling Eyes Club (TEC)

We have all sorts of clubs and societies nowadays. Each one caters for different interests or groups. It may be a particular sport or hobby or may be aimed at a particular age group or income bracket. Clubs and societies can play a valuable role, bringing together experts or people who share interests in common. But suppose we expanded that principle so that everyone shared what they most have in common—their humanity? We are all already members of the "club of human beings", sharing all that this planet has to offer us.

I was thinking about this one day in 1991 when I was in Washington D.C., talking with my friend Bill Halamandaris[44]. We were just discussing this issue of clubs and organizations, when I smiled at something he said, and he commented in jest, "You've got twinkling eyes!" I said, "So have you! Maybe we should set up a club for twinkling eyes people![45]" We were just joking about it at the time but afterwards I started to think how great it would be to establish a non-exclusive club and aim to make all six billion-plus human beings on earth into members. So I decided to create the Twinkling Eyes Club (TEC) and make it open to all members of the human family.

I got the idea of drawing a smiley face on my thumb and then transferring it to other people's thumbs to make them members. I thought that the TEC could aim to spread awareness of the power of a smile, as smiles make life easier and more agreeable for everybody.

We all know that an inspiring, authentic smile with twinkling eyes that comes from the heart can make us feel good and help us through the day, and that smiles can help to deepen friendships and experiences, too. I also later became inspired to create the slogans, "Miles of Smiles" and "Sprinkles of Twinkles" and made stickers and T-shirts with these words to spread the message about the club. A few years ago my wife Chris also presented me with balloons, pens and travel tags with twinkling eyes symbols, which I have given out to people around the world when making them members of the club. Members have been initiated into the Twinkling Eyes Club for over fifteen years now, so there must already be many thousands of members and the numbers are growing all the time.

Members also appear in the most unlikely places, as illustrated by the following story: My step-daughter Mel, who lives in New York, was in Central Park some time ago with a girlfriend, when they stopped at the small café.

---

44 Together with his brother Hal, Bill Halamandaris is the founder of the Caring Institute in Washington D.C.
45 "Twinkling Eyes" is a metaphor for our inner smile and need not be taken literally. Thus it particularly welcomes sight-impaired people within its membership.

Most of the tables were taken, but they saw a space where there was a good-looking guy sitting. Mel asked if they could join him and in talking to him found out he was Dutch. She jokingly asked him if he was a member of the Twinkling Eyes Club. To her amazement, he responded by opening a book he was holding to reveal a Twinkling Eyes Club sticker on the inside!

LEFT *Jane's "Miles of Smiles" birthday present*

BELOW *detail*

Another wonderful thing about this club is how the smiles you send out have a way of coming back to you in all sorts of unexpected ways. One birthday, Jane Goodall came to see me with a roll of wallpaper, fifteen meters long! Unraveling it, I could see how she had pasted hundreds of smiley faces on to the paper, making "miles of smiles" for my birthday!

To top it all, she had put a little mirror at the end, to reflect viewers' own smiles back to themselves. Jane had put so much love and care into her gift. It really inspired me and I was deeply moved.

HOW TO JOIN THE TWINKLING EYES CLUB

Wouldn't it be great to belong to a club that was for everyone? We are all already members of the ***"club of human-beings"****, sharing together the gifts of all that this planet has to offer us. So why not join the Twinkling Eyes Club, the only non-exclusive club in the world, and spread miles of smiles around the globe?*

HOW DO I BECOME A MEMBER?

Touch the pad of your thumb to the smiling face symbol on the thumb image . Then draw the smiley face onto your own thumb with a ball point pen to confirm your membership. At the same time repeat to yourself, ***"I am now a member of the Twinkling Eyes Club and I will make other people members too."***

You are now a member and can start spreading ***"miles of smiles"*** *and* ***"sprinkles of twinkles"*** *amongst others! Whenever you have the opportunity, redraw the smiley face on your thumb to refresh it.*

HOW DO I MAKE OTHERS INTO MEMBERS?

First ask the other person if they would like to become a member of the Twinkling Eyes Club, explaining that it is for everyone and costs nothing to join and outlining the club's philosophy to share miles of smiles between all six billion plus members of the human family.

If they say "yes" redraw the smiley face on your own thumb with a ballpoint pen, then draw another smiley face on their thumb, pressing your two thumbs together.

As the smiley faces join together you can tell them, ***"You are now a member of the Twinkling Eyes Club!"*** *and watch them smile! Ask them to repeat the phrase,* ***"I am now a member of the Twinkling Eyes Club and I will make other people members too."***

Then invite them to spread ***"miles of smiles"*** *and* ***"sprinkles of twinkles"*** *to everyone they meet and to repeat this procedure themselves often!*

Twinkling on the South Pole; Robert Swan (center) and two others

WARNING!
Like love, your smiley face needs maintaining, so re-draw your thumbprint often and pass it on whenever you can! (It is not a good idea to tattoo it because, like love, it is better when it is fresh and spontaneous!) Create as many new members as you can wherever you go and amongst whoever you are with.

IS THAT ALL I NEED TO DO?
Yes, life can be that simple! It is said that the purpose of life is not just to reach goals, or arrive at the end of the road, but is to be aware of the journey, enjoying the walk and living in the moment here and now. So just enjoy the process and have fun!

Remember anybody can become a member, so spread these inspiring smiles and the club's philosophy as widely as you can.

WHAT ARE THE ADVANTAGES OF MEMBERSHIP?
Whenever you have a bad day or the going gets tough, just remember all the smiles you have spread and all the smiles you carry with you. This can lighten your load, bring a smile to your face and brighten your day.

And remember that by joining the Twinkling Eyes Club you are helping to spread "miles of smiles" and "sprinkles of twinkles" around the earth. Help us to reach our target of making everybody on the planet into members by joining up new members today and every day!

Everyone Can!

Anyone can join the Twinkling Eyes Club. It costs nothing and is fun to belong to. Or you could think about starting up something yourself that is simple and costs little yet will bring people together. It just needs a bit of imagination and a willingness to think "outside the box". Everyone can create wondrous things in their lives if they wish to. To become a member of the Twinkling Eyes Club follow the instructions on the previous page or go to *www.Fredfoundation.org*.

2. Creative Simplicity

The way each one of us lives has an impact on the planet. There is a great deal we can do to follow the natural rhythm of life, learning both to give and receive from Nature with awareness and respect. This involves both letting go of excess and developing ways we can nurture the planet's resources. Living simply but well frees us from the endless distractions of consumerism. It creates a space where we can focus on what is really important to us and our planet.

One inspiring example of this was told to me by Hamid Hossaini, whom I met once through my friend, Jane Goodall. Hamid told the story of how he grew up in a farmer's family in rural Iran but secured an educational scholarship.

He chose to study in India rather than at a prestigious university in the US, as he wanted to be in touch with people who lived simply. There, he met a man who became his teacher. Later he found out that this man was one of the very wealthy in India but he never realized this at the time as the man used to walk around in an old coat and give his money away. The question he always asked himself was: "Can I do without it?" Yet, his life was one of joy, not deprivation. He had chosen to dedicate himself to a high ideal and had within him an inner richness that shone quietly.

When I heard this story from Hamid I felt it was a really useful yardstick to carry throughout life. It inspired me to sell my second car (a Mercedes Benz) as I realized I could do without it. I donated its value to a charity connected to Jane Goodall's work for the environment. The other side of "creative simplicity" is to find ways of helping preserve our natural resources or of utilising them effectively. For example, utilization of the humble alfalfa plant. While in Moscow in 1991, visiting several of the hospitals that were recipients of our Foundation's aid, we saw first hand the problems of inadequate nutrition.

This gave me the idea of introducing an alfalfa seed program, as I had already learned about its easy cultivation and potent nutrient content. As with the oral re-hydration programs that I had been involved with for the Red Cross, I realized that this simple, inexpensive intervention could have profound effects. The same year I wrote about this idea in a Dutch national newspaper but, to date, it has not yet been taken up, even though it could have quite an impact on malnutrition for a relatively low cost.

GROWING ALFALFA

Alfalfa seeds are packed with nutrients and are a source of high biological value protein. They can easily be grown in glass jars and require only light and water to germinate. The seeds need to be rinsed twice daily and left to drain. Within four to six days they sprout into nutrient- and chlorophyll-rich shoots that can be added to salads or sandwiches or simply eaten as a snack. The seeds can be stored for many months, or even years and can be used to provide a good source of nutrition all year round—even in sparse winter months. Nutritionists working with alfalfa in India have found that just the simple dietary change of consuming a handful of alfalfa daily can contribute to decreased infant mortality, and improved maternal and infant health. Therefore, this simple, low-cost seed has a very high potential. It can give health and power to people, empowering the poor and underprivileged, even in crisis situations when people are starving, giving them a self-sufficient source of good nutrition.

There all sorts of different ways we can choose to live more simply in harmony with Nature—taking less, growing more. We can free ourselves from the consumerist mindset and create our own path in deciding how best to live on this planet.

3. Keep Heaven in your Heart and your Feet on the Ground

Taking the Peace Flame to Sarajevo

In the early 1990s, as Yugoslavia was breaking up, wars broke out in the various states. In Bosnia, Serbs, Croats and Muslims were engaged in a bloody civil war. Its capital city of Sarajevo was laid under siege for almost four years[47], during which time electricity and water were cut off and food and medical supplies dwindled. The city was reduced to rubble and people were struggling to survive. In fact, so many had died that a football field had been converted into a cemetery to accommodate all the deceased.

Day after day, pictures of the devastation and suffering appeared in the TV news. On one program, I saw the football field cemetery, and behind it, I caught a glimpse of the stadium where Sarajevo had hosted the Olympics in 1984. On February 18, 1994, while watching another news item on this topic, I was struck by an idea:

Here's what I later wrote about what happened:

I am at home.
8 o'clock news.
Again images of the war in Bosnia.
A few minutes later an item celebrating the Olympics in Lillehammer (Norway).
A flashback: ten years ago the Olympic games in Sarajevo.
Lillehammer now. Sarajevo now.
Sarajevo then. Sarajevo now.
Two comparisons.
Two, or rather, three realities.
How in the world is it possible that these co-exist?
The violence of war and the joy of sport?
What does the Olympian in Lillehammer feel right now?
Does he think of his own performance?
Or does he think of the people in Sarajevo?
of their pain?
of their deep suffering?
Maybe he has all these thoughts?
Maybe he feels confused. Like me.

47 The Siege of Sarajevo lasted from April 5, 1992 to February 29, 1996 and was the longest siege in modern history. It has been estimated that 12,000 people were killed and 50,000 wounded during the siege—85% of them civilians—and that the post-war population decrease was 64%.

Then a plan came to me:
We'll go to Sarajevo with ten gold medalists from Lillehammer and ten from the Sarajevo Olympics of 1984.
We'll light the Peace Flame as a sign of our empathy, as a remembrance of the eternal flame that burns in all our hearts.
Peace Flame '94 was born.

I watched the news images showing the winning athletes proudly receiving their Olympic medals in Lillehammer. Next, current images of Sarajevo (1994) were shown; ravaged by war and reduced to rubble with people struggling to survive and in fear of their lives. This made me think back to the Sarajevo Winter Olympics in 1984 and triggered my idea to take the Olympic Flame and Olympic athletes back there. We could then stand in solidarity with the suffering people there and remind them that we had not forgotten them.

Rationally this was a seemingly impossible task, since Sarajevo was still a war zone and the logistics for making such a plan happen were mind-boggling. Yet I felt sure it could succeed. I called a Norwegian friend, Katarina Thome, who put me in touch with the Olympic committee in Lillehammer and promised to help in any way she could. Within two weeks I found myself outlining my plan to the Head of the Olympic Committee in Norway.

He liked the idea and gave the OK for the flame to be taken. Even though we hadn't yet got permission to fly into the war zone, he asked me to announce the plan at the Closing Ceremony for the Olympic games the next day. It was quite an experience to deliver this speech in front of the ten-thousand-strong crowd, including the King and Queen of Norway and the President of the International Olympic Committee, Juan António Samaranch.

I watched as a flame was taken from the Lillehammer Olympic flame, just before being extinguished at the end of the games, ready for us to take to Sarajevo. As we were not allowed to refer to it as the Olympic Flame we renamed it the Peace Flame.

Now all the details had to be rapidly finalized. Katarina continued to work on the project and, with her wonderful help, athletes were contacted and we started negotiating a plane and flight crew and trying to obtain a permit to land in the war zone from the UN. We needed the co-operation of the UN forces in Sarajevo, had to find musicians and organize the ceremony, and had to contact local people in Sarajevo who could publicize and participate in the event. This all took place in the days before mobile phones or emails were in common use, so the arrangements were very time-consuming and communications were not

Driving in an armed vehicle through Sarajevo, 1994

easy. The arrangements were also fraught with difficulties. At first we were told that only planes with anti-missile detection systems were allowed to land in Sarajevo, yet we were unable to gain access to one.

However we discovered that the very UN official who had dictated this requirement to us had been permitted to land in a plane without such a system! When we presented this information to him he agreed that this requirement could be waived for us.

In the end the Dutch government agreed to provide us with a military plane and crew, although the mission would not officially be done in their name. Then it was agreed that we could take off and land from Belgrade airport, and arrangements were made for the athletes and musicians who had agreed to participate, and the Olympic flame, to be flown there from countries all over the world. Yet just one day before departure, this permission was withdrawn and we had just twenty-four hours to find a new airport, make the travel arrangements and find accommodation for all the participants coming from many different countries—as well as rapidly rescheduling bringing the Peace Flame from Norway. Many obstacles like these—too many to mention—presented themselves, but a way through them all was found.

Finally, on March 29, just thirty-nine days later, thirteen Olympic and Para-Olympic gold medalists, three musicians, and various other supporters took off from Ascona airport in Italy en route to Sarajevo[48].

I remember the plane weaving down to land in Sarajevo airport, which was being held open by peace-keeping forces. It was swinging from side to side as it descended. We were not sure if this was to avoid making the plane a target for missiles, or if it was because the pilots were hung over—we had, to our great shock, found them very drunk in the hotel the night before take-off! I needed to go to the plane, ahead of our group in the early hours of the next morning, to check that they were ready and fit to fly, as their behavior had nearly jeopardized the entire project.

On agreeing to participate, each person had been required to sign a declaration confirming they understood that their safety on this mission could not be guaranteed. So we descended into Sarajevo knowing that our landing was potentially dangerous. Once on the ground, we were moved rapidly across the tarmac to get behind a wall of sandbags and then immediately placed into armored vehicles and driven in a convoy straight to the city square, where our event was to be held. As we peered out of the windows we saw destroyed buildings and rubble in every direction. It was deeply shocking to see the extent of devastation that the brave people of Sarajevo were being forced to endure[49].

March 29, 1994
39 days and 390 near dead-ends later we were standing there. In the middle of Sarajevo. In the midst of around 2,000 people; the women, men and children of Sarajevo.
The sun shone.
There also stood thirteen Olympic and Para-Olympic medalists and three musicians.
Sixteen wonderful people.
Our message:

> *We want you to know that we have not forgotten you.*
> *We know that you are in great pain, although right now things are a bit calmer.*
> *We cannot really experience your pain*
> *Yet we want to give you sparks of light and hope.*

---

48 The medalists and musicians who participated are listed in Appendix B on page 147.

49 Reports have stated that shell fire in Sarajevo was so heavy, with an average of 329 shell impacts per day over the four years and 3,777 impacts on one single day (July 22, 1993), that virtually all buildings in Sarajevo had suffered at least some damage and an estimated 35,000 buildings were completely destroyed.

While we were surrounded by many UN soldiers
We have also seen trees and bushes starting to bloom.
Signs of new life.
Through every barrier, be it earth, asphalt, rock, hate, jealousy or anger, the life force still asserts itself.

It is this inspiring force, which is beyond growth, flowering and decay,
that I wanted to remind the people of.
New connections are made.
New friendships sealed[50].

At the square, all had been prepared for us. There were around 2,000 local people, plus a ring of 400 UN soldiers for our security. We went straight onto the stage and told the crowd that we wanted to let them know they were not forgotten. We wanted to support them in this difficult time. Each Olympian spoke briefly, saying why they had been inspired to come. The musicians played and sang; local children staged a dance display, and various local people spoke. Then the Peace Flame was lit from the Olympic flame that had traveled by plane all the way from Lillehammer. It was placed on the bridge as a symbol of our united hearts and minds. It was heart-warming to see the joy in the faces of everyone present, especially at such time of suffering and struggle.

At the end of the event, I promised the people that we would come back and help them restore peace and harmony. As soon as the ceremony was over, we were whisked away, having been shown some other parts of Sarajevo en route. We saw the market that had been hit by shelling, with more than 80 people killed in one missile blast the month before. We also visited the Olympic stadium from the Games ten years before, including the indoor ice skating rink. This had been partially demolished in the fighting, a point that particularly forcibly struck the two skaters in our team who had won medals on that very rink. Then we were returned to the airport and flown out. The day was so full it went very quickly. On the return flight we quietly absorbed all the emotions we had experienced as well as our feelings of hope for the future.

50 Diary entry written at the time.

Addressing the crowd in Sarajevo, 1994

The Peace Flame House in Tuzla

Our visit occurred during a lull in the fighting, but the Siege of Sarajevo continued for another two years. I had made the promise to the people that I would not forget them, and soon after I had the idea of creating a center where their pain could be acknowledged, accepted and released. I thought that this could be helpful to the survivors in Sarajevo who remained deeply traumatized and emotionally scarred by their experiences of war. With this is mind, our Peace Flame Foundation was established in 1994 with the aim of contributing to sustainable peace in areas of conflict. Therefore we began negotiations with the authorities in Sarajevo for building such a center. However, after almost eight years of negotiations, we had still not been granted permission due to all kinds of red tape and some corruption, too. As an alternative, Maurits van Heek, a co-worker with considerable experience of the Balkans, suggested building the center in nearby Tuzla instead. This town had a history of inter-racial harmony and a mayor who was well-regarded for his reconciliation work, so it seemed a good choice.

The Peace Flame House in Winter

In due course we had permission to build in Tuzla and over the next eighteen months the project was realized. My friend, the Dutch architect Ton Alberts[51], known for his beautiful organic designs, which mirror natural forms, very kindly agreed to design the building as a gift. Ton very sadly passed away on August 19, 1999, just after completing his sketches for the Peace Flame House. However, his colleague, the architect Marius Ballieux, from Alberts & Van Huut Amsterdam, and the Bosnian architect Kenan Haracic, did a great job in bringing Ton's designs into form. Lani van Petten, Ton's widow, painted the interior in natural colors in her unique style, and Isabel and Frans Smeets helped 200 children in Tuzla to design and construct a playful and colorful floor mosaic.

---

51 The innovative and beautiful organic architecture of the late Ton Alberts is well regarded in the Netherlands and abroad. He and his colleagues, Max van Huut and Marius Ballieux and their team (*www.albertsenvanhuut.nl*) have created many renowned buildings including the ING Bank Head Office in Amsterdam and the Gasunie Head offices in Groningen, in the north of the Netherlands. Ton's approach was based on the principle of "healing through form" and he once said, "A building only starts to live when all the materials together in harmony mean more than each of the materials separately."

52 *www.peaceflame.nl*

The Peace Flame House[52] was officially opened in October 2003, consisting of a 90-seater theatre, three therapy rooms, a studio for all kinds of creative activities, a multi-purpose room, and a kitchen. It was a great day, with people from different ethnic groups who had been set against each other during the war, all enjoying music, laughter, performances and refreshments together. I initiated many new members into the Twinkling Eyes Club that day, too, and miles of smiles were spread everywhere.

Since the opening of the Peace Flame House, it has hosted many art, drama and dance programs and other courses as well as therapy sessions. A documentary on sports activities for those with disabilities has also been made and shown on Bosnian TV. However, the center is not without its problems. I have observed that in countries that have been used to a Communist regime, where everything has been "taken care of" by the State, it can be quite hard for people to feel empowered and really take the initiative. The Peace Flame House itself was a gift but the idea was that it should slowly become self-financing and independent as regards maintenance and running costs. Though in principle the idea of becoming self-sufficient was readily accepted, it has been harder to put in practice. To date, this has not yet happened and it still relies on the Foundation for funding and guidance though this is scheduled to end in 2008. I still hope that this independence can be developed in the future and that more trauma-resolution work can also take place there.

Sarajevo Now

Although the Peace Flame House was finally built in Tuzla rather than Sarajevo, I wanted to keep my promise of aid to the people in Sarajevo, too. Therefore the Peace Flame Foundation committed funds equal to the initial cost of the Peace Flame House for supporting various other projects and initiatives in Sarajevo itself. These have included setting up a halfway house for children leaving orphanages at eighteen, which helps to prepare them for independent life in the outside world, and co-financing the Vladimir Nazor Center[53] for the education and rehabilitation of severely handicapped children. At the Center, the children are treated with love and respect and encouraged to develop new learning skills, while their parents are given some much-needed respite. Today, Sarajevo has been substantially rebuilt and the Peace Flame Foundation remains committed to playing a small part in aiding its recovery. Another halfway house is due to open next year.

---

53 Named after the Yugoslav poet and novelist, Vladimir Nazor (1876—1949) who was born in Croatia.

Official Opening of the Peace Flame House, 2003

Working With Mind and Heart

My decision to respond to the plight of the people of Sarajevo came from my heart. At the same time, I knew that I would have to be intensely practical from the outset for anything worthwhile to be achieved. Thanks to the team, we literally and metaphorically were able to get the project off the ground. The innumerable obstacles we faced required everyone in the team to stay very focused on our goal. Thankfully, we got through and were able to hold the Peace Flame ceremony in war-torn Sarajevo. It represented one small triumph of the human spirit against despair and isolation.

But our task did not end there. To make our contribution solid and long lasting, we had to negotiate the difficult process of setting up a center in Tuzla and supporting projects in Sarajevo. Hopefully these have contributed to improving life for those who have survived the years of bitter civil war in Bosnia. Yet, I have also learned another lesson of mind and heart: however much I might wish to see people empowered to shape their own destiny, I had to accept that the process takes time. I recognize the limits of how rapidly people can empower themselves when they have lived for so long under an all-powerful state.

I needed to be aware of my own expectations and not fall into a very common trap when supporting people: attachment to the result. Whatever I do, or seek to do, I take responsibility for it. But how others respond, the use they make of the opportunities given to them, is their responsibility. Confusing the two can lead to a great deal of unnecessary pain. If people are empowered to make choices, I must accept that not all the choices they make are going to be ones that I would be in agreement with. In the case of our projects in Bosnia, a great deal of good work has been done. But it will always be the local people who hold the key to the success of the initiative.

4. Finding the Space to Be

My Personal Journey to Peru

Turning sixty helped me reflect on my life—not only on what I had accomplished so far, but on what I still had to do. As a young man I had seen many friends set off on foreign adventures before finding their life's purpose. I had never really taken the time off to venture away from my responsibilities, family and full agenda. As much as I appreciated my full life, I yearned to know what it would be like not being "my mother's son", "my wife's husband", "my children's father", or "my employees' boss". Being interested in spiritual development, I felt that I wanted to discover my inner self further. So my sixtieth birthday was a good reality check for me; I was healthy, curious and realized that I still wanted to explore my dreams of traveling to an unknown territory and tasting freedom.

I wondered where I should go on this personal quest and, for some reason, Peru kept surfacing. I did not know much about its history and indigenous culture, nor do I speak Spanish, but still I felt strongly drawn to going there. I contacted a Peruvian friend who lives in Spain for advice on making such a journey and she suggested that I should meet Victor Estrada. She told me that he is a wise shaman (medicine man) from Cusco, a large city 3,000 meters above sea level. I still had not decided my plans when Victor's name came up again via another friend. It struck me that this was perhaps more than just a coincidence. Out of all the people who lived in Peru, what were the chances of the same person's name coming up twice? I took this as a sign that I was to meet him.

Through a series of further synchronicities occurring a week prior to my departure, I began to trust this intuition even more. I happened to be in touch with a Belgian woman who was an experienced guide for remote areas of Peru and who gave me further suggestions about places I should visit. I was also able to speak with Victor on the phone and arrange to stay with him. He also arranged for an interpreter to travel with me.

Everything seemed to be falling in to place without much effort. I had experienced this sort of thing before in my life, and it felt right to go with the flow and allow my journey to unfold.

Encountering Obstacles

When I first set out to meet Victor in Peru, I encountered a number of obstacles. Just before my departure from the Netherlands, I suddenly experienced intense abdominal pain. It came right out of the blue and was so severe that I could hardly walk and couldn't even put my socks on!

Eventually it was diagnosed as a muscle problem in my abdomen, and with a mixture of orthodox and alternative healing, I was fit enough to travel, albeit in some discomfort. I don't know if this was meant to be an inner test of my resolve or pure chance, but it was the first of a number of strange experiences.

When I reached Lima, the Peruvian capital, I went to the home of two artist friends who had kindly agreed to have me stay for a few days. We would meet once a day for lunch, and the rest of the time I stayed mainly in my room, meditating and writing while they were out at work. Nearly all houses in this part of Lima are fenced in and have guards, and I felt this created quite an oppressive atmosphere. Yet during my stay, I was inspired by reading a book describing one man's experiences with the Indian guru, Yogananda.

One day I decided to go for a short walk and tried to open the door to get out but it wouldn't open! I tried it again and then realized that I was locked in the house compound. I couldn't get out or make any contact with the outside world, since every room was sealed with separate locks. My hosts were not due back until the evening and there were no people nearby to call out to—and in any case I don't speak Spanish—so I was imprisoned there.

This felt strange, but as I tried to make sense of it, I realized that both my abdominal pain and now my "imprisonment" could be interpreted as obstacles or "tests" on my way to greater things on my journey. So I decided to just accept my confinement and settled down to a day of more reading and quiet contemplation until my hosts returned home that evening. When they did, they were shocked to discover that their housekeeper, unaware that I was inside, had locked me in!

Meeting Victor

After four days of resting and acclimatizing in Lima I flew to Cusco, with Mary-Ann—a healer and translator who kindly agreed to accompany me—to meet Victor Estrada. Victor was waiting to greet us at the airport. He looked like a friendly man and had short, dark, curly hair and clear, dark eyes. As we drove through town I began to feel the effects of the high altitude and the heat. Cusco moved at a much slower pace than Lima and seemed to be filled with tourists. We parked on the dirt road next to Victor's large house. He opened the big, solid doors and I found myself in a dark hall from where they also sold handmade jewelry. After putting my things in an upstairs bedroom, we went to the kitchen where Victor's wife, who was busy cooking, greeted us. We sat together around the table and drank the coca tea[54], which many people drink in Peru as it is thought to ease altitude sickness and other ailments.

Victor invited me to come up to the top floor of his house, where he has a room for teaching and holding ceremonies. We sat down and talked via the interpreter so that we could get to know one another a little bit better. He said that he had to get a sense of me in order to determine which sites to take me to and what experiences I could benefit from.

Afterwards he stood up, selected some feathers, stones, and beads, and then chanted some words in his language. He performed a short ritual to prepare the path for me and then we sat in silence and meditated together.

Touching the Volcano

Victor planned a trip for me to experience some of the ancient spirituality of the region. The morning we left I was woken at 5 A.M. We ate a hearty breakfast, as we would travel far that day. Victor's son-in-law drove us and Mary-Ann joined us as translator for the journey. We drove through the lively and chaotic city to an ancient sacred site higher up in the Andes. It was once the center of Inca rituals, but was now filled with ruins. Victor asked me to enter a circular area, marked by standing stones, and to stand in the center. He told me to raise my arms horizontally and to spin to the right while holding my breath. When I had done this he asked me to do it again and he continued to do this several times. Then I found myself spinning effortlessly. It seemed that I was "being spun", faster and faster until I fell to the ground. It was as if the spinning had accelerated everything within me and then released it so I could be in union with the earth, the sky and everything beyond. My awareness shifted and I felt free from limitations. A few days later we traveled a long distance and it was pitch dark when we stopped the car. Victor said we were at the spot where the three mountain ridges of South America joined. In the meantime we were surrounded by ground fog .We stepped out of the car while our driver waited for us. While standing there for a few minutes we felt the silence enveloping us and the solitude of the place. We walked through the darkness and ran into a fence. Walking along it, all of a sudden we arrived at a gate. Victor shouted a name, we heard some noise and then we saw a weak flashlight coming out of a hut. It was an old woman. She and Victor greeted each other like old friends and then she opened the gate. We walked across a grassy field towards a small

---

54 Coca tea, also called Yerba mate, is a herbal tea made from the leaves of the coca plant.

hill about six meters high. Mary-Ann waited there while Victor and I crept up on our bellies. At the top of the hill there was an opening with a diameter of about two meters. Victor looked at me and said in Spanish "This is the womb of the earth".

In the meantime the mist cleared to reveal a sky full of twinkling stars above, like I have never seen before. Then Victor said if I was lucky, the dormant volcano that formed the crater we were on the edge of, would talk to me. This sounded odd yet after my earlier experience I was curious. Victor and I lay on our stomachs leaning into the rim of the crater as the sound of distant bubbling came up from below. Suddenly Victor said, "Fred, did you hear it? It is saying your ancient name. Listen well… it is meant for you." Victor explained that this was a gift from the core of mother earth.

Its vibration translated into ancient Inca language and was meant for me to repeat to help reclaim my inner power and strength. He motioned to me to put my hands inside the "womb", the crater. I slipped my hands over the edge into warm liquid at the top of the crater. I felt a part of this warmth and softness, beyond words and time.

When it was time to leave the crater, our walk back was easier, as the mist had cleared. The old woman was waiting by the gate; she opened it for us to pass through and then closed it behind us.

As we headed for our car we noticed a bright light shining in the sky. Its brilliance was outlined against the mountains yet the form was hard to distinguish. Victor immediately knelt down on the ground and started to offer coca leaves toward the light while passing leaves to Mary-Ann and I so we could do the same. Then he stretched his hands out and said, "We are open for contact". Later he told us that "they" were aware of our presence, and that this was not an unusual occurrence. I was curious and also felt calm. This light seemed very real— all four of us saw it but were unable to identify what it was. After a few minutes of it hanging in the sky, with the mountains as background, it suddenly moved off soundlessly. We watched it drift away with the light getting smaller and smaller, rather like a falling star.

We could find no words to describe what we had seen and got back into our car and began to drive away. There were no other cars on the road and as we drove we saw the moon coming up over the mountain ridge on our left side. A few moments later, Mary-Ann called out: "Look on the right, there they are again. They are following us." Indeed the light had reappeared and for a short time it seemed to follow us, at a distance about a mile away from our jeep. Then, as suddenly as it had appeared, it vanished. I was never sure what was the explanation for what we had seen.

On one of our last days, we drove out to the site of an old, ruined temple. While walking between the remains of this sacred site, some memories started coming back to me. After being with Victor had begun to trust this process within myself and knew that certain places activated inner experiences. I felt more in touch with the subtle energies there and as I came near some trees on the edge of the grounds, I particularly felt drawn to a large standing stone. It was as if it was silently calling my name. I sat on the ground with my back against it and felt its warm embrace. It felt so natural and safe and I allowed myself to dissolve and let go. Tears began to flow as colorful images from different parts of my past began to surface. I had an intense feeling when I saw my former wife, Ineke, with whom I had had such a difficult and painful divorce. Yet in this moment I met her again and experienced her innocence and her original sparkle. I was able to feel her pure heart, honesty and the trust that we had shared in the beginning of our marriage. Our divorce had not only divided our family but had left a scar in my heart. I allowed myself to follow this wound and, as my tears flowed, I was able to forgive the pain I felt over not being able to bridge our differences. My unconscious attachment to these unresolved issues began to disappear along with my tears. The man in me began to feel happy and free again. Afterwards Victor told me that I had been sitting on a very special spot. He said that the stone I had been leaning on is known as Kialla Rumi, which means "moon", or "mother" stone. On the way back to town, I continued to cry. I felt compassion from Mary-Ann and Victor's son-in-law and I sensed that in their wisdom they saw that my tears were a release of old pain. They came up with me to my hotel room and gave me some healing by laying on of hands.

Machu Pichu

For many who visit Peru, Machu Pichu is a must—and that included me. With my backpack on, I boarded a train full of fellow tourists from around the world. After our arrival at the railway station, we were immersed in a bustling village with a colorful market packed with all kinds of tourist souvenirs. I headed for the bus that was going up to Machu Pichu. It was also very crowded and had seen better days but it managed to slowly chug up the narrow dirt road. After our arrival we disembarked like a herd of sheep on to the sacred grounds of one of the world's most breathtaking sites. I stood in the midday sun trying to take in the panorama of the peaks of Andes Mountains that provide the background to this ancient Inca site.

I had been advised to book a place in the only hotel at this altitude. Checking in, I saw it had a large dining area that was packed with people enjoying the incredible views. That night in my room, I watched the classic film, *Gandhi*. I was moved by the simple, peaceful and effective methods that Gandhi used and how he did not allow obstacles to block his truth. I went to sleep full of these impressions of Gandhi's life and work, and these still resonate with me today.

I woke early and walked to the site of Machu Pichu. The sun had just risen and the majestic Andes Mountains seemed to be reaching for the sky. Being there and seeing this ancient city took my breath away. Without a soul there in the stillness of the morning, it felt like such a gift. I climbed on to the different terraced levels and looked at the remains of some of the grey stone houses and temples. The buildings no longer had roofs and were open to the elements. I wandered along the maze of small paths amongst the ruins and found a place to sit on the dry, clay ground. I leaned back onto a small rock wall and closed my eyes, feeling the sun's heat getting stronger. Thoughts surfaced of the many challenges the Incas endured to build this city. If occurred to me that perhaps they wanted to live on these precariously high terraces, where edges fell away into sheer drops, as a sign of their devotion. Waves of gratitude passed through me to have had this time here. The sound of distant voices came closer and I realized the first buses had arrived. It was time for me to go.

After my time in Machu Pichu, I stayed on in Cusco for a week. I wanted to have some quiet time to absorb my recent experiences and to have the opportunity to write and read. I learned how the Incas had been overcome by the Spanish Conquistadors who destroyed their temples and built Catholic churches on their foundations, which must have been very intimidating to the indigenous people.

These churches still stand to this day. While I was there, military parades took place on two days and, at the end of each, I was surprised to see Catholic processions of nuns, priests, voluntary groups, etc. carrying banners. This made me realize how powerful this indoctrination had been. The local indigenous people, the Quecha, have become regarded as inferior to urban dwellers and their native religion is no longer given any prominence whatsoever. This reminded me of the patterns of hierarchy and control that you see everywhere in the world; the local indigenous people are not part of the power structure and are excluded even though they carry many generations of wisdom in their culture. Yet this situation may also be changing—witness the dramatic election of a Quecha coca farmer, Evo Morales, as President of Bolivia in December 2005.

I also took time to take leisurely strolls through the city's colorful markets. My trip was about living differently instead of my usual active lifestyle and so it was nice to wander around slowly. Walking through the center of Cusco, I noticed that many people seemed to be leisurely chatting in cafés or sitting on park benches. They didn't appear to be caught up in the rat race as many of us are in the West. On one of the busy city squares I noticed an ATM cash dispenser at the entrance of a shop. As there were not many of these around, I decided to get some money out. I had been warned about pick-pocketing so I scanned the area to see if anyone was lurking who might want to take advantage of a tourist with cash. I noticed a thin, dark fellow leaning against the wall opposite. He didn't look that tidy nor did he seem to be doing anything in particular, which made me wonder about him. However I brushed off my feeling and went ahead and opened my wallet and inserted my card into the machine.

Then the thought surfaced—what if this man tried to take my wallet? I quickly punched in my pin number, took the cash and walked away. After putting the money deep in my pocket I heard a voice behind me calling out "Señor, señor!" I turned to see the same man and jumped to the conclusion that he must have seen me taking the cash and was now following me. So I kept on walking but so did he. When I eventually stopped he came up to me and to my utter surprise handed over my credit card. I had forgotten to take it out of the money dispenser and he had followed me to return it to me! I was so thrown off guard that I forgot to thank him before he walked away. As soon as I realized, I began to hunt for him in the crowd and was so happy when I managed to find him and could give him my heartfelt thanks.

Meeting the Shipibo

I next traveled to the jungle town of Pucallpa, a two-hour flight north from Lima, together with a translator, Mia. There we were met by our host Mateo who first took us through the busy town packed with noisy scooters. We then got in a car with five others and had a six-kilometer bumpy car ride to his home village of San Francisco. This area is populated by Shipibo Indians—a very modest, and delightful people with their own language, colorful clothing and rich culture.

Mateo's home is just a one-roomed hut with a thatched roof. Up to eight members of three generations of his family live there and they spend much of their time sitting together out on the front porch. The family were all very warm and hospitable and I was given an adjacent hut in which to sleep on the floor. Meals were taken on an outside table at the side of the hut. The dogs and chickens roamed freely around us and birds often alighted to share our meals. I was given the one chair to sit on but had to balance quite precariously, as much of the seat was missing! The others sat on a bench. One of Mateo's daughters did the cooking while the other had the job of washing both dishes and clothes.

Hardly anybody in the village has electricity, so after sunset it soon becomes pitch dark everywhere and during the evenings we took our meals by candlelight. There was no running water in the village. Water was drawn from the pump in the center of the village several times a day, brought to the hut and often used more than once. To my relief, the drinking water was brought in huge, sealed plastic containers collected once a week by Mateo from Pucallpa.

Most days, local women and children would come by the hut and urge me to buy their colorful bead necklaces—I ended up with quite a collection! I also walked in the village every day and would be accompanied everywhere by a flock of pre-school, bare-footed and smiling children. It was great fun to be with all these cheerful little children. They were very curious about my hair, the beard I had grown and the hair on my arms, as they are a smooth-skinned people. They constantly wanted to touch my hair and I must have seemed as if I came from another planet.

I learned a lot from being with the Shipibo people. I was particularly struck by how they never said anything bad about each other and how they rarely complained. For example in the village, which had around 2,000 inhabitants, there were blaring loudspeaker announcements that could be heard all day long throughout the village. The first announcements started at 6 A.M. and were about getting to school. Then at weekends an Evangelical group used another loudspeaker to dominate the village with their preaching. They held their services in a huge shed but normally only a handful of people turned up.

I found these constant noisy announcements very intrusive and they disturbed me quite a lot, but the Shipibo never seemed bothered by them at all. I was also impressed by their patience, modesty and simplicity. I found them to be wise and loving people.

During the three weeks I spent with the Shipibo, I was also grateful for the real sense of freedom that I experienced and the opportunity to get more in touch with my thoughts and feelings. Even after I returned home and resumed my daily life I found that the memory of this period and this sense of freedom would often sustain me.

Preparing for my Return

I loved the Andes Mountains but was not very comfortable in the jungle area where Mateo lived, as I found it so hot, humid and mosquito-ridden. While I was there, I began to long for the ocean, for fresh air and a sense of space, so I decided to leave a little early. I traveled back through Pucallpa and Lima and went on to the Caribbean island of Bonaire, which I had first visited in the 1960s with my father and mother.

It was wonderful to walk along the water's edge and feel the ocean breeze on my face. While walking I also really enjoyed listening to a selection of music compiled for me on an iPod given to me by my children before I left. The selection was wide ranging—from Billy Joel to Mozart. I've always been aware that music can have a very uplifting effect on me, even transporting me to different states of consciousness. In this context, it really revived my spirit.

While in Bonaire, my longing to see my wife Chris again became stronger. At that time she was doing a retreat in a place a few hours' drive north of Atlanta, Georgia, and my daughter, Lyke, also happened to be working in Atlanta then. So I decided to fly to Atlanta where it was great to meet up with Lyke and then I went on to where my wife was staying. In the time before her retreat ended, I thoroughly enjoyed walking in the wonderful, seasonal autumn leaves and after a week I had a heartfelt reunion with Chris at the end of her course.

We spent a few beautiful days together, and then we traveled back to Holland at the end of November. I was very much looking forward to seeing my other loved ones again but was also apprehensive about going back to the old routines of my Dutch life, as I had so much enjoyed my freedom. The challenge was going to be how to maintain this sense of freedom within the Dutch context. I had a few quiet days of adjustment before starting back at work at the beginning of December 2005 and tackling the pile of work that had accumulated in my absence.

Recharging Batteries

Going into 2006 I went back to work on existing projects but continued to reflect on my time away. I realized how low in energy I had been before my trip and how valuable it had been to have the opportunity to recharge my batteries and to reconnect with my inner self. I could see more clearly how important it is to have a balance between giving and receiving, activity and stillness and how in this stillness the Divine, or the Infinite, can be more readily experienced. I also continued to re-evaluate my life and took time to consider what should be my next step.

5. What Now?

Throughout my life, like many people, I ask myself how I can best make a difference and contribute to society. My trip increased my awareness of the need to utilize both inner and outer resources and to maintain some balance in my life. On the one hand I wanted to be less "busy" while on the other I still wanted to support and co-operate in different ways. I also wanted to be open to what the Infinite might send my way—to act according to whatever my "soul" purpose might be. Two things then became the main focus. The first was the writing of this book. I had been making notes on my philosophy and experiences for some time and the work of compiling them into a book was already underway before my trip. Now the challenge of completing this task became more of a focus. Synchronicity played a part and the right helpers and encouragement came my way to support me in this process and to convince me that the book would serve a purpose in inspiring others. My clear motive was to share experiences that I have had in order to inspire others to rediscover all our hearts so that we can co-operate to bring about change in the world. I did not feel that I held all the answers and have been aware throughout the process of writing the book of how much I still have to learn. I make mistakes and learn new things every day. I also believe that learning and caring and sharing together can help us make great strides forward together. I hoped that my book might play a small part in this. The second focus that emerged unexpectedly occurred as a result of a phone call from my friend Ray Chambers[55] in late October 2006.

Malaria no More

Ray invited me to develop a Dutch initiative as part of a wider campaign started in the USA to prevent and treat malaria[56] He told me that 350 to 500 million cases of malaria occur annually and that at least a million people die from malaria worldwide each year, most of them children under five years of age in sub-Saharan Africa. Yet, he said, malaria is both treatable and preventable by means of effective interventions currently available.

These include long-lasting impregnated bed nets and anti-malarial drugs such as Artemisinin-based combination therapies (ACTs)—that is, drugs based on an extract from the Chinese herb, *Artemsisia annua* (sweet wormwood). A big campaign, under the banner "Malaria no More", was being set up in the US and network partners were being sought in other countries to join the initiative. Would I like to be involved? I took some time to think it over. On the one hand, having just entered my 60s, I felt a strong desire to take more of a back seat and to simply focus on my existing Foundations and their charitable activities.

55 Ray Chambers is an American philanthropist, and the initiator of "Malaria no More USA". He was recently appointed as Special Envoy of the UN Secretary General for Malaria.

56 The United Nations Millennium Declaration in September 2000 set out eight development goals to be reached by developed and developing countries by 2015. The goals include targets for reducing hunger, lack of education, environmental problems and so on, with the overarching goal being the halving of poverty by the year 2015. Millennium Development Goal No.6 is aimed at health issues and, in particular, seeks to halt and begin to reverse the spread of HIV/AIDS, malaria, and other major infectious diseases. This has prompted a global campaign to control malaria.

On the other hand, I felt a strong pull to become involved, since I had myself miraculously survived a very severe form of malaria—*malaria tropica*—ten years previously. I was also motivated by my experiences with the Red Cross nearly twenty-five years ago, where I had seen at first hand how our campaign promoting oral re-hydration therapy salts had significantly reduced child mortality due to dehydration from diarrhea. I felt it would be marvelous if the incidence of malaria could also be reduced by means of simple interventions.

I felt that since I had been given my life back from malaria, I must help prevent others suffering and dying from this disease and help stop its spread. So I researched the topic a bit further and explored the possibility of mobilizing a team that would be capable and committed to establish the campaign in the Netherlands. After careful consideration, I decided to say "yes" to my American friend and set about establishing the Dutch foundation "Malaria no More!" The US campaign had decided to focus on the provision of bed nets, alongside education and monitoring, soliciting $10 donations per bed net with the concept that each gift of a bed net could save a life.

For the Dutch campaign, we decided to work closely with existing Dutch organizations that were already involved in implementing health initiatives at a grassroots level in Africa, such as the Netherlands Red Cross. A key characteristic of our approach is building bridges of trust through an attitude of true respect and patience, and the creation together of sustainable and effective methods for dealing with malaria in the context of primary health care in the most affected African countries.

As part of my commitment to the campaign, I attended the White House Summit on Malaria in Washington, in mid-December 2006. Ray had mobilized support for this initiative from influential circles. This initiative was launched by President George Bush and First Lady, Laura Bush, and it brought together 250 political and charity leaders, medical scientists and supporters from around the world to discuss new opportunities for combating malaria and to kick-start the combined public-private initiatives supporting the campaign.

Those present included: the US Secretary of State, Condoleezza Rice; many African representatives, such as the Nigerian Minister of Health Dr Eyitayo Lambo and the Principal Secretary, Ministry of Health and Social Welfare in Zanzibar, Dr Mohamed Saleh Jiddawi and many others[57]. This event helped

57 Melinda Gates, co-chair of the Bill and Melinda Gates Foundation has committed $83.5 million in grants to fight malaria. Ann Margaret Veneman, the Executive Director of UNICEF, is helping spearhead the campaign. Paul Wolfowitz, the then President of the World Bank and Dr. Richard Feachem, the then Executive Director of the Global Fund to Fight HIV/AIDS, Tuberculosis and Malaria, both headed organizations that are assisting with funding. There were also representatives of the American Red Cross, Millennium Promise, United Nations Foundation, the Global Business Coalition, United Way of America, and others.

to raise the profile of malaria on the global agenda and in the year since, more funding has become available and many more people have been mobilized to support the anti-malaria projects.

Dancing to the Music

As part of the Summit, we were entertained by some really good African musicians and singers, including Yvonne Chaka Chaka. While she was singing, an elderly lady, seated next to me, stood up and started dancing in the aisle to the music. I thought this was a wonderful response to the African music, so I got up and joined her but was surprised when no-one else followed suit. We danced to the end of the song and then sat down. Immediately after the song ended President George Bush walked on stage and addressed the audience, launching the initiative. Later someone came up to me and said, "That took some guts to dance in front of all those people and keep the President waiting!" I had no idea that was what we had done!

Starting the Dutch Campaign

In April 2007, on World Malaria Day, we officially launched the Dutch foundation, Malaria no More! (Netherlands)[58] in the Hague in alliance with the following Dutch organizations: the Netherlands Red Cross (NRK)[59], UNICEF (Netherlands), Médécins Sans Frontières (Netherlands) (AzG)[60], AMREF Flying Doctors (Netherlands), the Royal Tropical Institute (KIT)[61], CORDAID[62] Memisa, and "Drive Against Malaria". I feel privileged to be involved in this campaign and am delighted to work with a really committed Dutch team and a wonderful group of people on the Advisory Board, including Ruud Lubbers (Prime Minister of The Netherlands, 1982–1994), Jane Goodall, and the 1992 Nobel Peace Laureate, Rigoberta Menchú Tum. Together, with grassroots support and involvement, we hope to do a lot to help stop the spread of malaria and to prevent death and morbidity due to this disease. Perhaps, as a result of reading this book, you may like to join in this worldwide campaign and become involved, too? You can find out more on *www.malarianomore.org* or on our Dutch site, *www.malarianomore.nl.*

---

58 *www.malarianomore.nl.*
59 NRK is the abbreviation of Het Nederlandse Rode Kruis, the Dutch name of the organization.
60 AzG is the abbreviation of Artsen zonder Grenzen, the Dutch translation of "Doctors without Borders".
61 KIT is the abbreviation of Koninklijk Instituut van de Tropen.
62 CORDAID is the abbreviation of the Catholic Organisation for Relief and Development AID and Memisa is medical missionary action.

An Open Future

Last year one of my daughters got happily married and now she is expecting her first child. It fills me with great joy! My generation is stepping back, hers is coming up and the one after peeks around the corner. I am often in wonderment and learning. I am still trying to find a balance between maintaining my inner peace yet also dealing with my responsibilities and requests to be involved in new initiatives. I am learning not to over-stretch myself. I am mainly occupied with my philanthropic activities but also continue part-time involvement with my business interests. I am entering a more reflective period where I prefer to carry out supportive, advisory roles rather than more active ones. I continue to try and integrate my mind and my heart and to grow spiritually. With my trust in the Divine, I continue on my journey as a student of life…

Reflections
Making a Difference

The experiences in my life have come from seeing potentials and possibilities and then allowing myself to be inspired. When this inspiration fills my heart it seems to offer me a type of courage that doesn't entertain doubts. I can then enjoy being part of this process of co-creating.

I am not saying that all my adventures and ideas have always worked out because they haven't. Much of what I have been able to accomplish has been through co-operation with other inspiring people. Looking back on various projects that I have been involved with, I can see that sometimes even the simplest ones can have the best effects. For example, The Twinkling Eyes Club idea requires only the willingness of two people to share and to have a pen. Yet it provides a light and humorous way of reminding us that we're all part of one human family and one planet. It's a way of remembering the inner smile; the soulful spark that lies inside, which connects us all.

Traveling to Peru was, for me a way of going beyond my daily patterns and normal comfort zone. On my journey, I was blessed to be with wonderful people whose close connection with Nature and the Divine inspired me to see the world in new ways.

KEY 7: *We can make a difference.*

AFFIRMATION: *My personal development is linked to global transformation and I am aware that each one of us counts. I honor the global family of which I am part and cherish the home planet that we all share.*

Seven Keys to Personal and Planetary Transformation

KEY 1: *We can trust in the guiding hand of the Divine.*
AFFIRMATION: *I trust that everything has a divine purpose from which it is possible to learn and grow.*

KEY 2: *We can free our minds to explore new horizons.*
AFFIRMATION: *I can go beyond my conventional belief systems and open up to infinite possibilities.*

KEY 3: *We can rediscover our hearts and serve humanity.*
AFFIRMATION: *By expanding my consciousness I can integrate my mind and heart and serve humanity compassionately.*

KEY 4: *We can empower ourselves.*
AFFIRMATION: *I choose to free myself from fear to allow changes within and without. In supporting myself and others in this process, we can together develop a caring and sharing society.*

KEY 5: *We can live in the spirit of unity.*
AFFIRMATION: *By learning to integrate different parts of my being and focusing on our common humanity, I can work for the interests of all.*

KEY 6: *We can find our own path to truth.*
AFFIRMATION: *May I have the courage to explore the mysteries of life and seek the truth without judgment.*

KEY 7: *We can make a difference.*
AFFIRMATION: *My personal development is linked to global transformation and I am aware that each one of us counts. I honor the global family of which I am part and cherish the home planet that we all share.*

Downtown shopping center, The "Hilvertshof" Hilversum

APPENDIX A
The Shopping Centre "Hilvertshof" and Football Stadium "Galgenwaard"

"Hilvertshof" Downtown Development

In the early 1950s, my father had been thinking about creating a new project to rejuvenate the center of our hometown of Hilversum. He started acquiring land for this from the early 1960s onward. The challenge was to create a business environment that would serve the needs of the people of Hilversum and the surrounding area, and which would be economically viable. Given the high cost of land in the town center, this was no easy task.

We had been thinking about this project for some time but had been unable to come up with a successful formula for realizing it when I suddenly had a flash of inspiration. At the time, I was twenty-three years old and happened to be in Glasgow on a trip to Scotland with some colleagues on a shopping center study trip. In one moment, I realized we could solve the problem in Hilversum

With my Father at the Opening ceremony for the "Hilvertshof"

by creating a multi-layered building that would have different activities going on at different levels, including shopping, thus making best use of the available space. The new construction would be carefully integrated with the existing buildings around it. At this time, Hilversum had a population of 90,000 and a catchment area of 300,000 consumers. The idea was that consumers could start their shopping trip in the very center of Hilversum by parking on the top floors of the building. They could then walk down through the shopping floors below and also visit shops in the surrounding old parts of the town via linking pedestrian alleyways. The center also contained a large fitness club to help meet the health needs of the local population—at that time a new concept in the Netherlands.

We needed to get the agreement from the public authorities as well as the cooperation of existing stores and businesses. Some saw the opportunities it would provide straightaway, others were more cautious. But in the end, we secured the necessary consent both at local and national level and we got planning permission for building the new shopping center, "Hilvertshof". It was a very risky project, as we had to start the building work before having the leasing and finance in place, in order to complete it within the time limit of

The Galgenwaard stadium, Utrecht, in 1980

the planning permission and the deadlines of government subsidies. It was built in 1971–2 and opened in the spring of 1973. Today, these kinds of inner-city projects are common. However, around 1970, this was a very innovative approach. At that time in the Netherlands, enclosed malls did not really exist. In fact, our Hilvertshof project was, to my knowledge, the first Dutch multilevel, major, inner city, enclosed shopping center that was not attached to a major railway station.

Over thirty years later, it is still a hugely successful shopping center. Our company developed many shopping centers (twenty during my time with the company), as well several thousand homes, recreational parks, many office buildings and even a football stadium designed with integrated office space.

An Innovative Football Stadium, "Galgenwaard"

In 1981 our company developed and built an—at that time—rather innovative football stadium: the area under the stands were designed as office space. In addition, four office buildings were built at the corners of the stadium. The use of the different functions of the building complex provided optimal use of the parking facilities: when there were soccer matches on Sundays and evenings, the parking facilities were used by the supporters and players. During office hours, the parking was available for the office workers. This timesharing of the parking as well as the use of the space under the stands would be commonplace nowadays, but at the time it was totally unique in the Netherlands and, to my knowledge, in other countries.

I really enjoyed this creative aspect of the work and we also had very capable people in the business, who dealt with the building side of things, which did not interest me as much. Throughout this work, I experienced huge support from my colleagues on the board and from the other members of the staff and project teams. To this day, I feel very grateful for all this co-operation and support that enabled me to play a part in many useful and rewarding projects.

APPENDIX B
Olympic Medallists in Sarajevo—Peace Flame

Gaetan Boucher—Canada
Marjorie van de Bunt—Netherlands
Yvonne van Gennip—Netherlands
Stine Lise Hattestad—Norway
Paul Hildgartner—Italy
Bill Johnson—United States
Eirik Kvalfoss—Norway
Kristin Otto—Germany
Adrienne Rivera—United States
Alexander Spitz—Germany
Vegard Ulvang—Norway
Bart Veldkamp—Netherlands
Cato Zahl Pedersen—Norway

Others:
Lenny Kuhr—Netherlands *(Singer)*
Noreen O'Ryan—Eire *(Singer/Musician)*
Markus Stockhausen—Germany *(Musician)*
Kai Tidemann—Norway *(Paralympic Committee)*
Fred Matser—The Netherlands (*Initiator*)

Rediscover Your Heart

PART II

Exploring the Infinite

Going Beyond your Conventional Beliefs

Introduction

The philosophy I have developed has emerged from my life experiences. In some cases, it was a matter of reflection on past events. For example, thinking over the lessons that I have learned in my private life, business dealings, and philanthropic endeavors. I have also learned from many inspiring teachers, some of whose names are to be found in the pages of this book. Then there were moments of revelation, a sudden illumination when everything became clear and all the pieces of the jigsaw fitted into place. Amongst these were the life-changing moments when I experienced the Infinite. For me, this is the door that opens all other doors. The Infinite encompasses all dimensions and all possibilities and without this overarching vision of the Infinite, it would have been impossible for me to have a glimpse of the workings of our universe.

Because we are used to living in the finite world, finding the words to describe the Infinite is a challenge in itself. How can we describe a larger concept in terms of a smaller one? Logically, we can realize that the Infinite can encompass the finite, though not the other way around. It is rather like those Russian dolls that fit into each other. The large doll can encompass all the smaller ones but the smaller ones can never encompass the outer, large one.

Yet this logical explanation hardly does justice to our sense of awe-inspiring wonderment as we open to the Infinite. This is why, during the course of this book, I have sought to describe the Infinite through my own experiences. There was my first experience during a healing session that opened me up to dimensions beyond the so-called normal day-to-day life. Then there was the moment when I sat in the concert hall and suddenly became one with the music and entered an altered state of consciousness. Another similar experience happened one morning when I was just driving to work in my car and stopped at a traffic light. It was a beautiful day and the sun was shining, and I was just looking out of the window appreciating all the beauty of Nature and the dancing sunlight when, all of a sudden, I again had this overwhelming experience of oneness. I lost my immediate physical presence and instead my consciousness was one with the universe. Once again, this experience probably only lasted for a couple of seconds in our finite world yet my experience was of entering a timeless state of bliss.

From these experiences, I gradually developed a personal philosophy to try to explain how the finite and the Infinite interact and how we relate to them. Access to the Infinite is open to all, and every experience is unique to each person. Others may experience the Infinite in different ways. So, too, their conclusions may differ. What I offer here, therefore, is the fruits of my own journey. I am just a student of life. I have done my best to write down and explain quite a complex subject. I am myself developing each day, as is my philosophy. I don't claim to have all the answers, yet this is the way that I look at the universe and beyond. People may choose to work with my philosophy as a whole or select those parts to which they feel most drawn. More importantly, my hope is that it will encourage and support readers in their own reflections and above all their own experience of the Infinite. I have found it fascinating to read accounts written by others that have so many elements in common with my own.

1. EXPLORING THE INFINITE

We tend to prefer to live safely within our familiar comfort zones, treading the same paths, doing the same jobs, following the same routines day after day and holding onto the same beliefs and patterns of behavior. There is nothing wrong with following these routines, as they often give us safety, security, and comfort, but it is also important to be open to change and to be willing to explore what is outside our normal experience of life and not be scared of it. Although life is all about change and openness to the new, we often try to resist it. Yet new experiences give us a chance to evolve in consciousness.

Being open to new experiences is an important step in our personal development. It means being willing to explore beyond the confines of our limited belief systems. These beliefs come from the attitudes that we develop as a result of the choices we have made in the past and the experiences we have had. These determine our perceptions of what works, or does not work, for us. Our thoughts and actions come from the framework of our belief systems, and so they, too, have limitations that affect every aspect of our lives.

We often handicap ourselves by accepting only information that we can explain in so-called scientific or rational terms yet exclude the inexplicable, which can also provide valuable information and which occurs daily in all our lives. We so often reject these phenomena outright, labeling them as unreal.

However, by having the courage to be open minded and go beyond our conventional belief systems into the unknown we may discover new knowledge. Indeed, we may have an experience beyond knowledge. This might feel uncomfortable at first but, on the other hand, it may lead us to new levels of understanding that we never even imagined. Have we perhaps limited ourselves by trying to explain everything in finite terms rather than encompassing such infinite possibilities? By this exclusion we rule out wider concepts of reality. This is like those who were convinced that the world was flat and who initially greeted the idea that it was round with disbelief and ridicule! We have to remember that this occurred only a few hundred years ago. Yet our thinking and understanding has expanded rapidly to encompass ideas that could not even have been dreamed of in the not -too-distant past.

Many of us have experiences that make us re-evaluate the way we think about life. It could be a serious illness, a major sporting success, the loss of a loved one, a huge win of money, etc. Or we may be fortunate enough to encounter teachers who lead us to new understanding, beyond the everyday world of our five senses. These experiences can enable us to go beyond the fear of the unknown, to look at life in a completely new way and to change our attitudes. It was a single life-changing transcendental experience that was my route into the new world of the Infinite. This spontaneous experience had taken me completely outside of my normal belief systems, and I could not rationally explain what had happened. For me, the experience was so simple and fleeting and yet so magnificent, that I could not forget it. I started to look at life quite differently

A Journey beyond the Finite Universe

We are all familiar with the finite world. It's the one we experience every day as we go to work or meet our friends, complain about our problems or celebrate a success. It is the world into which we were born. However, encompassing our small finite universe, is the Infinite. To experience it is to experience a moment of illumination, when we sense that everything is connected, everything is alive. Above all for me, it is an experience of Unconditional Love.

Most of us spend our lives in a finite universe unaware of the Unconditional Love that surrounds us or any of the other marvelous wonders of the Infinite. We have become so used to it that it is almost an addiction that blinkers our consciousness. It is as if we have lived in a box, the four walls of which were formed by conventional thinking. However these are in truth not solid walls but curtains, and we may draw them aside at any time to see the world that exists beyond it. Of course this requires letting go of the illusion of security that the box provides. It might mean letting go of low self-worth, rigid forms of thinking, or limiting self-belief. Above all, it would mean letting go of the fear that underlies such thoughts and emotions. As a consequence, we might have to let go of our finite attitudes and behaviors such as:

- *Fear of death*
- *Always being in a hurry*
- *Having no time for one another or oneself*
- *Values being expressed in terms of money, rather than love and care.*

What a sacrifice we would have to make! It is strange how we can become almost addicted to our old ways, even when they leave us disatisfied or miserable. We do have a choice. I have summarized my conception of the Infinite in Figure 1.

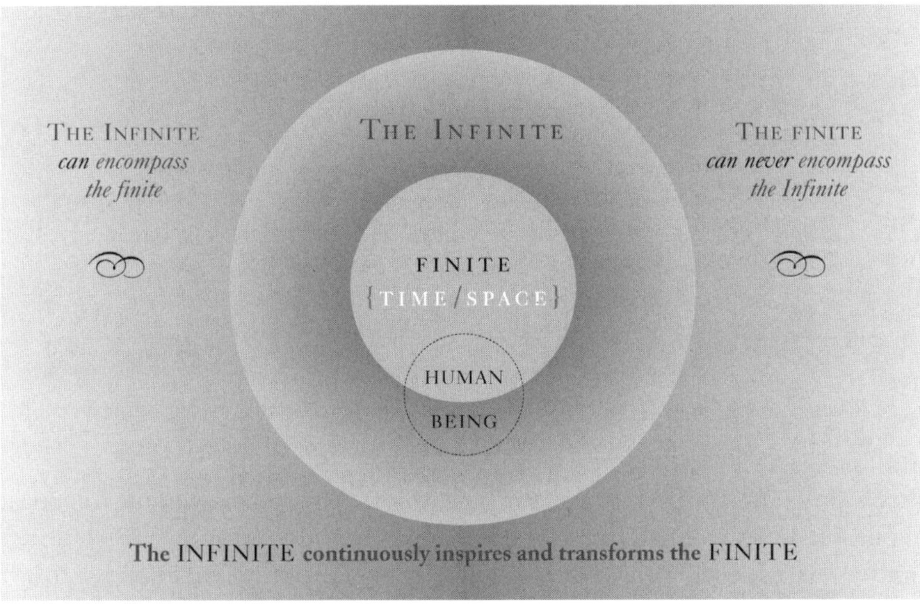

Figure 1: The Infinite in Relation to the Finite

Being a Human Being

One way to understand this transformation from the finite to the Infinite is to look at our nature as human beings. When we were born on this planet we came from the Infinite into the finite. So within each one of us is the essence of the Infinite—Unconditional Love, a sense of connection with the Divine, a feeling of oneness. However, this needs to be expressed through our ordinary human consciousness. Put another way, as human beings, our "*beingness*" (infiniteness) is expressed through our "*human-ness*" (finiteness). Yet because so many of us have forgotten about our "*beingness*", everything has become reduced to "*human-ness*"—to the exclusion of the Infinite. The whole finite universe with all its galaxies in which our planet exists is an expression of Infinite creation and yet we are hardly aware of it. This idea is represented in Figure 2 on page 154.

It is interesting to note that the roots of the verb "*to be*" encompass those of "*to exist*", "*to come into being*" and are linked to the Sanskrit words *bahavat*

"AS HUMAN BEINGS, OUR "BEING-NESS" (INFINITENESS) IS EXPRESSED THROUGH OUR "HUMAN-NESS" (FINITENESS)"

Expression of the finite:	*Expression of the Infinite:*
Human	*Being**

**To "be" = essence*
Essence = The Infinite
This could be summarized by saying: ***We human beings lost our "being"and became merely "human" by excluding our "beingness".*** *These days everything is so "human" and anthropocentric but the "essence" is so often left out. Yet we can all re-introduce this Infinite essence into our lives and embrace our real "beingness" and become human beings again.*

Figure 2: The Meaning of the Human "Being"

(becoming) and *bhumi* (into the earth or world). Yet we have almost forgotten about our Infinite existence and have tended to reduce our world to finite, limited experiences. However, based on my own experiences, I believe that if only we can expand our belief systems from the finite to the Infinite, then our whole perspective of life and death will dramatically change.

A Journey from the Infinite

Most people, including me, at one time or another ask themselves: "Why are we here?" It's one of the great mysteries of life, and it may be that we can never understand fully the answer whilst we are limited by our human consciousness. One way of approaching this question can be to see it in terms of our journey from the Infinite to the finite.

I believe it may be hard for us to conceive of the fact that we, living in the finite, are also a product of the Infinite: the great creative force termed by some as the Creator or God. We are part of an ongoing, inspiring process and we were born from the Infinite into the finite for a purpose. We came to experience all the gifts of life, the greatest of which is Unconditional Love. Yet strange as it may sound, we can only experience this by contrasting it with the fear that is found in the world of the finite. Similarly we can only learn about transcendence through the limitations of our daily lives, here on earth.

In my view, we can only truly experience our sense of connection within the Infinite when we have experienced the feeling of separation on this planet—above all the sense of separation from God. In other words, we are evolving through the experience of opposites—love and fear—or at least what appear to be opposites. For, in truth, Unconditional Love has no opposite. We are part of Creation and our connection with our Creator is never lost. Rather, we are learning through a kind of cosmic theatre; one in which we are both the actors and the audience. Like all good theatre, it has both meaning and purpose. We may experience all kinds of reactions as we watch and participate in the play. It may provoke many thoughts or provide any number of insights. Or we may stubbornly refuse to learn anything, sitting there with our minds firmly closed. Or perhaps we may try to sleep through the whole performance!

If we choose to believe in only a finite universe and exclude the possibility of contact with the Infinite, we may not even be aware of its presence. However, as a human being we can come to realize that existence is both finite and Infinite. As we awaken to the knowledge that we are actually one with the Infinite, then we may be able to let go of fear and experience this Unconditional Love. In such a state, we are fully experiencing our human (finite) "beingness" (Infinite). So the paradox is that the path to Unconditional Love is found through the experience of the fear in the finite. In this sense, love is more than simply "letting go of fear"; it is the process of going, with trust, through resistance and fear to dis-cover—"cover" being a characteristic of the finite universe—and to experience Unconditional Love. Thus we can go beyond seeing love and fear as opposites to embrace the whole, which has no opposites—only the oneness of Unconditional Love.

2. INFINITE HEART

For me, to receive Unconditional Love, I need to open my heart completely to the Infinite. We have an opportunity as human beings to express that love in a finite world. It means letting go of fear and all which binds to it. In the same spirit, we let go of judgment and replace it with discernment, wisdom, and compassion; we can evolve through our emotions and allow our feelings to shine through. We can also learn to value the heart and what it can teach us. We can integrate it with our mind so they can work together harmoniously. In a wider sense, we bring together the male and female sides of our being. In my view this is a journey of rediscovering our hearts.

Letting Go of Judgment

Letting go of judgment does not mean we stop seeing people as they are, with all their qualities and challenges. In fact, we may see them even more clearly. To me, this letting go means that we are no longer drawn into their personal drama. To take an example: we may see someone who bullies and cheats their way through life. We see the fear that tells them they must always put down others first, lest they be put down themselves. We see them believing that they must win at all costs, no matter how, so they can stay on top, terrified of the humiliation of being ranked below. We see how this behaviour is fed by their sense of worthlessness. At the same time we may see deep inside a small, frightened child feeling—or made to feel—that they are not good enough as they are. In truth, they are a precious child of God, loved beyond measure by their Creator, but they cannot, or will not, allow this realization.

Seeing all this play out, we can let go of our anger or sense of judgment. We can feel simply compassion. It does not mean that we think bullying or cheating is defensible or that their pain justifies what they do. However, we can see another struggling soul, one very like all the other billions on this planet. We may then support them wisely, lovingly, and with detachment. We can also pray for them. Using our discernment, we may create opportunities for them, while also letting go of any attachment to the result of our efforts. We can allow them to take responsibility for their own life without trying to fix their life or feeling the need to do so. This is Unconditional Love expressed in the form of loving detachment.

Freeing Ourselves from Fear and Emotional Attachment

How do we reach this point of loving detachment? I believe the first step is to let go of our own fears. It is important to realize how much fear can permeate our lives without us being aware of it, affecting our daily behavior, relationships, and creativity. There are many different expressions of fear; I list some of them in Figure 3. Fear can serve a useful function, such as keeping us out of danger. However, in many cases it works against us.

In many of the words in Figure 3, the connection to fear is obvious. We have already seen how fear can lead to deception and aggressive behavior. Laziness and procrastination can mask the fear that we will not succeed at our enterprise. Yet what about being in love? At first glance, this seems to make no sense. Surely, love is the reverse of fear? We all know that being in love is the most

Examples of Manifestations of Fear

Arrogance	*Jealousy*
Greed	*Addiction*
Anger and aggression	*Deception*
Laziness and procrastination	*Doubt*
Stress	*Lack of confidence*
Impatience	*Guilt*
	Being in love

Figure 3: Examples of Manifestations of Fear

wonderful feeling and a marvelous gift. However, if we look deeper we can also see that it may cloud our clarity. Being "in love", as opposed to loving someone, brings us into the world of emotional attachment. In our lives, when we are emotionally attached, everything is seen in terms of ownership and possession. You are "my partner", this is "my toy/property/town/nation", and so on. Here, we no longer love freely and unconditionally, but rather we experience a love that is actually based on fear. As a poet once wrote: "Love is a constant terror of loss."[1]

This is because emotional attachments are linked to a belief system that is exclusively anchored in the finite. Seen from this point of view, emotions can be regarded as limited, as they exclude the Infinite, and are ultimately expressions of fear. Even an emotion that might normally be considered marvelous, such as "being in love", also has a fearful aspect—it is simultaneously associated with attachment and the fear of losing the person who is loved. So, being "in love", although also a wonderful feeling, can actually create a kind of emotional tunnel-vision where clarity of mind and heart is lost. Maybe we are meant to transform our feeling of "being in love" into the next level of love: Unconditional Love.

In my own experience of the Infinite, I found there is no fear—only this Unconditional Love. So by accessing Infinite Love, it may become possible to go through fear, let go of it, and reach a state beyond it. Yet how many of us have achieved this type of fearless loving in real life? In fact we can consciously choose to let go of our emotional attachment, and of the fear which underlies it, right now. Instead we can learn to love freely.

1 Kazimierz Wierzyński, *A Word To Orphists*.

An example might be a situation where a man is jealous of his wife, fearing her unfaithfulness, and the possibility of losing her. If he can lovingly focus his attention on the jealousy and explore it, he might discover that it springs from a fear of loss that he developed after being rejected, for example, by a girlfriend or parent in the past. At that time if his sense of self-worth was defined by such relationships, then being rejected would lead to a sense of worthlessness and emotional pain. By becoming aware of and understanding this process, he may become able to dissolve the emotional block caused by the jealousy, move on and re-anchor his sense of self-worth in himself. In this way, the emotion has enabled the man to learn about a blockage that he needed to work on and to evolve through the experience.

Freeing ourselves from emotional attachment has wider implications for us in our daily lives. This principle of attachment—that is, having fears, judgments, and opinions expressed through emotions—is used by industry on a massive scale. Through the manipulation of emotions, desires, and wants, people can be triggered to purchase goods and services that they may not need—a kind of emotional blackmail if you like. This manipulation and binding of people diminishes their autonomy; it clouds their consciousness and takes away clarity of thought. On the other hand, if we can reconnect with our pure feelings and have a clear mind, we can enter a state of real being-ness. When I sat in the concert hall in Amsterdam and had the experience of merging with the music as I listened to it, I felt a wonderful sense of detachment, not devoid of feeling but rather experiencing pure feeling without the clouding influence of emotions.

If we could become better at, and find new ways for, integrating our thoughts with our feelings, free from emotional attachments, then maybe feelings could once again become valued as subtle information carriers that can guide and inspire us. This peeling away of emotional attachments may well be a life-long process! I have encountered a good example of just such detachment when the renowned Indian yogi, the Maharishi Mahesh Yogi[2], was asked in an interview how he felt about the death of somebody he was close to. The interviewer asked the Maharishi, "Did you cry?" The Maharishi answered, "No", and when asked, "Why not?" he said, "The sun goes down at night and the next morning it rises."

This answer seems to convey a transcendental view of life and death, namely that the individual is seen as a drop of water returning to the source, or ocean. Since the yogi experiences himself as at least part of the time in the Infinite, he feels no need to have emotion, fear, or attachment to humans. He knows that the connection with the Infinite is there before life, through life, and after life.

2 Who passed away in February 2008.

The Difference between Feelings and Emotions

These experiences highlighted for me the difference between emotions and feelings. For example, we may hear some music, smell a rose, or feel the coolness of a gust of wind. The resonance of the musical notes, the scent of the flower, or the movement of the wind, in its purest sense, is devoid of opinion or emotional content. You could say we are simply allowing ourselves to "be felt". In a way, our body is used as an instrument.

Emotions, however, can cloud our clarity of feeling and thinking. Our mind can no longer simply register the sensation clearly once emotions, for example, in the form of fears or judgments, are attached to the feeling. At this point, our mind is no longer clear and open; the emotion blocks our perception and limits our understanding so that we can no longer perceive the whole picture. We may be allowing ourselves to react emotionally rather than allowing ourselves to "be felt". At the level of feelings there is no judgment—just consciousness and discernment.

At this level, as I see it, our "in-vironment" (heart and mind—our inner landscape) is fully connected with the "en-vironment". However, as emotions surface, linked to fear, judgments, and opinions, our attention is drawn away from the whole and we can become disconnected from it. In a way, these emotions are dysfunctional because they are blockages that prevent us from being in full consciousness and linked to the Infinite. Emotions are based on our responses to past events or future expectations. Feelings are based on the present moment. However, from another perspective, I believe that emotions can also serve a useful function, as we can learn to understand what blocks our real feelings.

I find an analogy of a cello and chewing gum helps to explain these concepts (see Figure 4 on page 160). If some chewing gum (representing fear and emotions) is placed in the cello, it can no longer resonate clearly, but when the gum (the emotional blocks) is removed, the sound produced is clear once more. So too, as our emotional blocks are removed, we can allow feeling and full consciousness.

Removing Emotional Blockages

If we can understand the issue that created the emotional block, then we can start to dissolve it. We can begin by first accepting the emotional block. We do not suppress or deny the emotions but instead, in the words of Deepak Chopra, we "become friends with our shadows." By recognizing the fear or emotional attachment underlying it, we can, in the light of greater consciousness, express

Figure 4: About Emotions

gratitude for how it has served us thus far. Then we can let it go, as we do not need it any more, and we can replace it with thoughts or behaviors that come from this new level of consciousness. The key point to bear in mind is that all emotional blockages and attachments are based on fear. So to free ourselves from the dominance of our emotions, we need to free ourselves from fear. There is a process we can work through in which we can deal with our fears:

1. We can first recognize and acknowledge that there is fear and bring it into our full awareness rather than denying it.
2. Next we can unravel the kind of fear that often hides its true nature. Rather like unwrapping a present, we can strip it down and shed light on the main issue(s) underlying the fear.
3. By shining a light—paying attention—to reveal the real underlying issue behind the fear it begins to dissolve.
4. After some time (it may be almost instantly or it may be a while later), the fear will dissolve completely. Then we can express gratitude for the learning from it, say goodbye to it, and at last be free from it as the resistance dissolves and the fear is transcended.
5. We can then use an affirmation to take the place of the fear. For example, if we have let go of the fear of having to speak in public, we might say, "Now that my fear of public speaking has been dissolved, I fill myself up with the joy of sharing information with others."

Bringing Heart and Mind Together

Releasing ourselves from fear and emotional attachment creates a greater clarity in our thinking and feeling. In doing so, it paves the way for bringing heart and mind together as one and we learn to value both.

An important milestone in this process for me happened one ordinary workday in the latter part of the 1980s. I was just sitting at my desk in the office, about to dictate a letter to my secretary, when out of the blue the following expression just popped into my mind's eye: "The chaos in the world (en-vironment) is a reflection of the disorder in our minds and hearts (in-vironment)."

I was a bit surprised at first, but then I could see its meaning as I looked out of my office window and saw stressed car drivers scurrying about in traffic, fighting for space or to speed ahead of other cars. So much time was being spent doing and so little in simply being.

As I pondered these words more deeply, I started to think about how much our modern world is dominated by the intellect and what comes from it. Yet we also all have feelings! I thought to myself, "Feelings are sensors too! Don't they also tell us important things? Why do we take our intellect so seriously and yet not our feelings? Aren't they equal but different?" Then I thought, "Why have we put the intellect on a pedestal and regard it so highly, while feelings are so undervalued?" If feelings had a personality, I imagined they would "feel" rejected and dejected! Yet, for me, the reality is that allowing and trusting our feelings can enable us to connect with higher dimensions where, at times, the most important information may reside.

I wondered if there could be a way in which our feelings could become as valued and well regarded as our intellect. It became clear to me how important the balance between the two must be for our well-being.

This is something that could be addressed from our earliest years. We come into this world as newborns with our senses and faculties open, and this continues during our time as infants. However, in the West, from the age of four or five, we enter the formal education system, where the mind and the intellect are more valued and highly trained while feelings tend to be undervalued and neglected.

We are taught to evaluate, analyze, and criticize but are not educated in how to feel and trust our feelings, or how to be compassionate, kind human beings. Nor are we encouraged, or sometimes even allowed to explore a sense of openess to the possibility of other dimensions; an openess which seems to be quite natural in children who have not yet been "en-veloped". This can limit our understanding of the dimensions of reality and so, in the process of growing up, it could be said that we human beings lose our "being" and may start to develop into human-"havings" instead, concerned more with materialistic outcomes than with personal or spiritual development.

We may also lose confidence in our ability to express ourselves. This is illustrated in my version of story about Mary, which I once heard on a tape by Barry Neil Kaufman, the co-founder of the Option Institute in the U.S.A.[3]

Mary was a toddler aged around two years old. She woke up early one sunny morning and, seeing a box of crayons on the floor, started to spontaneously express her feelings of happiness and joy by drawing lots of colorful squiggles all over the wall in her bedroom. In a way, she was at one with her creation and was so totally absorbed in and enjoying what she was doing, that she did not hear her mother get up and come to her room.

When her mother opened the door, Mary turned to her with a beaming smile, ready to show off her creation. However, her expression of joy froze when she saw the angry look on her mother's face as she towered over her. "Mary,

---

3 *www.option.org*

what on earth do you think you're doing, you naughty girl!" cried her mother as she grabbed the crayons from Mary's hand and told her severely, "Get back into bed! We have only just decorated your room and now you have ruined it!"

From this experience, Mary learned that expressing her feelings was bad, so she shut off her heart and suppressed her feelings and instead focused on her intellect, which was praised by her parents. She became a straight-A student and went on to great academic success. Yet, in doing so, she became cut off from the creative power that underlies her feelings and heart while focusing only on her mental activities.

How different her life might have turned out if her mother had opened the door, sat on the floor at her daughter's level and said something like, "What a great picture! Next time it would be better to do your drawings on paper. We can go and buy you a sketchbook, as that is a good place to put your drawings in future." I have been so struck by this story because it resonated in some ways with my own childhood. My parents did their very best in raising their children, but they found it difficult to express their emotions and feelings, which affected us all. In my case, this meant that I also found it hard to connect with, and express, my own emotions and feelings. It was only much later that I reconnected with this power and have become more able to express and share my feelings. This is something that I continue to progress with, too. Another powerful learning experience for me happened ten years ago when I took part in a workshop on living and dying.

During the course of it, we were given an exercise where we were asked to lie down and imagine that we were going to die in twenty minutes. One workshop participant was asked to "sit by our bedside" to hear our "last words", while another was to sit on the other side simply as a silent witness. When it was my turn to lie down, I had no difficulty imagining this scenario; and almost immediately I had the overwhelming realization that there were so many things that I had not yet shared with my three daughters.

I had not told them enough how deeply I love them and was aware of how I had allowed barriers to remain between us. This ignited huge emotion and great sadness in me and my crying was so intense that I could not speak. As the waves of emotion eased, I was able to speak to the workshop participant joining me in the exercise, as if speaking with each of my children, and expressed my deep feelings of love to them. I also thought of my wife Chris, and felt the profound love connecting us and had a wondrous sense that there was an easy flow of this love, with few blockages between us.

My mother, who is still alive, was also in my consciousness at that time, and with her I felt our long-established love for each other, which has had full expression. My father, who had passed away, was part of the process as well and I saw his smile. This profound experience, amongst others, taught me how important it is not to miss opportunities to express love fully toward loved ones; not to procrastinate or hide our feelings. After this experience I realized even more the many opportunities that I have to express my love, in many different ways, toward my loved ones.

In contrast to Mary's story, I remember Jane Goodall telling me how her mother supported her adventures. For example, Jane, as a young child, was curious about where chicken eggs came from. So she got up very early one morning and went inside the family's hen house to sit and wait and to watch for the eggs to appear. Meanwhile, her mother woke up and found her daughter missing and looked everywhere for her.

On finally finding her, instead of being angry or fearful, she listened enthusiastically to Jane's story about her discovery of where the eggs came from. Jane told me how much this experience, and her mother's encouragement on many other occasions, stimulated her to explore and ultimately led her to travel to the forests of Africa and study chimpanzee behavior. It is so important to nurture and encourage children to express their feelings and to explore and be creative, as this enables them to stay in touch with their inner nature, and true self.

Overvaluing Thoughts and Undervaluing Feelings

As adults we of course have the capacity to both think and feel, yet in our society, the power of thought and the intellect tend to be the most highly regarded. Why should this be so? Perhaps it is because thoughts can be externalized, and the products of our thinking can easily be ordered, compared, and therefore communicated. Feelings are just as real as well but we often do not know how to handle them, since they cannot easily be measured or compared externally; they are experienced in the moment, basically in our own personal language and so cannot be communicated easily to others.

We have no real point of reference for feelings outside of ourselves, but we can compare them internally; for example, we might determine that "I feel better today than I felt yesterday." People often say to one another, "I know how you feel." Yet can this really be true? While we may relate to a person's experience and what this triggers in our own emotions about similar experiences, can we ever feel exactly the same as another person?

Yet feelings also serve a vital function, namely as subtle information carriers, transmitting and receiving messages to the body. For example they may be feeding back to us that we are in harmony or out of balance. Or, they could be giving us information about our surroundings as we enter a room with people or letting us know how we respond to a person as we make eye contact and, maybe unconsciously, also communicating something back to them. Therefore, it could be said that "brother thought" has a wonderful "sister feeling". But thought tends to dominate feeling and be overvalued, since it can readily be externalized and measured, while feeling remains internal and undervalued. For me, feelings can serve us by connecting us with the silence that lies within. Feelings encompass both the normal senses and the more subtle ones such as intuition and the so-called paranormal senses, such as extrasensory perception. Figure 5 summarizes some of my ideas about thoughts and feelings.

Integrating the Male and Female

Bringing together the heart and mind is part of a wider process of integrating the male and female sides of our being. I see the concepts of the male and female principles as going well beyond the idea of gender. Rather, these are different qualities that exist in both men and women, to a greater or lesser extent, and they are interconnected and in a constant dynamic interplay with one another.

THINKING	FEELING
• *Thinking is real*	• *Feeling is real*
• *The products of thinking can be expressed in comparisons or equations*	• *The products of feeling cannot be expressed in comparisons and/or equations*
• *Because of this we can communicate about thoughts*	• *Because of this we cannot deal with feelings as we do with the products of our thinking*
• *We can compare with one another*	• *We cannot compare with one another; we can only compare with our own experiences in the past*
• *We can agree or disagree with our thoughts*	• *We cannot agree or disagree with our feelings*

Thinking ◄——— *of equal value* ———► *Feeling*
External ◄——— *measurement instrument* ———► *Internal*
OVERvalued ◄——— *belief system* ———► *UNDERvalued*

Figure 5: Thinking and Feeling

These qualities are also described in ancient Chinese philosophy as Yin, associated with female qualities of softness, darkness, stillness, and receptivity; and Yang, traditionally linked to male qualities such as hardness, lightness, movement, and action. This is often represented in the well known Tai Ji symbol shown in Figure 6.

Figure 6: The Tai Ji/Yin Yang Symbol

I also associate the male principle with the (over-valued) mind and intellect and the female principle with the (under-valued) feelings, intuition, and the heart. Examples of words representing "male" and "female" qualities are given in Figure 7. Because the "male" principles have so often been over-valued, they have become dominant. I believe this has led to an imbalance between the "male" and "female" principles in our society as a whole. This affects the way in which we live our lives. "Male" qualities, especially the dysfunctional ones, such as competitiveness and dominance, are more valued and rewarded in both men and women. Thus we are encouraged to compete with each other on an individual, group, national, and global level. It also affects how we as businesses and nations exploit the natural world; we are focused on selfish needs, scarcity and on "taking". For example, we exploit all the oil reserves that we can, profit from water resources, carve up the rainforests and so on.

Yet we can rebalance ourselves both as individuals and as a species, developing the "female" side of our nature as well, such as our sense of sharing and caring. For example, we can ensure that we replenish and put back what we take away from Nature. In our personal lives, we could create greater harmony by creating a balance between these principles; for example, between giving and receiving. It is said that in giving we receive and vice versa; for there to be a dynamic balance with an exchange of loving energy going back and forth, we need to both give and receive. A person who simply takes all the time could be regarded as selfish and self-centered, but equally someone who always gives is denying others the pleasure of giving and could also eventually become resentful or burned out, too.

Expectations and values are also important in this dynamic. A person may give because they expect something in return, but this is not the same as unconditional giving, with no expectation of any reward or return. Being able to both give and receive unconditionally without any expectation could be seen as an example of living with the values of the Infinite in a finite world. These same principles are at work between the finite and the Infinite in every area of life.

Let's take the idea of life itself. For many scientists, life is perceived as a given, a natural fact of biology. Yet for me and many others, life can be perceived not only as a given but rather as a gift. In my personal prayers, I acknowledge and thank God, the Creator, for the receipt of this gift of life. So I receive life, born from the Infinite in the ultimate sense, and I give thanks from my finite universe back to the Infinite, from whence my life came. This is therefore an example of the dynamic connection between me, the human (finite) and my being (merged with the Infinite) in the cycle of life. Similarly a dynamic balance between thinking and feeling, and giving and receiving can play a role in our relationship with God. We may receive inspiration and ideas from the Infinite and use these to give birth to our creativity here on earth. In return we give thanks and then receive further and so on.

Synthesis

The polarity between heart and mind, or female and male principles, are manifestations of the finite universe. For this is a world of opposites, or at least what appear to be opposites. In reality, everything is connected; everything is part of the oneness of the Infinite. By opening, and valuing, our hearts as well as our intellect, we have the opportunity to unite these apparent opposites into one harmonious whole. In this way we can bring the values and clarity of the Infinite into the finite. We can do this by letting go of judgments and emotional

MALE	FEMALE
Mind	*Heart*
Intellect	*Feeling*
Analytical ability	*Intuition*
Giving	*Receiving*
Active	*Receptive*
Having an "overview"	*Attention to detail*
Focused	*Multi-tasking*
Comparing	*Sharing and caring*

Figure 7: Examples of Words Representing "Male" and "Female" Qualities

attachments, and by forgiving both ourselves and others. In this way we can receive, and become a channel for, Unconditional Love. Looking back at my own experiences in this regard, these are some of the lessons I have learned:

- *Releasing ourselves from emotional attachment, judgment and fear frees us to love unconditionally.*
- *Integrating thinking and feeling enriches our lives.*
- *Balancing male and female principles, in both men and women, creates harmony both in ourselves and in society.*

3. INFINITE MIND

The Infinite is full of endless possibilities. Once we have opened the door to it, we can explore the unknown territory beyond our five senses. We have only to free our minds. For this, the same principles apply with our minds as with our hearts: freeing ourselves from fear and emotional attachment to bring clarity and loving detachment to our minds. This holds true not only for us but also to all seekers of the truth, whether in the field of science and/or religion. For everyone, scientist or religious scholar, layman or professor, is subject to the same human tendencies that can cloud our perception of reality. Yet by opening up to the Infinite, we can expand our consciousness and access ideas and information from higher dimensions.

Accessing Ideas from the Infinite

As humans we have become so attached to our minds and physical bodies and all the material manifestations around us, we can forget to view these as expressions of the Infinite. For, apart from accessing the everyday world of information all around us we can also learn to access information transcendentally. Let me explain what I mean by this:

By believing *only* in conventional forms of learning; we have become trapped in our limited world of perception and so we tend to focus on accessing information from the obvious sources around us. This includes the information we glean directly through our five normal senses: sight, hearing, smell, taste and touch, as well as the information we gather from the radio, TV, newspapers, books, the internet, and conversations with others.

We have become dependent on, and maybe even addicted to, finite sources of information to the exclusion of the Infinite. However, I believe that we can also access information from beyond these normal sources. For example, we may be able to access information received while in a relaxed, meditative or dream state, via the so-called paranormal senses.

One example is the case of Galileo, the renowned Italian physicist, astronomer, and philosopher who lived in the seventeenth century. I read once that, when he was searching for the solution to a scientific, astronomical, or philosophical problem, he would sit in a rocking chair holding a ball balanced between his fingertips. He would then rock to and fro, to the point where he became relaxed and was almost falling asleep. In this relaxed state, he would often get great inspirations and solutions to problems, but if he fell asleep, he would be unable to recall them fully.

By holding the ball, just as he was on the point of falling asleep and forgetting them, the ball would drop from his hands and this would return him to a waking state. He could then recall the ideas and think them over. In this way, you could say that he was being informed from beyond the here and now of his conscious mind (the finite), by the Infinite (accessed via his subconscious or supra-conscious mind)[4].

Brain research has long shown that different patterns of electrical activity predominate in our brains when we are engaged in different types of activities. Four main types of what are popularly known as brain waves have been identified[5]. The beta brain wave predominates when we are in an active mode and focusing our minds on a task such as speaking, concentrating, thinking or worrying about something. Slower *alpha* waves occur when we have completed a task and are resting, relaxing, or walking in Nature. As we get drowsy and start to daydream or go on automatic pilot, such as when jogging or while soaking in the bath, *theta* waves start to predominate—at this time we often get our best ideas and feel positive. This state also occurs when we first wake up, yet we are not fully awake. So it seems likely that by relaxing and rocking in his chair, Galileo was shifting his brain from a conscious *beta* brain wave state to a slower, predominantly *theta* one, where he could go beyond thinking and allow himself to "be thought", thereby accessing new ideas.

Then as the ball dropped the *alpha* and then *beta* brain wave activity would have been reactivated, enabling him to concentrate his conscious mind on the new ideas. *Delta waves* occur when we are asleep, with the faster waves associated with dreaming and rapid eye movements (REM) and the slowest of

---

4 Supra-conscious mind is for me higher consciousness and is linked to the Infinite.
5 Beta "brain waves" are fast, with a frequency usually above 12Hz (12 cycles per second) and low in amplitude. Alpha waves are slower (usually 8–12Hz) with a higher amplitude. Theta waves are slower still (4–8Hz) with a greater amplitude, while delta waves are the slowest of all (up to 4 Hz) and have the greatest amplitude.
In very deep sleep states, delta frequencies may drop as low as 2–3 Hz but they never reach zero, as this only occurs with brain death.

all with deep, dreamless sleep. These different brain waves occur in all human beings, regardless of race or culture, and although a given brain wave may predominate at a particular time, components of all the brain waves are always present in different areas of the brain.

Dreams are also valid sources of information, and we have the choice of whether to pay attention to them or not. Yet dream information is never on the curriculum as a part of formal education in the West! Some information that arises in dream states may be coming from hidden memories or buried thoughts, but it cannot always be so obviously or easily explained. Certain dreams appear to have an element of premonition or pre-cognition, and there are various accounts of such dreams actually occurring later in real life. No one knows exactly where such information may come from, but I wonder if in the dreamlike state, we are able to go outside the limitations of our normal range of thoughts and emotions and somehow tap into the Infinite mind?[6]

Connecting with the Infinite opens up a whole new experience of thinking and feeling. For the bridge between the finite on one hand and the Infinite on the other hand is expressed through thinking and feeling, alternately allowing ourselves to "be thought" and "be felt". This is represented in figure 8.

Yet no one really knows exactly how information is accessed in these different states and where it comes from. Interesting work on brain waves, which are imaged electronically on a screen (neurofeedback), suggests that it may be possible to retrain the transition from one wave pattern to another, for example enabling a shift from say, *alpha* to *beta* brain waves. At the

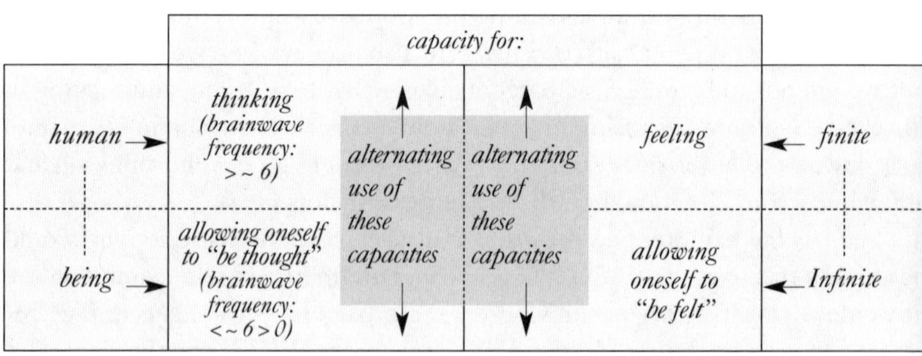

Figure 8: Sources of Information

6 This may have links with what psychologist C.J.Jung called the "Collective Unconscious", or what the Cambridge scientist, Dr. Rupert Sheldrake has termed "Morphic resonance"–that is, collective wisdom and learning that we may all tap into. It may perhaps go even further on many, many levels, ultimately to a Divine power at the source of creation itself.

Neurofeedback Center[7], which we established in Hilversum as an offshoot of one of our Foundations, we have seen dramatic, therapeutic results using neurofeedback, especially with children suffering from attention deficit hyperactivity disorder (ADHD).

Since all brain-wave frequencies operate at all times, maybe we can train ourselves to even switch from one predominant frequency to another at will. In this way, perhaps we could even choose to allow ourselves to be informed transcendentally from the Infinite, and then use our thinking capacity, regulated by *beta* frequencies, as well as our feeling capacity, to express thoughts and feelings about this information and to determine appropriate actions. Thus the Infinite could be used as a source of vital information.

In another example, we might consider the individual genius of someone such as Mozart. Most people probably regard him as a gifted prodigy who just happened to be able to write wonderful music from a young age. However, perhaps he was able to easily enter a *theta* brain-wave state and thereby have ready access to these wider fields of information, enabling him to compose wonderful music far beyond the normal abilities of someone his actual age.

Einstein and Michelangelo are also examples of people who may have been able to access fields of information beyond their normal mental processes, to inform and inspire their great works. A further example is Nicola Tesla who, in the earlier part of the last century, is said to have received some visions of different types of devices, which he then constructed on the basis of what he had seen. It is said that it was only after these devices were actually built that he was able to fully understand and explore their use.

I believe that these transcendental fields of information are potentially open to all, and I have experienced glimpses of them myself. I have found that if I wish, I am able to empty my mind—not thinking of the past nor having any expectation for the future—but simply being fully in the present, free of fear and emotional attachments. It's simple but not always easy! When one does empty the mind, it is possible to enter a state of quietness. Brain-wave analysis has shown that in this state, brain-wave frequencies slow and the *theta* range predominates. I feel that when I open myself up in this way, it is as if I am directing my human "antenna" toward the Infinite, or for me, God, and I am then able to receive help and guidance from that source. We can receive a lot of inspired ideas in this state and we can also access information in dreams or during meditation. Once this information is received, it can then be brought into the world of the finite and used creatively.

7 The Neurofeedback Center continues today as a privately run clinic under the guidance of Guusje Roozemond, who was, for many years, a highly valued co-worker within our Foundation.

However, I believe that we have to be willing to be open in order to receive information in this way. We have to go beyond our normal belief systems and be willing to enter the unknown. Otherwise, it is rather like God calling us up on the phone but constantly hearing the beep-beep-beep of the engaged tone, because we are so busy thinking our own thoughts that it is just impossible to get through! To make a phone connection, the line has to be accessible and so, too, we have to open our minds and hearts if we want to access these transcendental fields of information. It appears that this connection occurs most often when we are in a relaxed state with low levels of brain activity.

The process for allowing ourselves to be informed and inspired from the Infinite can be compared to us being satellite dishes. We can direct our satellite dish horizontally to detect and gain information from anything or any living being around us in the finite world. However, we can also direct it upwards (or transcendentally) to create a connection and access the Infinite power. We each have the power to direct our own antenna and to allow ourselves to be informed directly from the transcendental rather than just from the finite world around us. These two ways of accessing information can successfully be integrated, as symbolized in the form of a cross, whereby "horizontal" thinking, accessed from the finite, can be integrated with "vertical" or transcendental thinking (or "being thought"–see Figure 8 on page 170), accessed from the Infinite. Our connection can enable us to "go with the flow" of the Infinite.

In addition, I believe we have all had experiences of accessing information by going beyond the usual five senses, even though we may not have been fully aware of it. For example, we may "sense" a person and then receive a phone call, letter, or e-mail from them almost immediately afterwards; or two people may suddenly, simultaneously get the same inspiration; or intuition may suddenly prompt us to do or say something without really knowing why, and yet some time later it is revealed to have had a definite meaning or purpose. It is strange that we take for granted the operation of phones, televisions, satellites and other technological wonders and yet barely explore the power of our own minds and consciousness in sending and receiving "signals".

Accessing information transcendentally and in other ways may be an ability that can be developed. Like being able to listen to music while performing a job, maybe we can learn to "tune in" and alternate between receiving information from the finite world and also information accessed in other ways through intuition, dreamlike states, meditation, prayer, and so on. In so doing we can bring transcendental information into the finite. By developing the ability to access transcendental information, not only will our perceptions change but we may then also increase our respons-Ability in relation to each other and to God.

Even when using the finite senses, there have been some extraordinary examples of people who have developed them to go beyond what we conventionally imagine is possible. One such case is the blind Belgian detective Sacha van Loo. His sense of hearing is so acute that it is apparently used to gain vital information from wire-tapped terrorist phone calls. For example, it is said that van Loo can listen to the tones being dialed and identify the actual number. Also, by hearing the sound of a voice echoing off of a wall, he can deduce whether a suspect is speaking from an airport lounge or a crowded restaurant. If the suspect is calling from a car, he can deduce its make from the sound of the engine. He can also identify people's native tongue even when they are speaking in a foreign language.

Religion and Science

Traditionally, people seeking answers to the deeper questions in life have turned to science and/or religion. I believe both science and religion serve us in many different ways, helping us make sense of our existence and perhaps giving meaning to our lives. Yet neither have all the answers, and each has its limitations.

In seeking truth, their approaches seem at first very different. Religion relies primarily on Divine revelation, with varying amounts of room for interpretation according to the particular school of thought. It also relies on tradition, built up over the centuries through religious scholarship. Religions, in general, claim to have found absolute truth, and in that sense the human quest is about working out that truth within our individual lives.

Science, on the other hand, seems quite different in its methods. Truth is meant to be found via a process of rational thought and experimentation. A theory is put forward and put to the test under controlled conditions. Proof is determined when a set of circumstances can be repeated under specific test conditions. Theories are revised in the light of new evidence. Truth is thus constantly evolving. Many people consequently revere science as the absolute truth.

However, the conditions and the parameters of scientific experiments are created within a certain agreed standards advocated by the scientific community at any given time. This can mean that there is a tendency for scientists to find the results that fit into the predetermined limited worldview of conventional science. When Columbus set sail across the Atlantic to find the westward route to India, he decided that the islands that he came across in the Caribbean must be part of India, because that's what he expected to find. In the same way, scientists may tend to find the kind of things they are looking for.

Scientists can become emotionally attached to their own theories and may experience alternative ideas as a personal or professional threat. Disputes between scientists leading rival camps can become ill-tempered, and may block illumination of the truth. Established theories can develop into scientific orthodoxy, with new ideas being seen as heresy. Original thinkers have sometimes paid a heavy personal and professional price for sticking their necks out against the prevailing winds of opinion, like Galileo in asserting his new discoveries about the earth's orbit round the sun. Equally, some of the great breakthroughs in science have come about by intuition or accident rather than standard scientific procedure. Thus the "truth" of science is relative.

For its part, religion does not necessarily have the rigid "once-and-for-all" revelation of the truth that is sometimes portrayed. Religious doctrines evolve, and a new consensus amongst scholars emerges. Individuals will always seek to find their own way to God, whatever the prevailing dogma. What seems to be true, however, is that an open heart and an open mind in the quest for truth will almost always bring the scientist or religious seeker into conflict with the established authorities.

St Francis of Assisi, one of the greatest Christian saints, hovered on the borderline between orthodoxy and heresy. Similarly, a scientist such as Dr. Rupert Sheldrake has found his breakthrough work, on what he terms "morphic resonance", frowned on by the scientific establishment as going beyond the boundary of their orthodox beliefs.

This should not surprise us, as fear of change and the need to control are part of a finite mentality that excludes the Infinite. A free-thinking scientist willing to go beyond the accepted conventions, or the mystic whose spirituality leads them beyond the confines of dogma, are both on a journey to experience the Infinite, albeit in different ways. As they do this, they seem to converge. Religious commentators have long observed how mystics of different faiths seem to experience their spirituality in similar ways. Take, for example, these two extracts written about the experience of union with the Creator:

> *"This highest stage of union is an indescribable experience, in which all idea of images and forms and differences has vanished. All consciousness of self and of all things has gone, and the soul is plunged into the abyss of the Godhead and the spirit has become one with God."*

> *"I have ceased to exist and have passed out of self. I am become one with Him and am altogether His."*

The first is from a fourteenth-century Christian mystic, Suso[8], in his Book of Truth. The second is from Rabi'a of Basra, the eighth-century Muslim mystic, in one of her poems. This convergence may also be taking place between spirituality and some areas of science. In 1975, Fritjof Capra wrote a book, *The Tao of Physics*, pointing out the parallels between quantum physics and eastern mysticism. Though controversial, his book has inspired many, among them the Nobel prize-winning physicist Brian Josephson[9], who decided to explore paranormal phenomena, even though these are usually considered off-limits to reputable scientists.

In an interview in *The New Scientist*[10], Professor Josephson explained that he had started to feel there was more to reality than conventional science allowed. Yet he ran into an attitude of mind from the scientific community, which he summed up in the statement, "Even if it were true, I wouldn't believe it." In other words, the idea of paranormal phenomena is so abhorrent to conventional science that some scientists are unwilling to look at the evidence with an open mind. Josephson believes some scientists think that when an experimental result can't be repeated, it is not evidence of a real phenomenon[11]. Such an attitude becomes like a religious creed, where you have to conform to the correct position.

Another inspirational figure is Dr. Hiroshi Motoyama, scientist and Shinto priest. He has developed what he calls "subjective-objective science", that is, science that goes beyond its normal conventional outlook to incorporate understandings of reality gained from direct spiritual, paranormal, and even psychic experience. He argues that the way to achieve this can be based on trying to integrate science and religion, or rather spiritual experience that goes beyond the confines of religious dogma. Put another way, both science and religion could integrate their male and female aspects, using intuition as well as the intellect, inner experience as well as outer observation.

The Search for Universal Truth

There are scientists who hope to formulate a "theory of everything" that would explain the workings of the Universe, and some religious leaders may claim to have found an explanation through Divine revelation. Yet can either system of thought hope to aspire to absolute truth?

8 Heinrich Seuse, a fourteenth-century Dominican friar.
9 Currently leader of the Mind-Matter Unification Project at the University of Cambridge.
10 See *The New Scientist*, December 9, 2006, p56.
11 In *essence*, nothing is replicable.

Many people regard scientific truths as absolute and base their worldview on scientific facts. However, in my view, science does not represent absolute truth. Rather it is a wonderful tool that can help us to explore and explain the finite, physical universe but is, by definition, only a partial view of the whole.

So, though science helps us through its inventions and discoveries, and in the creation of ever new and different perspectives, it may also limit our belief systems to the finite universe. Though some of the greatest breakthroughs have come from scientists using their intuition, the more conventionally-minded usually limit themselves to only using their intellects, which may handicap them in opening up new horizons.

Similarly, religion, or spiritual beliefs, can be the basis for our perceptions and worldviews and our understanding of truth. Yet, if religion is experienced only through the intellect as a doctrine, and/or purely emotionally rather than in terms of real inner experience, this can lead to a competitive approach between the followers of different religions.

When religion limits itself through fear and emotional attachment to the finite, it inevitably leads to rivalry and the need to control. As a result, people debate the superiority of different religions and even fight wars over them. One of my friends and teachers, Peter Goldman, once told me, "If religion is experienced, it can never be the subject of fighting or discussion; when religion is subject to discussion you can fight about it and it is not experienced."

However, if religion is fully understood and experienced beyond the finite, then the "being" of the human can be revealed to each of us individually, and no thought of competition, or the superiority of one religion over another, remains. Just as it wouldn't make sense for everyone who was unwell to receive exactly the same medicine regardless of their condition, so it doesn't make sense to insist on the same spiritual medicine for everyone. What works for one person may not work for another.

In the same spirit, in the scientific world, maybe we can start to go beyond our finite view of reality whereby Western science is often seen as having all the answers and as being automatically superior to say indigenous beliefs. In the so-called civilized world, we have a strong belief in science but we sometimes forget that it may be based on concepts that are specific to our own culture. We may also focus on finer and finer details and lose sight of the whole. An example might be scientific research into a particular drug and its action at a cellular level. We think that we understand the workings of the drug and yet, when it is tried on a whole person rather than cells in a petri dish, it can have unpredictable results.

In traditional cultures the emphasis seems to be more on the whole person and there often seems to be a deep understanding of the way the universe works. This may include family relationships both with the living and sometimes with the person's ancestors, as well as the cultural environment in which they live.

For example, when I have listened to Peruvian shamans talking, they have no knowledge of quantum physics or modern medicine and yet their understanding often seems to embrace and even go beyond both of these disciplines. Western scientists may regard the views of indigenous peoples as unscientific and disregard them, but perhaps they also have elements of the truth in their concepts about the universe.

To me, scientific ideas represent particular viewpoints held at certain points in time within the finite, and shared with others within a certain scientific community according to mutually agreed rules and terms of understanding. Yet throughout the history of science, we can see that science evolves. That is to say, as scientists deepen their understanding of the finite universe, what was perceived to be true a thousand, a hundred or even ten years ago, is not necessarily perceived to be true today. Similarly, what is believed to be true now may be disproved in ten, one hundred or a thousand years from now. So we might ask ourselves, what in human thinking is really true in the finite universe?

Instead of trying to find absolute answers about our existence through conventional science or religious doctrine, we could seek them from other levels, such as in the Infinite. For what we perceive as truth on earth is merely an expression and a part of a greater creative blueprint from an unseen world; the world beyond the limited dimensions of the finite.

This blueprint is for all the forms of creation in our finite universe and explains how they interact. If we choose to open ourselves to the Infinite, then a totally different awareness can be experienced. As our perception changes, our under-standing (stands-under-God) and inner experience of creation or reality also changes. In this way, we may be able to go beyond the finite to embrace unity rather than always focusing on the things that divide us. I believe ultimately that truth is only fully accessible in the Infinite.

Experiencing Time and Space Differently

Contemplating the Infinite opens up another key area of our perception of reality—time and space. One of the apparent certainties of the finite is that it is determined by time and space. We look at our watches and see the minutes and hours tick by. We rest secure in the belief that everything happens in a time sequence, one moment after the other. Our perception of space also gives us a sense of order. We can measure distances, know where things are, and learn how they constantly move and change. Thus we see time and space as fixed phenomena that we can rely on and arrange our lives by. However, this is only part of the story because time and space are, in fact, relative.

What do I mean by this? I am not a physicist but I have found that Albert Einstein's Theories of General and Special Relativity help us to understand time and space differently. With these theories Einstein showed that time and space form a continuum and that time, far from being universal, actually passes at different rates. As I understand it, the rate depends on both velocity (the rate of change of position of an object in terms of its speed and direction), relative to the speed of light, and the strength of gravitational fields. According to these theories, moving clocks will tick more slowly than "stationary" ones (time dilation) and the lower the gravitational field the more slowly time will pass.

I was discussing this with a friend one day and he suggested that a way of understanding relativity in practical terms is to consider satellite navigation devices; these are used, for example, in vehicles to determine locations at particular points in time. The devices pick up signals from satellites controlled by the Global Positioning System (GPS) center near Denver, Colorado in the U.S.[12].To work correctly, the master clock on the base has to be exactly synchronized with the clocks on the satellites orbiting around the earth.

However, according to Einstein's theories, the clocks in the satellites are affected by their speed and gravitational field and as a result they fall a few microseconds behind the master clock each day. They therefore have to be pre-set to run slightly slower than "earth time", and are closely monitored by the GPS center, as otherwise all the navigations systems would be awry! This is therefore one example of how time, as measured by clocks, is not always the same even though we are conditioned to think that it is.

If we relate these ideas about time and space to the finite world then it can be seen that every person, animal, plant, mineral, element, atom, molecule and so on, occupies its own space and has its own time; it cannot occupy the space and time of any other expression of creation. The concept of everything having its own "space" can, I think, be easily understood; we can readily accept that, in the universe, every expression of matter, from subtle to dense, occupies a different physical position in regard to any other. However, understanding the concept that everything has its own "time" is, I think, more difficult for many people, including myself.

---

12 Schriever Air Force Base.
13 This system was described by Dr. Brian Cox in a recent BBC *Horizon* television program.

Again, I have found that Einstein's theories are helpful here. He suggested determining time in terms of the speed of light and the reference point of the observer. So, for example, if someone is standing in front of me, say a meter away, and a light particle is emitted from the sun, millions of kilometers behind that person's back, it will travel towards us and will reach the person in front of me before it reaches me. Since light travels in a straight line at the speed of 300,000 km/sec, the time difference is infinitesimal, as we are only a meter apart. However the fact that there is a difference is crucial to our understanding of time.

According to this understanding, there is also a time difference between any two points on my skin, or between my two nostrils, or between whatever elements we define in time and space. We too easily take the objects around us for granted.

This understanding of time and space had dramatic consequences for me. I came to realize how each one of us, each particle in the universe, co-exist in the universe, each with our own unique place in the matrix of time and space. Also, as each point in space-time is different from any other, I realized that, of course, we cannot compete for it; a person can never sit on exactly the same spot on a bench at exactly the same time as their friend—and there is no need to, as an abundance of points exist in space-time. This made me think how, at the deepest level of reality, there is no competition or scarcity.

HUMAN CONSCIOUSNESS

Human consciousness is defined as awareness of one's own existence, sensations, feelings, thoughts, and surroundings.

(+)	(-)
*positive, * "male" principle*	*negative, * "female" principle*
dense energy	*subtle, fine energy*
mental/mind	*feeling/heart*
giving	*receiving*

** These expressions imply no judgment about male or female, or plus (+) or minus (-) negative or positive. They are just a description of physical phenomena; for example, we see this represented in electrical circuitry, or with magnets that have a positive and negative charge, or pole. Both the terms negative and positive are free from any association with good or bad, but are of equal value as building blocks of our very existence. The male and female principles refer to different qualities, present in both men and women to varying degrees, rather than differences between the sexes, and are all manifestations of consciousness.*

Figure 9: Defining Human Consciousness

I also concluded that as we learn to experience time and space differently—not simply as defining borders of our world—we learn to expand our consciousness and, in my view, grow towards a greater understanding of the Infinite.

Synthesis

Our minds shape our perception of the world we live in to a degree which is hard to conceive. For the mind does more than simply record external events. It interprets all the information it receives through the senses, ordering it into categories. This includes not only deciding what kind of phenomena is being experienced, such as sorting things into animal, vegetable, or mineral categories but also determining values, such as good or bad, pleasant or unpleasant. It will also place events in sequence and understand them in terms of cause and effect.

From this we can see that the way the mind experiences our inner and outer environment—our consciousness—is key to our personal development. Consciousness incorporates awareness of one's own existence, thoughts, feelings, surroundings and so on. This can be related back to the concepts of "male" and "female" principles discussed earlier, and is represented in Figure 9 on page 179. If we can expand our consciousness we can enter more deeply into the Infinite. This is the invitation that lies before us. Drawing from all these observations, the lessons that I have learned from the Infinite Mind include:

- *Information and ideas from the Infinite can be accessed transcendentally.*
- *When consciousness touches science and religion, then the doors to true wisdom will open.*
- *Every element and every person co-exists in space-time with every other element and person, so in essence there is no competition or scarcity.*

4. INFINITE WILL

For me Infinite Will is the same as God's Will; all-encompassing power that works through certain laws. I will term these "Divine Laws" for the purposes of this book. I see these Divine Laws as cyclical and evolutionary, guiding natural creation and the natural flow of life on earth. As human beings we are part of natural creation and thus also subject to these laws and, in fact, an expression of them in time and space.

I see Divine Law as different to man-made laws in several ways. Man-made laws are: more narrow and rigid; relate specifically to a given culture, population or region; incorporate the concepts of obedience, consequences and punishment if not followed; and are based on an anthropocentric view. In contrast I see the Divine Laws as: broader; universal in their application; and related more to "cause" and "effect", self-development and self-responsibility. The concept of "cause" and "effect" has been well described in Indian Philosophy as the so-called "Law of Karma", that is, any action will also create a response at some point in time. Therefore, according to our level of development, we need to take responsibility for our thoughts and actions and the effects that they will produce.

This links to the concept of functionality. If we think in terms of machines or systems then, to be functional, they simply need to fulfill their intended purpose. Yet, if we think in terms of human beings what does this really mean? To fulfill our intended purpose must also involve understanding our deepest reason for being here in the finite universe. Maybe our purpose is to follow Divine Will or, in the Christian concept, to allow that "Thy will be done". For me this means attempting to be a hollow reed for God's love or, in other words, allowing Infinite Will to be expressed through us. To achieve this I believe we have to find ways of putting aside our blocks of fears, emotional attachments and judgments and allowing our thoughts and actions to be informed and guided transcendentally. The spiritual experiences that I have had, and reading of the experiences of others, have given me a glimpse of how this might work.

Now let us consider in a bit more detail the cyclical and evolutionary nature of Divine Law.

Cyclical, Evolutionary Law of Natural Creation

Divine law is expressed in patterns, which we see at work in Nature. These patterns are expressed as the *Cyclical, Evolutionary Law of Natural Creation*. Their fundamental principle is that all life evolves through a series of cycles. We can see this if we look at the life of a deciduous tree. Each spring, buds appear on its branches, from which leaves grow that are shed in the fall. Thus, each season represents a cycle of birth and death. Yet there is another aspect to the life of the tree with each different season. During its lifetime, the tree will grow larger and its growth will be affected by the seasonal elements—in other words; there is an evolution through the cycles of the seasons. The life and death of the tree itself forms part of a wider cycle of evolution in Nature. On a larger scale, the continents on which we live were once united in a single supercontinent, Pangaea. These drifted apart over hundreds of millions of years to form our present landmasses and are now slowly coming together again. Geologists estimate that c.250 million years hence, there will be a new supercontinent. The process of continents breaking up and coming together again but in new forms—cyclical evolution—has happened many times before and, as far as we know, will happen many times again.

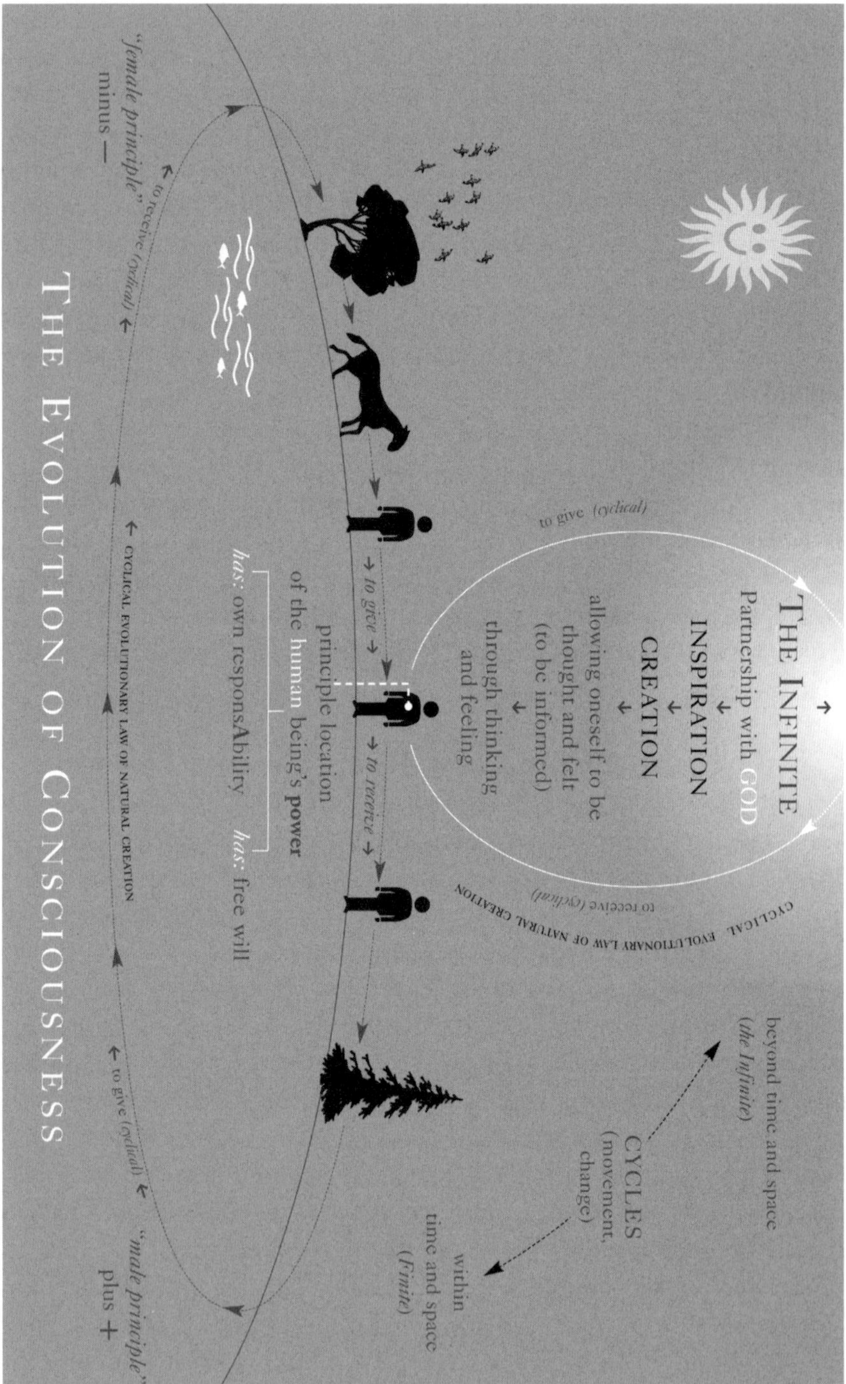

Figure 10: The Cyclical Evolutionary Law of Natural Creation. (Simplified version)

The Cyclical Evolutionary Law operates throughout Nature, governs our lives as individuals and works at the group level and in our consciousness. Throughout the universe, matter is in motion, moving in cycles. At the most fundamental level of atoms, there is a constant exchange of particles going from one place to another guided by these laws. Even in apparently empty space, a particle of matter and another of anti-matter (its mirror opposite) will appear, as if from nowhere, exist momentarily and then come together to annihilate each other. The cycle of evolution occurs at the cosmic level as stars are born, evolve, and die. So from the greatest to the smallest elements in the universe, the Cyclical, Evolutionary Law of Natural Creation is at work. Its pattern forms a spiral through creation as life evolves through its cycles.

These cycles occur in other more subtle ways, too, guiding the evolution of life at all levels. We have already learned of the polarity between the male and female principle. This is also part of a wider polarity found throughout the finite universe that manifests in many forms (see Figure 10). The key point to understand is that there is cyclical movement between these two polarities whether at the level of an electrical circuit or any other phenomena. All matter is in motion, irrespective of whether it is subtle or dense, and this motion exists in cyclical polarities moving from + (known as the positive, male principle) to – (the negative or female principle). Between these two principles, there is a continuous flow of energy back and forth between the two poles. These connections are expressed as principles and can be perceived in the world through our five senses as well as those that lie beyond the normal range. They are all reflections of cycles that are at work from the densest to the subtlest levels. The Tai Ji symbol mentioned earlier also illustrates these principles.

Perhaps the most significant cycle of evolution is that which flows between the finite and Infinite, between ourselves and our Creator. That is, we come from the Infinite (as beings) into the finite (as humans), and then evolve in the finite as beings expressed through the human (i.e. human beings), only to ultimately return to the Infinite (as beings) from whence we came. This is both cyclical and evolutionary and, with increased consciousness, we can realize that while being human we still contain an essence of the Infinite within the finite. So there are, if you like, two cycles that human beings participate in: one, in the finite universe, is through Nature, along with all the other elements in the universe. There is another, going from the Infinite to the finite, giving and receiving at the deepest level through transcendental exchanges.

Learning through Resistance

We have already discussed in the earlier section on Infinite Heart how we experience the finite world of opposites—male and female, mind and heart—and integrate them in the wholeness of the Infinite. We can also learn from them, evolving through the cycle of interplay between the two polarities, expanding our consciousness. The push and pull between the two forces, attraction and repulsion, can be termed resistance. For example, if we go down to the gym and start lifting weights, we will encounter resistance—our arms pushing against the weight of the iron bar. This resistance enables our muscles to grow. In the same way, it is precisely because of the resistance that we encounter in the finite universe that our spiritual muscles "grow".

In fact, not only does resistance make our physical and spiritual muscles grow, it makes the whole universe grow. Without it, there would be no matter and thus no universe at all. The entire finite universe exists because of the phenomenon of resistance. Although at the deepest level the finite is part of the Infinite, it also exists in contra-distinction to it. We could say it represents resistance to the oneness of Creation and hence it is expressed in a world of duality or opposites.

To put it another way, it is our separation from the one God into distinct forms, such as our universe and all it contains, that makes life possible. We can see this at the cellular level, where the cell has a wall that separates it from the surrounding environment (or other cells) in order to function. Without the cell wall, all the necessary chemical reactions could not occur. It's as if the cell had built its own little chemical laboratory where it could do its work. This is how life began on this planet. So from the simplest single-celled organism to the most complex cellular structures of the human brain, all is an integral part of the phenomenon of resistance. Resistance is vital, too, for the development of human consciousness. We learn through contrasts, and the most profound in the finite universe is between Unconditional Love and fear. Resistance is the very essence of fear.

Reflecting on Jerry Jampolsky's *Love is Letting Go of Fear*, I saw how we are repelled by our fears and anxieties but also attracted to them. We allow them to determine certain aspects of our lives and find it hard to let go of them. If we can look at the phenomenon of fear with detachment, we can see that it is just a form of resistance and can deal with it by letting it go. By learning to do this we can experience Unconditional Love. In a way, we need the contrast that this resistance gives us in order to be aware of the difference.

I then came to see fear—resistance—as a gift from God to humanity. I believe that we chose to be born into the limitations of the finite in order to learn about Unconditional Love. The paradox is that Unconditional Love from the Infinite can only be recognized when brought into contrast by resistance. Though we are bound to the earth by the physical forces of gravity, attraction and repulsion, we are tied in this way so that we may learn about transcendence as well. That is, by working through our fears and emotional attachments, we may transcend them and experience the Unconditional Love of the Infinite.

We could say that as human beings we are operating at two levels. The first is learning through resistance; experiencing polarities of the finite universe and growing through cycles of evolution. On another level of awareness, there is no polarity, no opposites, and no resistance—just the oneness of Unconditional Love that is the Infinite. This concept is summed up beautifully in the introduction to the renowned text, *A Course in Miracles*, where it is stated, "*The opposite of love is fear but what is all-encompassing can have no opposite.*"

Learning about Unconditional Love

The process of learning about love generally goes slowly, one experience building on another as we progress through our life experiences. I believe that this learning process is also a gentle gift from God because, if we learned too fast to access Unconditional Love, we would not be able to handle it. We might literally "burn-up" in the process. It is as if we have been placed on this planet to learn at our own pace. We then have moments for reflection, assessing how we feel internally, which gives us the time and space to grow in consciousness.

I believe that we humans have chosen to lose our conscious connection with the Infinite and to exist in the finite, with all its limitations, so that we can learn about and experience Unconditional Love. The goal of this transcendence is to be able to live the Infinite in the here and now.

The lesson is to learn to live here, in the constant flow of all that we have been given, without being attached to any part of it. If we are able to be in this flow, then we may detach with love from our past, no longer bound to memories of it nor carry any guilt over it, and use our free will functionally.

Neither do we have any expectation for the future, not even hope in the sense that hope can just be another type of expectation that may prevent us from experiencing the now. I think, however, on another level, that hope can also be experienced as a functional state of being since it can express the memory of where we all come from—the Infinite—and where we will return to. This kind of hope is for me an inner knowing. In this sense, it could be called trust.

Free Will and Functional Choice

As we grow more aware of the Cyclical, Evolutionary Law of Natural Creation, we can use our free will to make ever more functional choices. As human beings, we have the gift of free will, and we can use it to make choices and decisions in our daily lives. Yet how do we exercise this free will and what is the nature of our choices? I believe we make functional or dysfunctional choices depending on our powers of discernment and our level of awareness of the Cyclical, Evolutionary Law of Natural Creation.

I see discernment as being free from judgment or emotional attachment, and it allows us to develop an open mind and heart to decide the appropriate course of action. I believe that as our power of discernment and level of consciousness increases, we become more aware and more able to make decisions and choices that are functional in nature. When I no longer have self-interest, then my interest merges with the whole. I would define a functional decision as one that is in harmony with the Cyclical, Evolutionary Law of Natural Creation, while a dysfunctional decision is not, depending on our level of consciousness. Put another way, we use our free will functionally when we align it with the will of our Creator.

Developing a Functional Culture

Nature existed on this planet, as an expression of Divine creation if you like, long before humankind appeared. When humanity came into creation, one aspect of our uniqueness was the ability to make use of elements from Nature. I sometimes think of these as elements that God gave us to play with, using our free will creatively to take them out of their natural context and make new combinations. That is, our intervention created what Nature could not, on its own, achieve. This gave us the choice of whether to use our free will functionally or dysfunctionally.

We could use our consciousness to utilize and interact with Nature with dignity, respect and understanding. An inspirational example was St. Francis of Assisi, who had an intuitive connection with Nature, preaching, so the story goes, to animals and birds. In his *Canticle of the Sun*, he celebrates "Brother Sun, Sister Moon, Mother Earth".

In contrast, dysfunctional use means harnessing and exploiting the elements of nature purely for financial profit, as in the case of some modern industries that take little responsibility for the damaging, environmental consequences of their businesses. Indeed, if we think of the planet as a business, The World Inc., we would see that our company is in bad shape since we have depleted our natural resources, threatening the future sustainability of the company. Our response-Ability now is to bring back into the natural cycle those elements that we have removed for human purposes and taken out of their natural context. As such, it could be said that we suffer from both egoism and anthropocentrism.

I understand egoism as an attitude that focuses on the end product for the individual and excludes consideration of the effects on the whole. Anthropocentrism is the egoism of the species: that is, viewing humanity (one of the billions of expressions of life) as the center of the universe and focusing on our own interests to the exclusion of those of other species, such as animals or plants, and other manifestations of nature. As a result, we tend to view other species and natural elements, such as the oxygen that enables us to breathe, or the force of gravity that enables us to stand upright and walk, as a given instead of also appreciating them as a gift. By using our free will in a functional way, we could develop a culture that is in harmony with the Cyclical, Evolutionary Law of Natural Creation. In this, I define culture as humankind taking elements of Nature out of their natural context and then recombining and utilizing them in new ways for our own ends.

To me, this type of "culture" can be viewed as either functional or dysfunctional. An example of a functional culture might be deciding to grow some alfalfa seeds. Within two weeks, by utilizing seeds, earth, water, light, air, and warmth, I can facilitate the creation of a highly nutritious food to maintain my health. This is a highly functional decision because I am using a tiny seed with a huge potential—one that is cheap, readily available, and easy to grow, to provide my body with valuable nutrition within a short space of time, while utilizing minimal natural resources and creating no damage or toxic side effect. Furthermore, the outcome of ingesting the alfalfa, which results finally in human feces, may be recycled back into Nature.

This brings the natural, creative cycle back full circle without any wastage. We can do this over and over again. Certain technological developments could also be regarded as functional if they operate within these principles, but some aspects of modern technology have contributed to both the functionality and dysfunctionality of our society—such as computers or mobile phones.

Dysfunctional culture is the utilization of elements of Nature outside of natural Laws with damaging consequences. An extreme example of this might be the creation and use of the atom bomb. We have no way of bringing these elements back into their natural cycles—in the case of the atom bomb, we cannot heal the damage caused by the radiation fallout and just have to wait for it to gradually dissipate over time.

Those involved in consciously deciding to act in this way bear the responsibility for such actions and their effects. Nature herself is not dysfunctional, since all Nature operates according to her Cyclical, Evolutionary Law. Yet we humans have implemented a widespread dysfunctional culture, and I view the serious environmental disturbances that we are currently seeing in our world, such as global warming and soil erosion, as Nature mirroring our dysfunctional culture back to us.

This could even lead to the extinction of the human species. We already are responsible on an almost daily basis for the extinction of other species that all too often disappear unnoticed from our planet. Many of us, as a species, seem to be indifferent to the suffering and destruction we cause. Yet I believe that, as human beings, aware of both our collective and individual responsibilities for the full cycle of effects from our utilization of natural resources, we can correct and prevent our dysfunctional culture of Nature, which is creating such problems today[14].

A functional example of this response-Ability is a company like the Body Shop, created by the pioneering Anita Roddick, who sadly died recently. The Body Shop offers refills for many of their toiletries and cosmetic products. There are also companies that use biodegradable materials in their products. An example of one of many deliberately dysfunctional choices can be seen in the mobile phone industry, where companies manufacture non-compatible phones and their accessories. They have generally taken little or no responsibility for the appropriate disposal or recycling of old phones, although, thankfully, this is beginning to improve.

The problem is that most of us see ourselves as the dominant species. This is yet another example of the over-valuation of our intellect and the technology to which it gives birth. In reality, we are actually the stewards of Nature, and I think it is our task to care for her with respect and understanding. As we are not educated to value our feelings and our sense of connection with Nature, we grow up increasingly disconnected from Nature and our sense of the Infinite. In the process we lose our "being-ness" and risk becoming "human-havings", rather than human beings. As a result, it appears the majority of decisions that affect our planet are ones based on taking and having. These lead to the destruction of Nature and a depletion of natural resources. Most of these decisions are made by working adults, such as politicians and businesspeople.

14 A good book on this subject is *Cradle to Cradle* by Michael Braungart and William McDonough.

On the other hand, children may still be in a state of being-ness, and elderly people may have moved beyond having-ness back towards being-ness and to a state of greater wisdom. Yet both groups are largely excluded from these decision-making processes. I've summarized how I see this in an age scale diagram below (Figure 11).

We come to a planet as human "beings" with open hearts and minds.

Between 6 to 18 years we slowly become human "havings"; we have less trust and wonderment and operate more out of fear and desire to control, possess and "own" things.

We retreat into our minds, as we approach our mid-fifties, and grow older, we tend to gradually become more mellow and may then start to return to a state of human-beingness where possessions, control and so on have less importance to us.

Alas, in so many governing bodies in the world, we are dominated by the human "havings"; they have the vote and hold the external power.

It might be good instead to work from both sides of the scale (see below), taking more account of the voices and views of the young and the elderly, empowering the human "beings" and reducing the power of, and transforming, the human "havings".

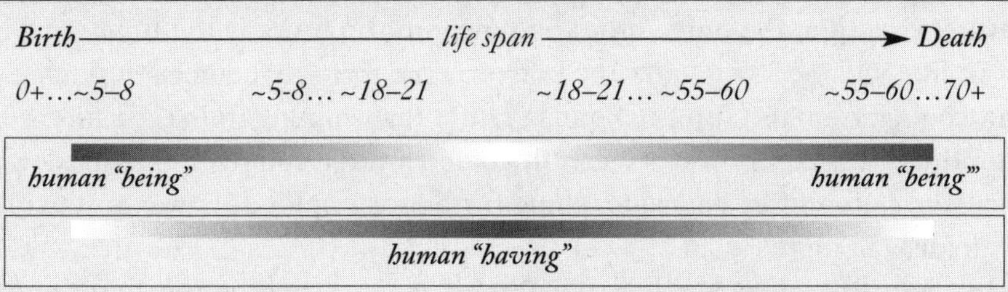

The human "havings" have the vote in so many of our "power holding" bodies, such as governments, companies and other organizations that affect all of our people's (including the human "beings") societies and our planet.

Figure 11: Age Scale and "Beingness" in Western Society

Authentic Power and Self-Development

How can we use authentic, internal power appropriately? When we act in the world, we bring into play our own power. Yet what power do we, one amongst billions, really have? And what is power in reality? For power is a term that is so often used and misused but seldom clearly examined or defined. Often it is understood in terms of the power of one person, or group of people, to dominate another person or group, or in terms of military might, or in sports prowess and so on. As a reflection of our collective belief systems, often reflected in the laws of a country, many of us have given our power away to leaders. In order to maintain their power and control over people, these leaders can create fear and anxiety and use it as an instrument through which they can manipulate their followers or the masses. In turn, people can buy into that fear and anxiety, as they have not yet learned to develop and rely on their own inner power.

Yet seen from an understanding of the Cyclical, Evolutionary Law of Natural Creation, the only authentic power in the finite is the functional use of our free will. So I would define power as the force that comes through each living being, from the Infinite Source, rather than coming from the finite world around us. It is the power we can develop through following Divine law, as discussed before. Let's consider some further examples of power and explore these ideas in more detail.

In daily life we often see transfers of power, such as the huge energy transfers from supporters to their sports heroes. They identify with their idols and try to imitate them and are focused on them winning. If the idol/team wins or performs well, then the supporter is happy or sometimes even ecstatic. On the other hand, if they lose, the supporter is downhearted and may even become angry and aggressive, as has often happened with soccer fans in Europe at huge cost to the police and to society at large. While it is, of course, fine to enjoy and be enthusiastic about a soccer match and the sense of belonging it brings, if the person's whole state of mind and well-being is dependent on the outcome of the match, this can hardly be healthy.

In relationships, we may also allow others to exert power over us, such as the man or woman who allows their partner to dominate or control them. All these kinds of relationships hinder us in taking responsibility for our own lives, since in this process we give away our power to others. These power transfers are dysfunctional for both the leaders and the followers, as the two are inextricably connected.

The way I see it is that, in essence, the need to control is based on fear. The need to be controlled is also based of fear of one's own authentic power. But if this dysfunctional bond is broken on either side, then a change towards a more functional relationship between people and with oneself can start. The process of leaving the apparent security and comfort of a dysfunctional relationship and standing on one's two feet can feel painful, but it can be very worthwhile.

Developing an awareness of our authentic power and allowing that to become stronger is an example of real, functional power. This type of power is the God-given power that resides in each of us, expressed as the functional use of our free will. Such power exerts no force or dominance over others and does not seek to manipulate or control. Rather it is a process of successful *self-development* that leads to calm self-assurance and inner strength, while at the same time retaining vulnerability. It understands that this power is gentle, humble and pure and connected to the source of all power, the Infinite. If we respect this power in its essence, then it cannot be misused. If we need to use our power externally, then we should do so with wisdom and restraint.

Self-development toward authentic power can be seen as *de-velopment* (rather than envelopment), which, for me, is the same as *evolution or unfoldment.*

Vulnerability, which is an aspect of the female principle, is often confused with weakness and thus labeled dysfunctional. Yet, we forget that out of this vulnerability comes the manifestation of authentic power; for example, an acorn falls on the earth and is vulnerable to moisture, temperature, nutrients in the soil and so on and yet it can grow into a mighty oak.

Touch is another example: we can push someone forcefully, or we might caress them gently and yet have a much more powerful effect on their being. However, physical strength, which is an aspect of the male principle, can also be functional. For example, it enables our bodies to work and exert force for the construction of buildings, bridges, roads, transportation vehicles and so on. The same strength can also be used dysfunctionally, for example, in an assault. The question is how to use this power.

If we are totally in our own power, then our mental clarity remains undisturbed and we are able to make clear, functional decisions with ease and carry them through powerfully, yet effortlessly. At the same time, we can feel our vulnerability and humility without in anyway being weak, as well as feel a connection with the creative force from the Infinite.

The traditional pattern of leaders and followers has brought us to our present-day situation. We can see all the progress that has been made, the magnificent projects that have been initiated, and the inspiration provided for future generations. On the other hand, it has been at great cost to humanity and the planet as well. Everywhere we see human suffering and environmental damage. This is because people allow themselves to be manipulated and are kept in ignorance about the true nature of reality. So they can suffer the consequences of the greed and selfish interests of some political and business leaders, or their organizations—sometimes in the form of monopolies or oligarchies. Quite recent examples of this are the American company Enron and the Italian company Parmalat, which kept their respective shareholders and the public in ignorance about the true state of their financial affairs in order to maintain their (false) position in the marketplace. This deception was discovered and led to criminal charges and convictions against corporate officers.

These examples of the misuse of power are well-publicized ones, but we can also see many lesser examples of such manipulation of individuals or the environment in everyday life.

The danger of the dysfunctional use of power is the reason why, in essence, I don't believe in the principle of leaders and followers. As I see it, leaders can take away power from their followers, while followers can give away their power to their leaders; it is a co-dependent relationship.

In our society, we have created many power structures based on a belief in this kind of power transfer, while not recognizing the power of the Infinite working through everybody. If we all had more real, functional power from within, then we might be less willing to step into these roles of followers and leaders.

Certainly some people take a more active role than others in different situations but those who have a deeper understanding of authentic power act more as guides, inspirers, or co-ordinators rather than taking on the role of dominant leaders for submissive followers. Their functions then reflect respect for the real, functional power of the other in their growth process, as their position is now based on a sharing of experience and wisdom.

An analogy might be the parent who nurtures and coaches the child but then at a certain point, like the parent bird, pushes them out of the nest, so that they can learn to fly.

Of course, I realize that it is not possible, realistic, or even desirable to change societal structures overnight; this is usually a gradual process allowing people to adjust. Yet, I do believe that facilitating changes in the inner attitudes of those who we call leaders or followers could gradually lead to a more functional society if the wish for change gathers sufficient momentum.

If we can work together to increase our awareness of these principles and develop real, functional power expressed through our free will for the benefit of all, then I believe we will be taking important steps towards transforming our world.

Synthesis

If we stand back for a moment and consider the wider question of the purpose of our presence here on earth, we see how these laws are vital for our development. From the human being's point of view, it could be said that we have been given this world, and beyond, as a teaching tool to develop our consciousness. In my view, the aim of this process of developing consciousness is to have an ever deeper, and wider understanding of the functioning of the Cyclical, Evolutionary Law of Natural Creation, and to use our free will with the awareness that this understanding brings. To me, an understanding of these laws underlies a sense of spirituality. One does not need to follow a specific religion to have an appreciation and a sense of wonder about this law or about the awesome universal power that lies behind it.

To paraphrase the words from the mystical book, *Mirdad*:

> "*The power beyond birth, growth, degeneration, death and decay is itself not born nor grows, degenerates, dies or decays. This is the power of God.*"

I feel that this sentence describes the Infinite well.

If we look at this in terms of the evolution of human consciousness, we can see that its source is the Infinite consciousness of our Creator. One could imagine this Infinite consciousness as a grid through which the infinite "electricity" of consciousness flows. Our human consciousness is like a light bulb that is plugged into the grid for the duration of our lifetime. It may burn brightly or, for example when we are ill, flicker. At the end of our lives this light is extinguished, but the "electricity" of Infinite consciousness flows on and will find other "light bulbs" through which to shine. How each one of us uses our time to shine is the question.

Infinite consciousness also expresses itself through animals, plants and minerals. This also extends to the planets and the universe. There are different levels of consciousness throughout the finite world that have their source in the grid of Infinite consciousness.

Looking back on my exploration of the Infinite Will, these are the key lessons:

- *Our inner nature is connected with outer nature and governed by the same Cyclical Evolutionary Law.*
- *We can make ever more functional choices if we utilize our free will with greater consciousness.*
- *Authentic power resides in each of us, rather than outside of ourselves, and can be reclaimed.*

5. LIVING AN INFINITE LIFE

Each of us has the potential to live a life in the Infinite. If we make the decision to do it, the process of transformation is set in motion from that moment on. Indeed, it is happening right now, for we are all evolving through a cyclical process all the time, whether we know it or not. The point is that by making a conscious decision to embrace this change, we are going with the flow of cyclical evolution rather than against it. As we open to the Infinite and follow Divine Law, our lives change. In an inner sense, the change can be immediate and profound. In an outer sense, it will take its own time to work through.

Our perception of the world will be transformed. Physically, you may live in the same place, you may meet the same people, walk the same streets, and you may do some of the same things. Yet, your experience of your life will be different. It is something that is beyond words and yet it is the most important thing I could share with you. I am aware that I am still learning every day, but I know it is a journey worth taking. Indeed, in the end, I think it's the only journey we can take.

Comparing and Sharing

As we change, our society changes, so this process of transformation has wider implications. Bringing our sense of the Infinite into the outer world will challenge its ways of working. A great deal of our society and culture today seems to be based on the concept of competition, exclusion, and of fears of scarcity, rather than on abundance. Yet on a planetary level, I would argue that there is actually enough to go around for everyone. The issue is more about how we share wealth across the whole planet.

If we cling to the belief that there is not enough to go around, each individual, group, or nation fights to get what it can at the expense of others, rather than realizing that there is plenty for all to share. I have witnessed and been part of this competitiveness for decades in the corporate world, where companies, including mine, compete to be the biggest, the best, and the most successful, fighting off competitors along the way.

Yet I have thought over the whole concept of competition for many years, and I am convinced that in the long run there is an alternative whereby everyone can benefit, rather than a few at the expense of the many. Let us explore this in a bit more detail.

Economics, as it is taught today, is based on the premise of scarcity, such as the scarcity of natural resources, resulting in the constant fighting for ownership or control of them. We have seen this clearly demonstrated in disputes over offshore oil rights and just recently in Russia's attempts to claim territory in the Arctic Circle, and thereby access to minerals, oil and other resources in one of the world's last remaining vast, wilderness areas.

If only we could realize that we all exist together in time and space, all breathe the same air, are all subject to the same gravitational pull and share the commonality of our human birth, then maybe it would be easier for us to share our resources.

Scarcity, as a concept, functions on different levels. Besides the belief system implanted in our minds, from which the idea of competition sprouts, there is also a link between scarcity and consumption. I realize that currently in many parts of the world, there are not enough resources to meet basic needs. At the same time in another part of the world, consumption goes beyond basic needs and so there is an imbalance. My core beliefs in this regard are:

- *In essence, scarcity doesn't exist and the false belief in it leads to competitiveness.*
- *If we can change this belief system, then together we can open up to abundance.*
- *With a caring, comparing and sharing attitude, no-one needs to go without.*

An example is world nutrition and the production, supply, and consumption of food. We know that the average male and female needs approximately 2,200kcal and 1,800kcal daily respectively to meet their energy needs. However, many Westerners now consume calories far in excess of these amounts daily, leading to an epidemic of obesity and associated health risks, while in other parts of the world people suffer and starve. When viewed in terms of global availability of food, this over-consumption can be seen to be parasitic, depleting global natural resources.

Other aspects of wasteful consumption are: excessive and unnecessary packaging, throwing things away needlessly, and all the goods that we buy that we don't need. Unfair trade practices by wealthier countries can also work against a more equitable distribution of the earth's resources. On the other hand the empowerment of food producers, for example by forming co-operatives, can help to ensure a fair price for all.

In addition, functional consumption, as in eating according to daily energy and nutrient needs for health and strength, avoiding excess packaging and so on, are inspiring acts that contribute to abundance since available resources can be spread more widely. When this attitude is combined with consciousness and gratitude, then the sum effect of these actions are greater than the individual outcome, since a contribution is also made to global consciousness as well as to our physical nutrition and life balance.

Another issue is that of food choices. Globally, one third of the world's cereal harvest is fed to farm animals, mainly cattle, and one fifth of the world's land area is used for livestock grazing; twice that given over to growing crops[15]. Meat-eating habits are therefore threatening food security as well as wilderness areas so choosing to eat less or no meat will, in the long-term, have a big impact on the overall supply of food worldwide. Similarly, over-fishing is depleting global stocks, so there are powerful arguments for a predominantly vegetarian diet.

In fact, nobody needs to go hungry or starve in this world. That there is starvation and hunger is a product of fear (in the form of greed, selfishness, and belief in scarcity) and the resulting dysfunctional economic policies. These include overproduction of certain foodstuffs, destruction and wastage of "food mountains" and national competitiveness over trade issues. If we can all take responsibility for caring, comparing and sharing and for sustainable farming and permaculture, then we could contribute to the eradication of scarcity and help to ensure there is nutritious food for all. The same principle can also operate for other types of resources such as oil and gas, if we are willing to ask ourselves, "Do I really need to travel?" and "Can I do so with the lowest carbon footprint?" This is something I am still working on in my own life.

Of course, there are many places in the world that do have a real scarcity of water, food and resources as well as funding, workforce, educational, and health care facilities at this time. Yet if we look at the planet as a whole, we can see that there are actually enough resources for all of these—it is just their distribution that is unbalanced.

Therefore, our challenge is to:

- *Empower people to find ways of distributing resources more equally.*
- *Ask ourselves, when we are about to acquire or buy something, "Do I really need this?"*
- *Develop an attitude of caring and sharing on an individual, community, national, and global level to empower our fellow women, men, and children.*

Also, it is reassuring to find that philanthropy is coming back into fashion. In the last decade, many individuals have given over large sums of money and given their time and attention to charitable activities such as Bill and Melinda Gates, George Soros, Warren Buffet, Ted Turner, Tom Hunter, Anita and Gordon Roddick, and many others.

15 Source: Food and Agriculture Organization (FAO) of the United Nations, (1995) & (1997).

Competition

Competition has produced many advantages for society at large. For example, competition has helped to improve the quality of many products and keep prices low. Competition can also produce greater efficiency and it has helped many of us, especially in the West, live a more affluent life. Thus we live in a world where competition is held up as being indispensable for society to function but do we really always benefit from it? At present, much competition could be said to be counterproductive. We can see the dysfunction of the game of competition as it is played, by using the metaphor of tennis.

To me, tennis is a game in which the Cyclical, Evolutionary Law of Natural Creation can be well expressed. I have been told that in the original scheme of the game, people played tennis co-operatively and tried to keep the ball in the game for as long as possible in order to help each other stretch and increase flexibility and to keep playing. The game, as it was played then, reflected the Cyclical, Evolutionary Law of Natural Creation; that is, to give and to receive as part of evolution of play; to keep in the loop.

Nowadays, however, the game has become competitive so that one plays in such a way that the other person cannot return the ball, i.e. deliberately tries to break the cycle of continuity of the game.

Not only does the person break the cycle, but she/he is also rewarded for doing so by gaining points, and finally the one with the most points is termed the winner. Where there are winners there must also be losers. Yet this is an illusion, for there are no actual winners or losers, just two or more people playing a game together, reflecting the cycle of life in different time-and-space zones.

Similarly, in business and in the culture of the celebrity, many people aspire to be the big boss, the top celebrity, the most popular recording artist, or to be the leader, the President. By creating such a system, we encourage people to want to be better, faster, richer, more beautiful or more powerful than another. Yet, in these examples, only one person can attain these positions at any one time, and so large numbers of others are left with feelings of dissatisfaction, disappointment, and even worthlessness.

When we expend so much energy on being better than somebody else, or when we lose so much energy by worrying that we are not as good as others, so much energy is wasted in the process!

Language can also reflect these attitudes and actions. It is fascinating to note how much corporate language is couched in terms of winning and losing and profit, rather than there being much mention of care, compassion, or virtue. This has been dramatically illustrated in a chart that I came across a decade ago (see Figure 12). I believe it came from the *Wall Street Journal* but its exact source is unknown to me. However, I am including it here as I think the message it conveys is important.

Perhaps this language is now changing in the twenty-first century as it becomes more fashionable for companies to have a caring face, showing concern for the environment and so on. Certainly many companies are now demonstrating their eco-credentials and supporting charitable initiatives, even though these actions may have been stimulated by consumer concerns and demands externally rather than internally.

From all this, it might seem I am against competition. In which case, I might be asked, how could businesses, mine included, survive without it? I believe there is nothing wrong with the functional, comparing aspects of competition as long as it can wisely stimulate creativity, innovation and efficiency. The reality is that we are all born on this planet and we all partake of its abundance, and we can enjoy the aspect of playful interaction of competition without becoming attached to it or identifying with it. The constant, natural cycle of creation, destruction, and recreation replenishes the planet and ensures that there is enough for one and all.

We can put a ceiling on our individual or national wants and share with others, even those with whom we are not directly connected. As an aside, it is interesting to consider that the earth has been created as a globe or a ball, rather than as a more rigid structure such as a cube or square with ends and sharp corners. This means its spherical structure is, in itself, a symbol of a never-ending cycle! We could go round and round the globe and never reach an end point; so our planet can be seen as an expression and a reminder of the Infinite. It is also a reminder that we are all one human family sharing the same planet in the solar system; how great would our power be if we could all cooperate together rather than compete? We can also compare with ourselves rather than compete against each other.

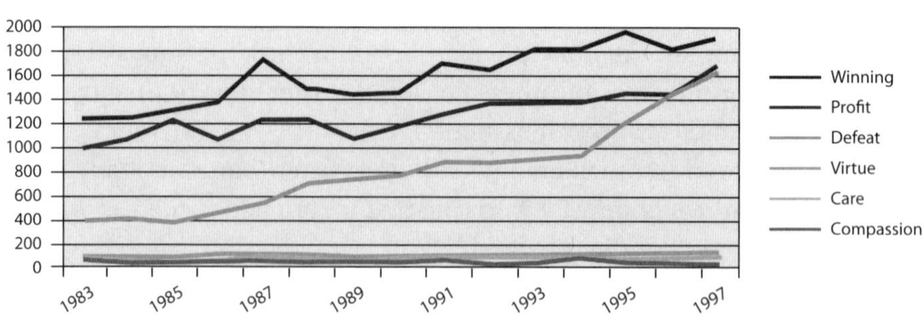

Figure 12: The Language of the Corporate World

Let me give an example of this in terms of a children's race at a school sports day. In such competition, children are encouraged to race against one another, and some come out winners and others losers. With comparison and sharing, the children would be encouraged to see how they can improve and get the most functional performance according to their ability when they race. In that way each child still puts in maximum effort but the comparison is with themselves and their own personal goals rather than competing against each other. In this way, a child who might have come in lower down in the ranks of the race, might instead compare his current race time with his previous ones and find that he was a winner, as he had improved and beaten his own record! If the child's consciousness is introduced to this concept and develops in this way from an early age, then the emphasis is on self-growth rather than competing to get the better of others.

So how can we resolve this issue and create a functional model for our own lives? So often our heart is forgotten in the way we relate to each other. Can't we allow one another some space to grow and develop? I would suggest that we can take the comparing elements from competition, to improve efficiency and performance. We can support one another in focusing on comparison and mutual caring and sharing, rather than competing at the expense of others. *To sum it up, the process of competition excludes while the process of comparing includes.*

To explore this further, you may like to think about situations in your own life where you are competitive. For me, it is sometimes when I am queuing in a shop, or heading off from traffic lights against other vehicles. How might your attitude and behavior be different if, instead of competing for things, you focused on comparing and sharing; what would the outcomes of this approach be? If you are a businessman or woman what would the effect be if you went and talked to your competitor and explored ways in which you might co-operate and share ideas for mutual benefit? It could open up a whole new way of doing business and, more importantly, of being in the world. Of course, this is already happening as millions of people worldwide are already working together in co-operatives.

Practicing this comparing, caring, and sharing attitude also means that we would feel less pressured and have less stress in our lives, helping to bring about a healthier, happier, society. These principles also extend to the workforce in a business. If we see our co-workers as valued fellow human beings, we can create a more functional organization where everybody benefits. Rather than trying to push the workforce ever harder, we could support them in their own self-development to achieve a good work/life balance, which is, in the end, in everyone's interest. For example, greater flexibility with hours of work, including time set aside for personal development, would produce a happier and more functional workforce. It would also be possible to gradually reduce hours of work as people reached retirement age, which would make it easier for those who wished to carry on in a part-time role to do so. So much experience and wisdom is lost when we get rid of the older members of our work team. An abrupt change from full-time work to retirement can also leave people feeling disorientated and lost. They can easily deteriorate physically and mentally at great cost to themselves and those around them as well as society at large. If we can see people as a whole, rather than trying to exploit the parts that seem of immediate usefulness to the company, we can receive the benefit of the whole person working in our company. There are many examples in this holistic approach in various businesses today, not least in my own country, the Netherlands.

Staying Connected and Living in the Present

The way I see it, living the Infinite life is not about floating in some dreamland far above the earth but being fully present each moment of the day. We can bring the Infinite into our daily lives (or if you prefer, allow the Infinite to work through us) in order to transform ourselves and the world in which we live. Staying as connected as we can with the Infinite will help ensure the "being" in our human being is alive and well and integrated with our human side. This sense of connection extends to all areas of our lives, including:

1. CONNECTING WITH OUR INNER NATURE.

   This in turn involves:
   - *Connecting with our whole being.*
   - *Connecting with our sense of playfulness and joy.*
   - *Connecting with our heart.*

2. CONNECTING WITH OUR OUTER NATURE.

Connecting with our Whole Being

In 1991, I took a course at the Schumacher College in Devon in the UK, given by Matthew Fox[16] and Satish Kumar[17]. I liked the teachings of both these men,

---

16 Matthew Fox was formerly a Catholic priest yet had the courage to explore the tenets and practice of Catholicism with great authenticity to find his own truth that went beyond religious dogma. For Matthew's story in his own words, please read his fascinating contribution on page 223.

17 Founder/Director of Programmes of the internationally renowned Schumacher College (*www.shumachercollege.org.uk*), nuclear disarmament advocate and Editor of *Resurgence* magazine. I kept in touch with both Matthew and Satish afterwards and was able to support Matthew in founding his original Center for Creation Spirituality in Oakland, California and to share a week of teaching with him there in 2001.

who have the courage of their convictions and are good at communicating them. One Sunday, Matthew had a public lecture in Dartington Hall with a few hundred people present. After half an hour of speaking he stopped and said, "You are all looking rather tired of listening to me—so let's do some exercises!" He then had everyone standing up and doing some exercises, and I was interested to see how it changed the whole energy of the place. I had never experienced a presenter doing exercises with the audience in the middle of a lecture! Yet I could see that it had a good effect, as everyone was laughing and smiling and energised by what he had done. Matthew's exercises illustrated the important connection between mind, heart and body and how the need to balance them is important in staying healthy and alert. We have seen how thought and feeling also need to be connected with each other. Our actions also work best when both mind and heart are engaged.

The challenge we face in modern society is to stay connected with ourselves, each other and our planet. In my view, anti-social behavior such as stealing or violence is in essence an expression of feeling disconnected from ourselves and our fellow human beings. Damaging our bodies by filling them with narcotics or excessive amounts of alcohol is a way of disconnecting ourselves from our feelings as well as the world around us.

Fortunately, we have the freedom to make functional choices and to choose self-development. We can nurture our bodies and our minds, eating healthy food, drinking lots of water, listening to music that relaxes and uplifts us and stimulates healthy brain-wave patterns. We can limit our exposure to external noise and information overload and instead be aware in meditation or quiet reflection of our inner selves and the beauty around us. Letting go of our fear, we can learn to live lovingly in the here and now and be in tune once more with the Infinite.

I once saw an image of a Buddhist monk meditating in the middle of a busy traffic junction in the U.S. The traffic was roaring all around and all the sights, sounds, smells, etc. could overload the senses, yet he sat totally calm. He had filtered out all these stimulants and was relying on inner information, his connection with the Infinite if you like, enabling him to access an internal sensation of total calm and peace.

Connecting with our Sense of Playfulness and Joy

It is important to remember that all our self-development can be put in the context of playfulness and joy. I am a great believer in having fun, joking and laughing, qualities that I maybe inherited from my parents and which I have enjoyed sharing with, and receiving from, children and adults in all kinds of settings. Even complete strangers can enjoy sharing a joke together. So joy and humor in any activity can lift the spirits and transform. Humor can be deeply healing, too. A friend once told me about an American who had a diagnosis of terminal cancer. He decided to banish all the long faces from his hospital room and said that anyone visiting him had to come with smiles, jokes, funny stories, humorous videos, etc.

His friends and relatives all did as they were asked, and the room was constantly filled with uproarious laughter. Everyone wanted to visit and join in the fun, whereas normally people feel more inclined to avoid visiting places of serious illness. Some time later it was discovered that the man's cancer had totally disappeared, to the utter amazement of his doctors. They could only explain his miraculous recovery as a spontaneous remission but we now know that laughter actually does precipitate the release of "feel-good" chemicals in the body. So perhaps all the joy and good humor that he shared with his friends somehow changed his body chemistry and healed him.

But the essential point is that, regardless of how he was cured of the physical illness, his changed attitude to life healed something within himself and those around him. We are all in the cycle of life and death. It is the attitude with which we choose to live and die that is the issue.

My friend, Patch Adams, is also renowned for his use of clowning and humor in his medical work and healing and many healers around the world have also been inspired by him and his work (see page 216 for his contribution to this book). My own love of fun gave me the idea of founding the Twinkling Eyes Club (see page 114 for more). I have had lots of fun spreading "miles of smiles" and "sprinkles of twinkles" around the globe. I hope you will become a member in the course of reading this book, too! I am sure that you must have lots of your own ideas for spreading fun and laughter too, dear reader, and I hope you put them into practice regularly!

Connecting with our Heart

I often remind myself, "The chaos in the *en-vironment* is a reflection of the disorder in our minds and hearts ("*in-vironmen*t")." I believe that it is through reconnecting our hearts with our minds (our in-vironment), through our feelings, that we can handle the chaos around us—including our damaged relationships with other people and other nations, global pollution, energy crises, global warming, etc. (our en-vironment)—and restore the balance.

We can stop competing and taking advantage of each other and basing our actions principally on our thoughts rather than both our mind and heart. If we could be more in touch with our heart and allow it to influence our thoughts and actions, we would then be more likely to be in tune with the Cyclical, Evolutionary Law of Natural Creation. This, in turn, could help make our world a place of balance, dynamic harmony, inspiration, and peace.

One way might be to give children and youth a greater voice, and to have more respect for the wisdom and voices of our elders and of indigenous peoples. Children often seem to have a greater awareness of their being (a "now" awareness) than adults. Elders, once out of the rat race, have a lifetime of experience and wisdom that they carry with them. Indigenous people also often have unique perspectives linked to living closer to Nature and being more in tune with the natural world.

Connecting With Nature

Connecting with Nature is a key element in our relationship with the Infinite. Yet most of our industries, governments, and other decision-making bodies are dominated by people who have become largely separated from Nature and who seem to operate from the point of view of "human-having".

Our leaders, living in urban environments, are often cut off from their own feelings and Divine inspiration. Removed from Nature in their urban offices, their environment acts like an anthropocentric screen, which stands between their inner nature and the outer natural world. They make decisions which often reflect dysfunctional culture. Think, for example, of how many governmental buildings in different countries contain little natural light or air and, of course, few plants, animals, children, or elders.

As leaders are often not connected with their inner nature or their authentic power, their decisions often reflect their numbed feelings and overpowered intellects. Yet they make decisions about our natural world and can sometimes even keep people in ignorance of the full implications of those decisions. We seem to accept this as normal conduct since we have mostly been through similar educational systems and have become accustomed to the same dead, urban environment. In actual fact, we could be living in a self-created prison and not even be aware of it!

Many people surround themselves with artificial, urban environments—living in cities, driving air-conditioned cars and residing in climate-controlled rooms and concrete buildings. These separate us from Nature and remove us from her inspirational power. Even urban architecture is dominated by unnatural right angles rather than more natural shapes such as the curves, circular and spiral forms found in Nature, as seen in trees, shells, and our own bodies. We have become so aligned with the urban environment, rather than the natural one, that it is now hardly possible to feel and absorb the vibrations of Nature in our daily lives.

Many of us spend most of our days indoors, being bombarded with "dead energy"—recognized as the so-called sick-building syndrome. The constant exposure to controlled air, artificial light, electronic machines and so on can leave us feeling tired or depressed, rather than feeling the vitality and invigoration so often experienced when out in Nature.

For me, it is often sad to see how decision-makers have created their own urban prisons. I spend a lot of time in such "prisons" myself. I am reminded of an international summit on the environment that I attended in 1993 where I was in a room full of influential people discussing nature and environmental issues. I observed that we were sitting in a room where the only aspect of Nature was a single, wilted plant in the corner. So we were actually totally divorced from the issues that we were discussing! I pointed this out and suggested that we reconvene the meeting outside, where we would be surrounded by Nature. While some people got the point of what I was saying, nobody took it seriously and the meeting simply continued in its dead environment. So, although there were people present who did care about environmental issues, the voice of Nature was not really heard.

To me, this meeting was quite symbolic, and it kindled my strong desire to facilitate greater contact with, and awareness of, the environment and to stimulate dialogue on this issue. To this end, under the auspices of one of my Foundations, I joined forces with Ria Lubbers[18], who has a long-standing interest in the environment and social welfare. We jointly facilitated the creation of an environmental booklet that was offered to all secondary schools in the Netherlands in 1989. It aimed to stimulate discussions and raise environmental awareness amongst children and their families, and encourage environmentally-friendly actions such as recycling. It also contained a specially commissioned musical score and tape based on the environmental message. Six hundred schools participated, and I attended one of the delightful and inspiring performances at the school of one of my daughters.

I have also been inspired to initiate and contribute to projects that actually take children out into Nature and even on wilderness expeditions. The Sacred Land Foundation, which was established in the early 1990s under the auspices of our Foundation for Environmental Awareness, helped many elementary school children to experience Nature. I believe that having such experiences as a young

18 For 12 years Ria was an active volunteer and board member of The Sunflower, a national association supporting people with physical disabilities. In 2000, she was awarded the Frekie Prize by the Netherlands Organisation for the Welfare of the Disabled in recognition of her work. She is the wife of the former Prime Minister of the Netherlands.

person is vital to stimulate an understanding and appreciation of Nature.

Fortunately, nowadays people are becoming much more aware of, and thus concerned about, environmental issues. Films such as Al Gore's *An Inconvenient Truth* and excellent environmental school programs, continue to help raise awareness and promote debate as well.

However, it still strikes me how sometimes awareness programs and environmental discussions may focus on intellectual aspects, while the participants are still divorced from actual Nature, including their own inner nature (which is waiting to be rediscovered as natural!). I would love to see men, women, the elderly and children all be together in Nature and take time to reflect on the environmental situation. This is not to focus on what has gone wrong or blame one another, but to talk together, to see if we can recreate our present and future, and bring our lives and environments back into greater harmony with the Cyclical, Evolutionary Law of Natural Creation.

Inspirational Figures

It can also be helpful to consider those people who have had the courage to go beyond the conventional mindset or to think how we have each been challenged to do this in our own lives. I can think of many marvelous people who, for me, demonstrate this in action. Several have already been written about in this book but there are some other people I would also like to mention.

One is a wonderful woman, Irene, who comes from an aristocratic background and yet has freed herself from its velvet shackles and followed her heart to write and teach about Nature. I met her in 1989 around the time that I was engaged in setting up various foundations related to harmony and the environment. I could recognize in her life a lot of the principles that were at the roots of my foundations and so we had an easy rapport with one another. I have been impressed by Irene's courage to pursue her own path and to inspire others with her work.

Another inspiring figure has taught me an important lesson about growing spiritually despite physical limitations. Many years ago, Jerry Jampolsky in the U.S. asked me to make contact with a Dutch lady, Debby Noordhoff, who had written to him about attitudinal healing. She had lived in California but was now living in the Netherlands. When I met her, she was very frail physically and needed help from her female companion Darby, to climb the stairs. She also had difficulty swallowing, problems with her vision, and had to spend a lot of her time in bed due to a muscle disease called Polymyositis. Yet I was struck by her wonderful spirit and great sensitivity; she seemed so in tune with

Enjoying Thor Heyerdahl's wisdom

everything that was going on around her. I felt uplifted by her presence and we have become great friends. I visit her once a year and enjoy our visits. To me, Debby is an example of how human consciousness and Divine connection is far greater than any physical limitations of the body. She makes a wonderful contribution to this book on page 254.

The late Thor Heyerdahl, with his great physical and mental fitness right into old age, has also been inspiring to me, as he changed my concepts of what I might expect ageing to be. I remember having difficulty keeping up with him on our walks together, although he was about thirty years older than me! His courageous Kon Tiki expedition challenged our conventional understanding of history, as did his discovery of pyramids in Guimar in Gran Canaria. This led me to develop my ideas on the ageing process itself. To me, ageing is natural, just like breathing in and breathing out. I think that the actual process of ageing is not as important as the way in which we relate to it. Some people invest vast sums of money into staying young-looking and the beauty industry promotes this. Yet the aging process can help us develop mentally, emotionally, and spiritually. If we allow this process to happen and go with the flow maybe we can cope with the physical changes better and in the end have an easier transition.

In my own case, I am so far fortunate to be in good health and do not have any particular problems with my ageing. I notice that I have a bit less energy, and I now value my afternoon twenty-minute power naps, as I find they give me increased vitality. I also feel the importance of exercising, if possible, on a daily basis in order to keep my body flexible.

When I see sports people in the peak of fitness, I sometimes miss having the athletic ability that I had in my younger days but, in general, my philosophy is to catch any negative thoughts about ageing, or anything else for that matter, and replace them with positive ones. Consequently, I have no fear of getting older. It is all part of the evolutionary cycle through which we pass in our journey to the Infinite.

Recently I had my 60th birthday and to celebrate it, I went out working on a social project with my wife and daughters. On my actual birthday, we sat outside at a simple wooden table enjoying a farmer's meal when my daughters surprised me with a wonderful medley of songs they had put together as a story of my life. I was so touched by their singing and by all the love that I felt from them that I was moved to tears. It was the most wonderful gift and I appreciated it more than I can say. I also loved receiving my step-daughter Mel's subsequent gift; a wonderful photo album with photos of the event. It was a true work of art and I was deeply touched by that, too.

Synthesis

Gradually I have come to understand that each of us, and all other forms of life on this planet, are expressions of Unconditional Love. Our lives in the finite universe are not only bounded by time and space, but also by the most fragile of ecosystems in which we live. We operate within a band of breathable air only a few miles thick. We can only function within certain temperatures. Even our sense of smell has limits—a sufficiently concentrated amount of manure can actually make people faint! Our planet itself orbits at just the right distance from the sun—making it neither too hot nor too cold—sometimes this is called the "Goldilocks zone." The physical forces that govern the universe, such as gravity and electromagnetism, are so finely tuned that the minutest change in any of them would fundamentally alter the cosmos and make life as we know it impossible. All the conditions that make life possible exist in a delicate balance. Truly our lives are a miracle. When I reflect on all this harmony, I am filled with a sense of gratitude for this Divine gift.

I respect this sacred gift—mine, other people's, life in all its forms—and make use of it as much as I can according to Divine law. Learning to co-exist with all these expressions of life is part of that process. We can also awaken to our connection with all creation as part of the Infinite. Finally, bringing our sense of the Infinite into the finite is a wonderful creative opportunity for us all. We can not only co-create with our fellow human beings but, in allowing the Infinite to work through us, we become co-Creators too. So these are some of the lessons I am learning in keeping my connection with the Infinite in a finite world:

- *Comparing, caring, and sharing can replace competing.*
- *Playing joyfully expresses the Infinite in our lives.*
- *Rediscovering our hearts can help heal ourselves, each other and our world.*

Are we Ready to Change?

I am keenly aware that accepting change is not always easy and so the implementation of the principles I have been discussing in this part of the book can be, for any of us—including myself—difficult. Perhaps the difficulty that we have relates to the ways in which we have been educated and to the types of belief systems that we have adopted. We may have been encouraged to think in a limited way rather than to believe in our ability to change and in abundance.

Yet, I do believe we can connect with the Infinite. In my experience, such a connection can be life-transforming. It can make us more peaceful, more loving and joyful and it can help us to make this world a better place to live for all its current inhabitants, as well as for future generations of all living beings. So the vital question to ask ourselves is "Am I ready to change?"

For me, the key consideration is having the courage to realize that human systems, based on having, and on power control, separation and exclusion, do not work anymore. With open hearts and minds, and with courage, we can now explore the creation of new systems based on an understanding of the need for empowerment and self-response-Ability for all human beings. I know I am just one human being, like you, dear reader, who cares about our planet, but I do believe that if we can join forces, we can make a difference for the good of all.

So I would like to invite us all to work toward developing a more functional society here on earth. Perhaps the key principles I have outlined in this the book and also the wonderful shared visions of the contributors that follow, may support you.

Please turn to part III and be inspired!

Glossary of Terms Used in Part II of the Book

ANTHROPOCENTRISM—The egoism of the human species that regards humans as the center of the world.

CULTURE—The taking of elements from Nature out of their natural context by humans, and then re-combining and utilizing them in new contexts and new ways to suit human purposes. Functional culture is the utilization of elements from Nature according to the Cyclical, Evolutionary Law. Dysfunctional culture operates against this Law.

CYCLICAL, EVOLUTIONARY LAW OF NATURAL CREATION—The Divine Law by which all creation evolves through a series of cycles. This Law works at the level of the individual, group, and the evolution of Nature and the entire universe.

DE-VELOPMENT—The process of opening ourselves to an ever higher consciousness, and to deepen our understanding and experience of the Cyclical, Evolutionary Law of Natural Creation. The opposite is "envelopment", which is the closing off of consciousness.

EGOISM—Selfishness and not harmonizing with the interests of others and Nature. The product of losing contact with our sense of connection with the universe and God.

EMOTION—Emotion is the sensation based on past experience or expectation that blocks our true feelings.

EN-VIRONMENT—All matter, whether subtle or dense, that exists outside of our own bodies (see also "in-vironment").

EVOLUTION—See "De-velopment."

FEELING—Experiencing fully in the present, and connecting with the inner experience and yet being detached.

(THE) FINITE—The physical universe in which we live. It is bounded by time and space in which each person, animal, plant, mineral element, or speck of matter occupies its own point in space-time.

FREE WILL—God-given power of discernment to make choices that are functional rather than dysfunctional; that is, not distracted by judgment or emotion.

FUNCTIONAL CHOICES—A choice, or decision, that is in line with the will of God as expressed in the Cyclical, Evolutionary Law of Natural Creation.

GOD—The Divine source of creation, or Infinite Being, also expressed in the finite (see also, the Infinite). God has both male and female qualities and yet transcends them both and thus is neither female nor male.

(THE) INFINITE—That which is the beyond the finite and yet also encompasses it. The creative source of the whole and all, which is God.

IN-VIRONMENT—The "inner world" of thoughts, feelings and emotions.

LAWS OF NATURAL CREATION—See under the "Cyclical, Evolutionary Law of Natural Creation".

LOVING DETACHMENT—Being able to use our hearts, feelings and minds with clarity and without the blocks of fear, emotional attachment or judgments.

"MALE"AND "FEMALE"PRINCIPLES—A range of interconnected qualities or aspects as in the ancient Chinese philosophical concepts of Yin and Yang. Yang is linked to male qualities of hardness, action, the mind and the intellect; Yin is associated with female qualities of softness, receptivity, feeling, intuition and the heart.

RESISTANCE—The dynamic, natural forces of push and pull or attracting and repelling by which the finite universe exists and is maintained.

RESPONS-ABILITY—Experiencing fully in the present, and connecting with the ability and willingness to interact with the world around us with the awareness that we are all part of the Infinite. Being accountable for our actions.

TRANSCENDENTAL—The ability to connect with the Infinite.

UNDER-STANDING—Used to refer to "standing-under God", that is, having a greater realization and awareness of the true nature of reality and of Divine creation.

UNIVERSE—The entire finite world.

Rediscover Your Heart

PART III

Visions for the Future

PART III

Visions for the Future

For this part of the book I invited friends and colleagues from all walks of life—men, women and children—both well-known and unknown and drawn from the worlds of business, politics, health, arts, schools, youth groups and so on—to share their visions and dreams for creating a more functional world. There are many others who I would love to have invited to contribute to this part of the book, but there just was not the space or time to do so! These shared visions, as well as your own ones and those of others around the globe, all play an important part, now and in our future.

Each contributor was asked to consider the following:

- *What are your visions/dreams for the future of the planet?*
- *How can you/we make these visions/dreams happen?*
- *What particular experiences in your life shaped your vision?*

Some people chose to answer each question briefly while others were inspired to write more. All contributions were written especially for this book and are truly individual. Some common themes also emerge.

I am grateful for all these contributions, which I have found truly inspiring and uplifting and a joy to read. I hope you will enjoy reading them, too, and will feel inspired to create your own visions for change, along with the will to put them into action for the benefit of all beings.

If you would like to share your vision, then I invite you to post a message on our website on *www.rediscoveryourheart.com*. This site is intended to share and inspire so that we can help each other bring about functional changes in the world.

THE CONTRIBUTORS TO THIS SECTION ARE:

1. Hafsat Abiola-Costello (Nigeria)—*Democracy Activist, Founder KIND (Kudirat Initiative for Democracy)*
2. Sipho Abram Nkosi (South Africa)—*Orphan and Student at Nkosi's Haven*
3. Patch Adams (USA)—*Medical Doctor, Clown, Performer, Social Activist, Founder and Director of The Gesundheit! Institute*
4. Roman Bumbi (The Ukraine/Netherlands)—*Student*
5. Antony Burgmans (Netherlands)—*Former Chair of Unilever LV and PLC*
6. Jan Ebeltjes (Netherlands)—*Aid Worker/Project Co-ordinator for the Fred Foundation*
7. Matthew Fox (USA)—*Educator, Author, Co-initiator of the YELLAWE Program in Oakland, California and Scholar-in-Residence with the Academy for the Love of Learning, Santa Fe, New Mexico*
8. Jane Goodall, Ph.D, DBE (UK)—*Founder of the Jane Goodall Institute & UN Messenger of Peace*
9. Azra Huzanovic (Bosnia-Herzegovina)—*Student and former Worker at the Peace Flame House, Tuzla*
10. Gerald D. Jampolsky M.D. (USA)—*Doctor, Author & Founder of The International Center for Attitudinal Healing, Sausalito, California*
11. Vandy Kanyako Jr. (Sierra Leone)—*Student*
12. Rola Khoury (Italy)—*Media Director and Public Relations Consultant*
13. Craig Kielburger (Canada)—*Founder and Chair, Free The Children*
14. Nsaa-Iya Kihunrwa (Tanzania)—*Member, Robert Swan's Inspire Antarctic Expedition 1996 and Worker on Dr. Jane Goodall's global humanitarian and environmental program*
15. Marc de Klerk (Netherlands/Bosnia-Herzegovina)—*Entrepreneur, (NGO) Project Developer & Freelance Consultant in the western Balkans*
16. Olesya Koba (The Ukraine)—*Fred Foundation Ukraine Worker & Translator*
17. Indra Kumari Khattri Tamang (Nepal)—*Housewife*
18. Ervin Laszlo (Italy/Hungary/USA)—*Author, President of the Club of Budapest*
19. Irene van Lippe-Biesterfeld (Netherlands)—*HRH Princess of the Netherlands, Chair of The Lippe-Biesterfeld Nature College Foundation*
20. Ruslan Lokotosh (The Ukraine)—*Ukrainian Orphan*
21. Ruud Lubbers (Netherlands)—*Prime Minister of the Netherlands 1982–1994 & United Nations High Commissioner for Refugees 2001–2005*

22. Chris Matser (Netherlands)—*Housewife*
23. Dr. Hiroshi Motoyama, Ph.D., Ph.D. (Japan)—*Scientist, Author, Psychic and Shinto Priest*
24. Caroline Myss (USA)—*Author, Teacher, Medical Intuitive*
25. Debby M. Noordhoff (Netherlands)—*Retired Person*
26. Thomas van Nouhuys (Netherlands)—*School student*
27. Rev. Alex L. Orbito (Philippines)—*Spiritual Healer*
28. Matthew Parrish LaCasse (USA)—*Student*
29. Jasmina Redzepagic-Avdagic (Bosnia-Herzegovina)—*Volunteer and Trauma Therapist, Manager of the Peace Flame House, Tuzla*
30. Floris Rost van Tonningen (Netherlands)—*Entrepreneur*
31. Marika Verheijen (Spain)—*International Co-ordinator*
32. Ernest Volosin (the Ukraine)—*Ukrainian Orphan*
33. Herman Wijffels (USA/Netherlands)—*Executive Director of The World Bank, former Chief Executive Officer of the Rabobank*, *Netherlands*
34. David R. Woollcombe (UK)—*Founder & President, Peace Child International*
35. Glynda Yoder (USA)—*Friend and Spiritual Teacher*
36. Michael Young (UK)—*School Student*

Afterword by: Dr. Deepak Chopra

1. Hafsat Abiola-Costello (Nigeria)
Democracy Activist; Founder, KIND (Kudirat Initiative for Democracy)

What are your visions/dreams for the future of the planet?
My current vision for the creation of a more functional society is one founded on the principles of solidarity. Among the South Africans are the Zulus who speak of the word "*ubuntu*". It translates roughly as "humanity towards others" and is the spiritual foundation of African societies that involves a belief in a universal bond of sharing that connects all of humanity. I would like to see a world where the mechanisms are in place to support fellow-feeling among humankind, a world where the mechanisms and incentives encourage people to share such that no child or adult goes hungry, dies from preventable diseases, becomes a victim of violence, or feels other forms of human suffering.

What particular experiences in your life shaped your vision?
I was raised in a family by parents with a strong sense of responsibility to their community. Although in his adulthood my father became materially wealthy, his measure of well-being was whether he was making a positive difference in the lives of vulnerable people. Among my ethnic group in Nigeria, called the Yoruba, there is a proverb that encouraged my parents' values. It says "people are the clothes I wear". The proverb affirms the belief that clothes (material well-being) is not so important; paramount is one's standing among his or her fellow people. My parents' values and commitment led them to participate in my country's democracy movement. Their efforts cost them their lives but the manner of their living on earth shapes my vision today.

2. Sipho Abram Nkosi (South Africa)
Orphan and Student at Nkosi's Haven

What are your visions/dreams for the future of the planet?
My dreams for the future of the planet are to see a high reduction of poverty in the world. I want to see a world where everyone should have enough to eat. I would like to see a world with equal distribution of world economy in my lifetime.

How can you/we make these dreams happen?
I am fortunate to belong to a group called the Teleios Korban Organization. In this group, we have already started to make a difference through the arts.

In our plays, we highlight the problem of poverty, especially among children, and we perform them to the various departments and bodies that matter to the community. Secondly, everyone comes from a community. It's high time we open our eyes to see people who are truly suffering from malnutrition and severe poverty and donate food to them. If all the food that goes into dustbins everyday is properly managed, hunger could be greatly reduced.

What particular experiences in your life shaped your vision?
I came from a family where I experienced what it means to go for the day without food or to depend on luck to survive. This happened particularly once I lost my mother and my dad was not available. I can't really imagine how life would have been if I hadn't encountered Mr. Isidore Martins Duruji, who introduced me to the group. It was through the help of this group that I met great people and especially those with Kidsright. That brought about a turning point in my life and the life of my family. Many may not be as fortunate as I am. Many have died from hunger, especially here in Africa, because they never met an important person who changed their life around.

3. Dr. Patch Adams (USA)
Medical Doctor, Clown, Performer, Social Activist, Founder and Director of The Gesundheit! Institute

What are your visions/dreams for the future of the planet?
My goals for planetary transformation are peace, justice and care for all people everywhere, at all times, and to live in harmony with the rest of nature as simply one of the members.

What particular experiences in your life shaped your vision?
The most significant pivotal experience of my life was at my birth. I had a fabulous mother who lived by loving others in every way. I never saw her otherwise. Being loved by her gave me self-esteem, so any time in life I have decided to do something, I was sure I could do it and did. As a schoolteacher, she filled me with a lifetime of exuberance, wonder and curiosity. I never saw her unkind, derogatory or rejecting in any way to other human beings, so I grew up loving people. All people. She embodied care in every moment. I recognised many years later that I am simply a reflection of her gifts of love to me. My father being a professional soldier led to another pivotal moment. When I was

16, he died as a soldier. It broke my heart. We moved back to the United States in 1961, to the southern States, which was in the throes of fighting racism. I immediately joined the Civil Rights Movement. I was frequently beaten up. These two events crushed my spirit and three times at age eighteen I was hospitalised because I wanted to die. I did not want to live in a world of violence and injustice. In the last hospitalisation, on a locked ward of a mental hospital, I realized that instead of escape, I could instead choose to be a political activist. I changed overnight. I made two decisions that changed me forever. I chose to serve humanity in medicine and have now been a free doctor for 35 years. I also chose, as a political act, to never have another bad day. I have lived a joyful life every day since, which has also manifested in my becoming a clown.

Another choice that happened at that time was to pursue a thoughtful life, seeking out thinking people and their works. This led to reading many thousands of great works and cultivating intelligence in everything I do. In this fertile soil ideas blossom and solutions are forged for whatever question or dilemma comes. A life in sensitivity has eliminated the possibility of burnout or discouragement.

One final pivotal choice that was so important was the decision to live communally, to be part of a tribe. Friendship is my spiritual path. I get my strength from the sweet embrace of friends. My two artistic creations, a free hospital and taking clowns (love) to places of horror (poverty, refugee camps war, etc.) have been easy because they are done by a group of committed friends. Tribe feels like the nest of our most ancient selves.

How can you/we make these dreams happen?

I think capitalism is the worst thing that ever happened in history. We could have chosen love, compassion and generosity as a value system. Instead, men have historically chosen money and power as their value system. As women more often choose the values of compassion and generosity, I would put them in charge of everything. Not the man-woman types such as, in my opinion, Margaret Thatcher or Condoleezza Rice, but women like those I've seen all over the world in orphanages and refugee camps, and teachers and nurses who exude love. I would take all wealth in people and corporations (that is not donated) to middle-class levels and use the funds to build this loving world. And I'd clean up our disasters to people and the environment. I would make our schools into temples of culture and our teachers into society's heroes (quadrupling their salaries until wages equalize). I would only use the TV for education and to help create a loving world for all people. Loving would be taught in schools every day, just like math is taught. Children would become excited to serve their society, like they are excited by sports now.

The internal combustion engine must go. As capitalism disappears and living and harmony become important for all, the pace of today would change. I see roads mostly returned to nature and, over time, people loving to live nearer to each other—interdependently—and cities as flourishing garden cities, with much land returned to nature and (communal) family farming. There would be no more than fifty weeks of "work" each year. People would have time to travel the world by bicycle, sailing ships and maybe even a trans-continental slide. As we get safe with each other we could stay in houses along the way and help out while staying there. Manufacturing would decentralise to local crafts and people would be "living-oriented" rather than "thing-oriented". Celebrity would disappear and ideas would become interesting.

Yum!
Let's do it.
Patch

P.S. This is an inadequate report on what methods we can use to transform the world, because an accurate answer by anyone who has thought about it for years would fill volumes, so this is just a teaser.

For more, see: *www.patchadams.org*.

4. Roman Bumbi (The Ukraine/Netherlands)
Student

What are your visions/dreams for the future of the planet?
My dream is that every child and every human has a family. Also, that there is no poverty any more, because the rich share their wealth with the poor. Then peace will come.

How can you/we make these dreams happen?
God is an example for all of us. When everyone is an example for others, there will be no poverty and sadness anymore.

What particular experiences in your life shaped your vision?
I was raised in an orphanage in the Ukraine. Six years ago, I came to Holland. I was and still am very ill. In Holland, I was blessed to experience the warmth and love of a foster father and a family. I have learned a lot from that love. It has enabled me to deal with my illness.

5. Antony Burgmans (Netherlands)
Former Chair of Unilever NV and PLC

What are your visions/dreams for the future of the planet?
The world needs more solidarity, a sense of mutual/ global responsibility; it lacks a communal sense. An example of this is the fact that the United States of America, responsible for 25% of the total global CO_2 expulsion, has not fully ratified the Kyoto Protocol. There should be a better balance between individual energy and global energy. This should replace the indifferent, anti-social and egotistical behaviour that seems to flourish nowadays. Indifference on a lower level creates an intolerable society.

The ultimate aim is to include society in its totality as well as to create space for individual and personal development.

The main task of any government is to create the right conditions for society and to keep it habitable. It's too easy to constantly blame the government. According to the democratic principles we ourselves agreed upon, everybody is to blame and thus responsible to solve the problems we all created.

People perceive nature as something outside of themselves, and as something of which they are not a part. Some global problems, such as global warming, for example, are frustrating because they seem to be irreversible and uncontrollable. What we need is a mature discussion between all parties, representing all different interests, and to combine our forces in order to get them aligned.

Very important in the creation of a more functional society is:

1. *investment in education*
2. *enhancement of respect for each other and nature*
3. *more focus on non-material things (we are numbed by luxury)*
4. *creation of true (world) leaders*

Our world today desperately needs authentic and profound leadership. Leaders who give perspective, who are able to think from different points of view (instead of only from a materialistic or mono-dimensional point of view) and who are capable of creating a communal sense/solidarity (thus overcoming individual or personal interests).

People should be taught to ask themselves: "Who am I in relation to my fellow human being, to nature, to the previous generation and in relation to culture?"

For me, Nelson Mandela is a very good example of a great leader. He has shown the world the importance of communal sense and has always promoted this, instead of focusing his interest on taking revenge on the people who locked him away for over 25 years.

Communal sense/solidarity can sometimes come about as a result of the course of history. Europe is a good example of a continent, once hopelessly divided by wars, that has managed to overcome separation according to different (border) interests and create a communal sense. It is very unfortunate, however, that Europe needed two World Wars and a Holocaust to establish this. Yet often, in the vacuum after a disastrous event, the greatest opportunities and higher forms of consciousness can develop. So this could be a hopeful example for the rest of the world.

What particular experiences in your life have shaped your vision?
A trip I made to the continent of Africa. This trip brought tremendous enrichment and awareness; the feeling of going back to one's roots. It showed me how essential nature is for our own, and for society's development. Most people in powerful positions live "outside" of nature and thus are infected with too much "urbanity".

6. Jan Ebeltjes (Netherlands)
Aid Worker/Project Co-ordinator for the Fred Foundation

Ukraine Story

For many years, the questions kept going round in my head: "What am I doing here?", "For what purpose have I been put on this earth?" I thought I would be able to find the answer in a successful business career, but I found it did not satisfy me. The more I strove for success the more I saw this effort and its result as forms of individualism and egotism. This insight often made me quite depressed. But what should I do? And how?

The answer came in 1992. I met some Polish youngsters and spent a few days with them. This led to strong ties between us, an overwhelming kind of friendship that I had never experienced before. I made time to visit my friends in Poland. I was aghast at the poverty in that country and felt I had to do something about it. Together with my Polish friends, we organised a number of aid expeditions for mentally handicapped children, who were living in an institution in the Polish village of Izdebnik. I was deeply touched by the gratitude of the children and the workers of the institution. All this rather complicated my life. My world had been one of production and profit-making, but my experiences in Poland had opened a whole new world for me. How could I combine these two worlds? I found a solution by spending all my free time on aid to Poland. With great difficulty I was able to live in both worlds at the same time.

In April 1994, I visited a children's home in Cinadiewo in the Ukraine. It is difficult to describe what I found there: 135 malnourished children, who were ill because of human faeces that were everywhere, psychologically ill from lack of (parental) love and maltreatment by drunken personnel. A little boy of six came up to me, looked at me inquisitively and whispered: "Are you my father?"

Completely thrown by this I returned to the Netherlands, horrified by the injustice and suffering of these children. Every day I heard the little boy's question in my mind and I longed to be able to do something for these children. But how? I created a Foundation and brought the plight of the Ukraine to the attention of people around me. Gradually, schoolchildren started to become involved and churches and other organisations contributed to the work in the Ukraine. This involvement got me even more fired up. My employer gave me the opportunity to work a six-day week, which enabled me to save time in between for my work in the Ukraine. I gained the trust of the people in the children's home and, more than once, I smuggled sick children out for hospital treatment in the nearby town of Mukachewo.

In 1996, I made contact with 320 orphans who had been housed in a home in Perechyn. I found out that the majority of these children had been abandoned by their parents. Conditions in the home were appalling; there was a serious shortage of food and the lack of hygiene was abominable. The mental suffering of these children was immeasurable. Over and over the children asked me if I knew where their parents were and whether I could perhaps search for them. I tried as hard as I could to become the answer to the little six year old's question: "Are you my father?" Meanwhile, the Foundation to help the Ukraine grew and opportunities arose to improve the living conditions of these children. As a result, we were able to achieve some good improvements in their health care.

The increasing work for the Ukraine created an imbalance between my two worlds. My work with my employer came under pressure and I no longer felt at home in the world of commerce, but resigning wasn't an option—after all, I had to make a living, didn't I? However, in January 1998 I did resign and chose to become an interim manager for an agency. I did temporary work for a number of companies and between each job I would be found in the Ukraine. In conjunction with Ukrainian organisations, I worked towards short-term solutions for the problems in the children's homes. And with everything I did, the question from the six-year-old boy kept ringing in my ears.

In 1999, I took two terminally ill children with me to the Netherlands for medical treatment. Volodymir underwent three operations and after a little over a year he returned to the Ukraine a healthy boy. Roman was said to be incurable but, against medical advice, I continued to care for him in the Netherlands. The stay of the boys in the Netherlands created a lot of media interest and this contributed to the development of a plan to bring Ukranian children to stay with Dutch families during their three-month summer holidays. Every year, around 70 children come to the Netherlands to become part of a family and, although it is only for three months, to have an honorary father and a mother.

I enjoyed my job as an interim manager particularly, as, in between jobs, I was able to devote myself to helping children in the Ukraine. However, this arrangement became untenable as I did not earn anything during my visits to the Ukraine. Finally, in 2001, I was forced to look for permanent work again. This was a hard decision: my work in the Ukraine would suffer if I resumed full-time work. but I could see no other way out.

During that time I had an invitation from Fred Matser to tell him something about my activities in the Ukraine. He was extremely interested and I was impressed by the way he communicated his attitude to things, and his understanding. When I had finished talking, Fred indicated that he wanted to support my work in the Ukraine and a few days later he donated funds sufficient to renovate a children's home.

A few weeks after that, I was offered a job as an office manager, but on the day that I was due to sign the contract, the phone rang. It was Fred Matser again. He asked if I would like to work for the Fred Foundation that he had recently set up. I was amazed. How was it possible that Fred, with this question, had unknowingly brought my uncertainties to an end by enabling me to join my two worlds together? With enormous gratitude I accepted his offer.

Within the Fred Foundation I was given full scope to further develop the work in the Ukraine. We started up the Fred Foundation (Ukraine) and decided to begin by concentrating on around 40 youths who had been locked up for years in a stable. They ate food that was intended for cows and pigs. They had no shoes or underwear. In short: they needed everything. We developed a living-and-working-plan for them. The Fred Foundation bought dwellings and apartments and, in consultation with the Ukrainian authorities, work was found for them. Now, a few years on, most of them are happily married and almost all of them have found their place in Ukrainian society.

The Fred Foundation (Ukraine) also set up a Crisis Centre in Uzhgorod and a Shelter in Vingradov for child addicts. Contacts were made with two psychiatric institutions where hundreds of people were housed. Renovations have been, and are being, carried out and hygiene is being improved. Every year, holiday camps are organised for children from problem families and aid is transported to homes in the Vinogradov region.

The Fred Foundation (Ukraine) also gives a great deal of individual support. We remain in contact with our original target groups, the forty youngsters in Perregrestya and the hundreds of people who are being cared for in the psychiatric institutions. Help also means being able to listen, give encouragement and offer a pat on the back.

We are concerned with street children, children who have become involved in prostitution, single teenage mothers and young people in prison. I often ask myself how I have come to be doing this work, but I am so grateful to be able to do it and I always keep in my mind the question of the little six-year-old boy. He is now 18 and is attending University in Uzhgorod. Whenever I see him he calls me "father" and his faith in me gives me the strength to continue this work for children who are so unfortunate.

I have now adopted Roman, one of the two children I brought to the Netherlands in 1999, as my son. We were so grateful when, a few months ago, he was able to have a successful liver transplant. Roman is now 17 and in his opinion people ought to work together more in order to tackle the problems of the world. "Together we are capable of so much more and when everyone works together there will be peace," says Roman. Is it possible to think of anything more beautiful?

7. Matthew Fox (USA)

Educator, Author, Co-initiator of the YELLAWE[1] Program in Oakland, California and Scholar-in-Residence with the Academy for the Love of Learning, Santa Fe, New Mexico

Transformation: my Visions and Experiences Yesterday and Today

When I look back on pivotal moments in my life that awakened me to issues of global transformation, there are many. Much of this is due to the generation of which I am a part, the times in which I came of age. I was twenty years old when John F. Kennedy was elected President and challenged my

1 Youth and Elder Learning Laboratory for Ancestral Wisdom Education.

generation to "ask not what your country can do for you but what you can do for your country." I was twenty-two years old when the beautiful Pope John XXIII wrote his amazing encyclical, *Pacem in Terris*, in which he called on all people of good will to make peace happen. It was the same year that Dr. Martin Luther King called for racial justice by filling the jails of Birmingham and arousing the courage of young and old alike to return violence with non-violence, hatred with love.

I was twenty-three years old when a family friend who was a graduate of West Point was captured in Vietnam by the Viet Cong and was killed in captivity—but who, just before he was captured, had sent a letter to the Maryknoll congregation saying he wanted to quit the military and become a priest missionary in Vietnam because he had fallen in love with the people.

Then, doing doctoral studies in Paris in the years 1967 to 1970, years that included the events of 1968, the student riots that brought down the de Gaulle government among other things, I had the privilege of encountering my mentor, the Dominican theologian Fr. Marie Dominic Chenu. Father Chenu was a "worker priest" theologian who worked closely with unions, and the Marxists in them, in France after the war. He thereby developed a methodology for *listening to the poor* that would later be basic to the methodology of liberation theology.

For his efforts on behalf of bridging Christianity and the alienated blue-collar workers of France, Pope Pius XII forbade him to publish for twelve years. But, under Pope John XXIII, and the Vatican Council that he launched in 1963 to "open the windows" of the Catholic Church, Fr. Chenu was rehabilitated and indeed it was he, more than any other theologian or "peritus" at the Council who was most responsible for its most radical document, *The Church in the Modern World*. This essentially told believers to get into the professions and into history and make a difference according to the Gospel values of justice and compassion.

It was Pere Chenu who named the "creation spirituality" tradition for me in my studies with him in Paris—a tradition that combines mysticism, art and social justice. It was he who, during our last visit when he was about eighty-eight years old, put his arm around me and said: "Never forget, the greatest tragedy in theology of the last 300 years has been the divorce of the theologian from the artist, the potter, the poet, the musician, the dancer, the film maker." Chenu died at ninety-five years of age—the very day Nelson Mandela was released from prison. Chenu was the effective "grandfather" of liberation theology. The first book on liberation theology, published by the Peruvian theologian Gustavo Guttieriez, cites Chenu many times.

Those heroic persons in Latin America, who were standing up to decades if not centuries of injustice and oppression by founding base communities and listening to one another's efforts to interpret the justice message of the Gospel—they were my heroes in my own efforts to take on unjust powers in my culture. Among these in the 70s were the issues of sexism and the rise of the women's movement (I taught for four years at an all-women's college near Chicago and learned much of what women had been going through). The gay and lesbian liberation movement and the environmental movement were also integral to my growing awareness and education in issues of global transformation.

What am I currently involved in and what have I learned from these decades of interest in global transformation?

1. With the passage of my sixty-fifth birthday, I looked forward to stepping out of administration of an academic institution, but I do not use the word "retirement". I prefer the term "Re-Firement". I think elders have a grave obligation *not to spend their lives on golf courses* but rather to *refire* and rekindle their hearts and minds. Never in history has there been such a deep need for elders working with and serving the youngest generation. Never before has more than 50% of the human race been under sixteen years of age. We cannot afford elders looking only to their own security and pleasure and financial investments. We elders must give back and do so creatively. Giving our time, our wisdom, our creativity, our ideas and—if we are so blessed—our money or connections to places of power. So that marks one of my current interests: awakening my "boomer" generation to our possibilities and responsibilities as elders, especially as to how we are serving the young.

2. A second passion of mine, closely related to the first, is to contribute to reinventing education. The Dalai Lama has wisely observed that "education is in crisis the world over". He is correct. Education is in crisis because our species is in crisis (and one reason our species is in crisis is because education is in crisis). For too many centuries we have been satisfied with educating people from the neck up; Descartes defined truth as "clear and distinct ideas" and Western academia bought this nonsense hook, line and sinker and called it "education". Now, with the destruction of the planet ("most of it at the hands of people with PhDs", according to Dr. Thomas Berry), the chicken is coming home to roost.

We must unite heart and head again in our education. This would mean we train people for wisdom and not merely for knowledge. A Native American teacher has said: "Only a mad man thinks with his head." Well, Western culture has been turning out mad men for centuries because the form or system of education has been trained too exclusively on the rational, on the heady, on the "left hemisphere" of the brain.

This can be turned around—I know this from years of experience. Thirty years ago I designed a model of education for adults (master's and later a doctoral program) that integrates right and left hemispheres of the brain, the intellectual/analytic and the heart/intuitive/mystical brains. It necessarily involves the whole body and all its chakras (the heart resides in the body after all). And it works!

It is energizing, serious, fun and joyful. Learning can be fun and joyful—indeed learning is one of the greatest pleasures humans can enjoy. The key to this education is the recovery of Awe and of Creativity and of our place in the Cosmos. I remain fully committed to reinventing forms and models of education and am currently completing a book on this topic called *The A.W.E. Project*.

3. Another passion of mine that I have been actively involved in for the past twelve years is the reinvention of ritual. Melidome Some, the African spiritual teacher, says "there is no community without ritual". Clearly our species has to rediscover community as a primary value. Indigenous peoples have a wealth of experience to teach us about that. Modern physics, with its teaching that the universe and the earth and our bodies are machines and that atoms are rugged individuals, not interpenetrating, took the rug out from under our awareness of community. Today's post-modern physics has a different story to tell: That, in fact, atoms link up with other atoms and form molecules; molecules link up with other molecules and form cells; cells link up and form organisms that in turn link up and form societies or communities. Contemporary science's rediscovery of the habit of "interconnectivity" in eco-systems and cosmic systems and microcosmic systems all set the stage for a revival of community.

But humans have to celebrate their interconnectivity: our shared joy and our shared grief. There is so much to grieve about in the world today—the loss of tens of thousands of species per year, war, poverty, abuse of many kinds—all this begs for rituals that gather communities to honour their beauty and to grieve their suffering; to bring out the artists and creative ritual-makers and to make ritual-making one of the great "industries" of our time, where true community is always participatory.

With this in mind, I have been working with teams of others to reinvent Western liturgy and to move it from sitting in benches and pews and being read to and reading to dancing and using the image-making potentials of the post-modern language of computers, fractal-making, djing, vjing, rap and other new languages to help us explore our hearts together. We call our worship experience the "Cosmic Mass" and we borrow much of the language from pre-modern sources and from rave, which is a kind of a global celebratory model that youth the world over are experiencing.

In our gatherings (unlike many rave happenings), drugs are not a part because they don't have to be if you connect valid forms of worship with ancient liturgical traditions. One gets very high without drugs. Canadian Television filmed a recent Cosmic Mass and that 14-minute DVD is available on our website at *www.thecosmicmass.org*.

I believe that when we dance again as a species and as communities, we will return to our lower chakras and get out of our heads and the rational madness that justifies wars and religious and imperial propaganda. This puts us in touch with the sacredness of existence and of the earth. The survival of our planet as we know it and the marvelous species that share the planet with us requires we do so.

4. Another direction for global transformation that calls me today is the issue of moving from Religion to Spirituality. We all need spirituality—that is, we need to calm that reptilian brain that is over 400 million years old and that is destroying the earth and one another through its overdeveloped sense of action/reaction response. This crocodile brain can be calmed by meditation. That is what meditation does: it calms the reptilian brain. Then our mammal brain—the compassionate brain of kinship and family and compassion (the Hebrew and the Arabic words for compassion both derive from the word for "womb")—can rise. Our third brain, our creative and intellectual brain, must be connected more profoundly to our mammal brain and be less occupied with reptilian responses.

Because I am a Westerner, my particular responsibility is to challenge Western religion, which today is at an all-time low as regards credibility, energy and spirit. Protestantism has practically lost its capacity for *protest* and, in my country, has pretty much rolled over and played dead for kooky versions of fundamentalist and reconstructionist Christianity, which dominate the air waves, television and politics itself. Coming from a Roman Catholic tradition, I must blow the whistle on the emperor (or pope) who has no clothes as well. The pedophile scandals in Catholicism represent just the tip of the iceberg of a tradition that has sadly invested so much in keeping its hierarchy all-male and all-celibate (or claiming to be such) and all-ignorant (the current pope dismissed and silenced over 107 theologians during his previous office, thus effectively closing down thinking in the Catholic Church). The hierarchy was in fact totally dumbed down during the previous papacy. Dumbed down leadership opens the door to folly.

To wake up both wings of Western Christianity, I went to Wittenburg, Germany at Pentecost, 2005, to pound 95 theses at the doors where Martin Luther began his Reformation five hundred years ago. We need a new Reformation in religion in the West. One that moves us from religion to spirituality, from patriarchy to gender-justice, from anthropocentrism to love of all creation, from preoccupation with sexual morality to preoccupation with ecological, economic racial, gender and gender-preference issues of justice. We have no time to waste. For more on the New Reformation, one can go to the website *www.matthewfox.org* or, if one speaks German, to *www.publikforum.de*. One can also look at my book, *A New Reformation!* available through my website.

I am, of course, very much interested in Interfaith or what I call "Deep Ecumenism" which is the subject of another of my books, *One River, Many Wells: Wisdom Springing from Global Faiths.* I agree with the Dalai Lama that the number-one obstacle to Interfaith is a bad relationship with one's own faith tradition.

Most Christian Westerners, for example, do not even know their own mystical tradition—great souls such as Meister Eckhart, Hildegard of Bingen, Nicolas of Cusa, the Celtic tradition, Jesus as Mystic, the Cosmic Christ, Thomas Aquinas as mystic. I have published books on all these subjects in order to awaken us Westerners to our own in-depth heritage so that we can join forces with Buddhists, Taoists, Hindus, Jews, Native Peoples, goddess worshippers and today's science to see a true renaissance emerge in our species. A renaissance is a rebirth of civilization based on a spiritual initiative. We need that today.

Many are the hands, heads and hearts contributing to the same. My friend Fred Matser, who has gathered the contributors for this book, is such a person, as are all the contributors to this volume. May the work continue!

8. Jane Goodall, PhD, D.B.E. (UK)
Primatologist, Founder of the Jane Goodall Institute and UN Messenger of Peace

What are your visions/dreams for the future of the planet?

In the world of my dreams all people have the opportunity to raise themselves from poverty and ignorance; spiritual growth is valued above the acquisition of material wealth; all children enjoy true childhood; no end can ever justify cruel or unjust means; people understand the interdependency of all life, and respect not only each other, but also animals and the natural world—and realize, too, that the heart is as important as the head in determining how we behave.

In this world, there is much laughter and singing and a sense of the Divine. And there is hope for lasting peace based on tolerance, compassion and love.

How can you/we make these dreams happen?

The world today seems to lie under a dark shadow of violence and war, cruelty, injustice, human greed and lust for power. Millions of people are living in fear, depression, apathy, or bitterness and anger. Millions have lost hope. Indeed, the problems to be solved are daunting. How to end mushrooming human population growth, raise the standard of living of the poor, and curb the unsustainable lifestyles of the wealthy? The answers lie with each one of us: for the collective power of "we, the people" is potentially unlimited.

We must stop leaving all the decision making to greedy, weak or corrupted corporate leaders and politicians. We must realize that each of us makes an impact on the world around us every day: all the little choices we make as to what we buy, eat and so on, affect people, animals, the environment—and the future of our children. We must support companies with sound ethical values and practices. Refuse to buy anything produced by exploiting children, the poor, and animals. Buy into the growing and eating of organic foods, adopt a mainly vegetarian diet. We must listen to our hearts, not only our heads.

We must also recognize the tremendous importance of early childhood experience, the need for wise parenting and a nurturing family. Nothing should be more important or worth spending more money on, than the preparation of the citizens of tomorrow.

Roots & Shoots, an education program that I established, now has some 8,000 groups in over 90 countries, and is growing. It emphasizes the value of each individual. It enables young people from pre-school through university and beyond, to chose and perform activities that will make the world a better place for people, animals and the environment, and helps to break down the barriers that we have built between people of different cultures and religions, and between us and the natural world. By partnering with other organizations that share our philosophy, we move towards creating a critical mass of young people—the next teachers, scientists, lawyers, businesspeople, politicians, parents and so on—who understand that they will not find meaning in their lives through simply acquiring money and *stuff* but that caring about and helping others makes the heart sing and that doing all this in a group is fun. They understand, too, that violence seldom provides lasting solutions to disputes.

What particular experiences in your life shaped your vision?

During years alone in the forest I became increasingly in awe of the mystery and beauty of that world, increasingly aware of the Great Spiritual Power that we call God, Allah, Tao, the Creator and so on. I occasionally had almost mystical experiences that left me feeling that I *knew*, deep within, more than I *understood* about the nature of God and human existence on earth. At the same time, the human population in the surrounding hills grew, refugees arrived who were fleeing conflicts in neighboring countries and suddenly I found that, beyond the boundaries of the tiny national park, virtually all the trees had gone. Desperate people, needing firewood and meat, were jeopardizing the sanctity of the park. In the villages I saw first hand the terrible results of poverty, overpopulation and lack of opportunity to create change. We developed a program (TACARE) that includes reforestation, new farming techniques, primary health care, micro-credit and information about family planning, HIV-Aids and soil and water conservation. I witnessed the dramatic change when people, especially women, received the opportunity to improve their lives. Now we are replicating the program in other places.

www.janegoodall.org

9. Azra Husanovic (Bosnia-Herzegovina)

Student and former Worker at
the Peace Flame House, Tuzla

What are your visions/dreams for the future of the planet?

Well, I am hoping for something big to happen that will change the whole quality of life that exists today. The established social order of things is such that the true virtues like humility, kindness, loyalty, etc. aren't recognized, causing real friendships and deep human relationships to be rare and short lasting. Put it like this—the most important things are put in the last place in the consciousness of the masses—and this has to do with the sort of life that's being promoted by the dominant societies (i.e. Western society). There are too many lies around us.

What particular experiences in your life shaped your vision?
I cannot think of any one particular experience. Rather, this is my view of the world after all that I have been through during my 20 years of life. It is also one of my favorite topics in my conversations with friends.

How can you/we make these dreams happen?
Everybody has to be aware about these problems. It is something that cannot be changed quickly. We have to find a way to teach all of us, and ourselves, what is good and what is bad, what is moral and not. The change has to start from the bottom, from the people... and then somehow I hope that the capitalistic and destroying mechanisms around us will start changing.

10. Gerald G. Jampolsky, M.D (USA)
Doctor, Author & Founder of The International Center for Attitudinal Healing, Sausalito, California

What are your visions/ dreams for the future of the planet?
My vision would be that each of us would begin to live as if the future and the present were one and the same and that we would live each moment as if it were an eternal never- ending moment filled with unconditional love. It would be for each of us to take responsibility for our own happiness and let go of the belief that the past was going to predict the future. It would be a moment where Love would be our only reality, and that we would live in harmony with each other and the planet we live on.

It is my vision that, as each of us heals our split mind, that the world we see begins to change. The world we used to see begins to disappear and we enter a world of no time, no space and only Peace and Love.

How can you/we make these visions/dreams happen?
Each of us can make this happen by making forgiveness as important as breathing. We can make a difference seeing our purpose as loving, caring, serving and helping others and experiencing and demonstrating Oneness. In other words, it is letting go of any illusion of any kind of separateness in the universe.

What particular experiences in your life have shaped your vision?
In 1975 I was introduced to some, then unpublished, writings called *A Course In Miracles*. In reading just one page I heard an inner voice for the first time in my life stating, "*Physician heal thyself. This is your way home.* I then had an experience that I have never adequately been able to put in words. I was an atheist at the time and what I experienced was the Peace of God and inner knowing that my life was going to be a life of service where God's Will and mine would be the same. I still remain today a student of this Course, which gives ways for letting go of the blocks that interfere with our experiencing unconditional love.

I continue to be a work in process and do my best in making decisions based on love rather than fear.

www.attitudinalhealing.org

11. Vandy Kanyako Jr. (Siera Leone)
Student

What are your visions/dreams for the future of the planet?
I dream of a future for the planet without the ravages of wars and environmental degradation. I dream of a world where the human race lives in harmony with one another and with nature, a world circumscribed by respect for diversity and cultural tolerance, a world where the beauty and nurturing care of mother nature is revered by the present generation and preserved for future generations.

I dream of a future in which the ever-widening gulf between the haves and the have-nots is addressed, to make it possible for those plagued by hunger, malnutrition and preventable diseases to be able to meet their basic dietary needs and have affordable, quality health care. I dream of a world where a sizeable proportion of the global poor are not forced to live on less than one dollar a day while governments spends billions of dollars on armament build-up. I dream of a planet where the world's massive technological advancement can be put to proper and effective use to eradicate famine, malaria, HIV/Aids, to name just a few. I dream of a future where the poor and the disempowered take control of their own destiny, a world where they choose their leaders freely and fairly. I dream of a future where people are judged by their ability rather than by their national origin, race, gender or sexual orientation. I dream of a future in which nations and communities resolve their differences peacefully rather than resort to the use of violence, which more often than not only begets more violence. I dream of a world in which the twenty-first century becomes more peaceful than the preceding century which by all accounts was the bloodiest in the history of humankind.

What particular experiences in your life shaped your vision?
The civil war in my native Sierra Leone (1991 to 2000) shaped my outlook on life in general. The conflict brought out the worst as well as the best in humankind. The rather senseless war claimed over 15,000 lives, left countless others maimed and scarred for life and the country's infrastructure in ruins. The social fabric of the society was torn apart as people's lives were disrupted and in some cases consumed by the carnage. Family members, friends, neighbors and colleagues whom I knew to be loving and caring in peace time, suddenly found themselves armed, on different warring sides.

The consequences were disastrous. I witnessed the radical transformation of once-peaceful communities as they degenerated into chaos and anarchy. The war also brought out the best in humankind, for, side by side with the ravages and brutality of the conflict, went the sacrifice, dedication and resilience of some individuals and groups (both local and international) to change the situation for the better. Some, such as the peacekeepers and humanitarian aid workers, put their lives on the line to end the human suffering. Others used their time, energy, expertise and resources to bring succor to the traumatized and war-weary population.

The bravery, commitment and dedication of such groups and individuals was critical to saving thousands of lives, including mine, and was no doubt a source of inspiration to those of us who have since decided to dedicate our lives to working for peace. Without such interventions and proactive stance, countless more would have died.

How can you/we make these dreams happen?
I have been a peace and human rights activist for most of my working life. This job has taught me several important lessons. One is that we all have the potential, as well as the responsibility, to make the world a better place. Indeed, both war and peace begins and ends in the minds of the individual. Being aware of the impact of our actions and decisions on the lives of others, both near (acquaintances) and far (strangers), will go a long way to creating a more peaceful world.

The second lesson is that we can indeed make dreams come true by being true to ourselves and to our individual philosophies. We can do this by putting into practice what we say, especially as we live in a world where a huge gulf exists between rhetoric and practice. This vocation offered me the opportunity to use my talent, skills and experience on behalf of the marginalized and the disempowered.

We have to bridge the economic divide by leveling the playing field at all levels of society: internationally, nationally, and in our local communities. Creating opportunities for young people is critical to achieving this goal. Some of the most unstable regions in the world, including mine, are those that lack opportunities for the youths.

Finally, we have to see the world we live in as a truly global village and to think of ourselves as global citizens. The latter sees humanity first before anything else.

12. Rola Khoury (Italy)
Media Director and Public Relations Consultant

What are your visions/dreams for the future of the planet?
I don't really rely on the future as much as on the moment, as my future will come in the form of this moment called NOW, and what I hope is only that I have my heart fulfilled in this moment and each human being, like me, will aspire to this most noble gesture, to pursue his or her heart fulfilment, now.

How can you/we make these happen?
KNOW THYSELF!! No two are alike, each one's needs are different and our hearts know our own truth. If I get to know myself and this becomes my goal, then I'm in charge and I can be responsible to make things happen, and thus express myself and be fulfilled. When I know myself and connect to the knowledge I am born with, I experience an intimate field of joy and peace that is immeasurable… if each of us concentrates on such fulfilment then we can ALL make it.

If you are not a lit candle, you can't pretend to light others, or inspire others to become lit, yet one bulb can light a stadium. If each of us cultivates our own light, then we can light the whole world.

Experience is something the heart feels. Some experiences, especially this one, are beyond words or manuals; they are simply experience.

What particular experiences in your life have shaped your vision?
Every breath that comes to me, and that is not wasted, is an experience of full joy and happiness. This life is a miracle and each breath is proof of an Existence

worth living. I don't wait or rely on circumstance and conditions outside of myself to determine how fortunate I am. BEING is already the biggest gift and miracle that is happening now.

13. Craig Kielburger (Canada)
Founder and Chair, Free The Children

What are your visions/dreams for the future of the planet?

My dreams for the future are rooted in one goal: that this be a world in which every child receives an education.

About 121 million children around the world between the ages of six and eleven have never stepped foot in a classroom. Two-thirds of these are girls. And yet education is the solution to everything: child labor, Aids, poverty, gender inequality.

An education means people can read the posters that provide health awareness and women and men get vital Aids education and prevention. Education is the key to women's empowerment so they know about their basic and inalienable rights. An education means parents are not putting thumb prints at the bottom of contracts they can't read, giving away their assets, their rights, even their children. Education allows democracy to thrive. It means a child can break out of the cycle of poverty.

Education means a child has a future.

How can you/we make these dreams happen?

Children must be at the forefront of making these dreams happen. They must challenge the adults of the world to take action.

Through Free The Children, more than 100,000 young people from around the world have raised millions of dollars to build more than 400 primary schools in developing countries, providing education to more than 35,000 children every day.

Children have collected more than 200,000 backpacks full of school supplies and created entire support programs, such as mid-day meal programs, which allow their peers to receive an education.

Youth have been at the heart of raising awareness and funds for clean water programs so that girls don't have to walk far distances to fetch water. Young people have built health clinics, so that students are healthy as they learn, and funded alternative co-operatives for women, so they can afford to send their child to school instead of sending their child to work.

Through Free The Children, young people around the world are helping to fulfill that dream of making education possible for every child.

What particular experiences in your life shaped your vision?
Through my travels to more than 40 countries, I've spent time with thousands of children in many slums, shantytowns and jails of this world. And whether it was a girl cutting sugar canes in the fields of Brazil, a boy pouring molten metal without any protective gear in a factory in India or young girls and boys fighting as child soldiers in Africa, they all shared the same dream with me: to one day receive an education.

Mary Smart was nine years-old when her family was killed by rebels in Sierra Leone, a country still recovering from a brutal eleven-year civil war in which more than 30,000 children fought as child soldiers. Mary lived in the bushes for months, always moving so that the rebels wouldn't capture her. She realized her only dream when she began attending a Free The Children school. Education gave her the chance to build a future while also giving her a safe environment in which to cope with the trauma of war and loss. We nicknamed her "Very Smart" because she graduated at the top of her class, becoming the first female in her village to go to high school.

For Mary, education is hope for a brighter future.
www.freethechildren.com

14. Nsaa-Iya Kihunrwa (Tanzania)

Member, Robert Swan's Inspire Antarctic Expedition 1996 and Worker on Dr. Jane Goodall's global humanitarian and environmental program

What are your visions/dreams for the future of the planet?
Currently the world's leading nations are bad examples of serious cases of systemic repression, human rights violation, acute injustice and inequitable and unfair economic treatment to poor nations. My dream for the future is for a more peaceful planet. I dream of well-accepted global ethics that will bring a lost vision for peace.

I dream that there will be a significant reduction in global conflicts, increased tolerance and understanding among nations and individuals, sustainable population growth, reduction in diseases and poverty, sustainable exploitation and use of resources, less greed and competition among nations and individuals on available resources.

What particular experiences in your life shaped your vision?

Conflicts & crises

My dreams are very much influenced by past and current personal experiences. Although conflicts and crises are part of life, wrong solutions have deliberately been applied in solving conflicts due to mediators' self interests. Be it in Africa, or elsewhere on the planet, I believe that personal interests, dogmatism and stereotypes of mediators are detrimental barriers in arriving at effective and sustainable conflict resolutions.

Greed forces nations to support conflicts in other places aiming at benefiting them. These conflicts create inequity among societies, which establishes competition. The world still has hatred and suspicion of ethnicity, religion, politics and class, which is arguably the result of mishandled conflicts. Unresolved conflicts and crises have resulted in a loss of vision towards peace. The justification of military force following a particular political circumstance and the approval of pre-emptive strikes accelerates fear and jeopardizes global peace initiatives tremendously.

Democracy

As a Tanzanian and a true citizen of the world, I question the existence of an effective, honest democratic election process. The recent elections in my country have left me with a big question. Will we ever have a 100% democratically elected government whereby citizens obtain a leader agreed by all to be freely and fairly elected? I am not yet convinced. Losers have the right to complain when they are dissatisfied at losing. Sarcastically we may be said to have a culture of complaining but in some cases complainants may have valid reasons. Yet their appeal progresses nowhere in a bureaucratic appeals process that is not independent. I wonder if elections that are said to be free and fair have final results that are actually genuine. Have the losers truly lost? I have lost faith.

Injustice & human rights

Is there justice? Thieves on the streets are killed or burnt to death by mob justice because of lack of confidence in the law-enforcing agencies. Participants of petty corruption are punished severely if found guilty, while players of white-collar crime and people who engage in grand corruption walk away freely. The poor are made poorer by the rich through various tricks.

Overpopulation, poverty & diseases

At over six billion, the world is unbalanced and overpopulated. My dream is to have a sustainable population growth that is equitably distributed for our own benefit. The past fifteen years, where I have been working for Dr. Jane Goodall's global humanitarian and environmental program, has exposed me to environmental issues, especially those of habitat destruction. I have witnessed thick forests turning into eroded bare land due to the development of settlements and the clearing of fields for agriculture. Hunting for scarce food has resulted in animals' extinction while overpopulation has lead to outbreaks of uncontrolled diseases. Since animals cannot talk for themselves, they continue to be exterminated and squeezed day after day.

Our resource requirements at six billion plus have increased dramatically. Overpopulation in Tanzania has brought about an increased consumption of resources and production of waste. The Government is concerned, with its limited capacity to provide basic services. Under-capacity has accelerated ignorance, resulting in poverty and diseases. With inevitable globalization, poor nations become weaker and will eventually fall prey if not harmonized well.

Understanding, tolerance & accommodation

In 1996/97, I was very fortunate to visit the Antarctic continent when participating in an adventure of a lifetime to celebrate 50 years of UNESCO. I was sponsored by Fred Matser's Twinkling Eyes Club—Miles of Smiles, and was among thirty-five young people from 25 different countries.

Among the many lessons learned was the way the Gentoo penguins living at Port-Lockroy (British Antarctic Survey Base) accommodated us. When a penguin is walking to, or from, the shore and encounters a stranger—as long as it is not a Leopard seal—they will stop and wait for the stranger to move off before continuing with their journey; a unique demonstration of accommodation.

The Antarctic, being very quiet, pure and peaceful, is a great place to learn about the interaction of fauna. If only all humans could have such tolerance and understanding and live with their neighbors in this co-operative way, then nations and all individuals would have a guaranteed peace for life. I oppose authoritarian rule, where an individual or nation thinks they know best, and forces others to adopt their way.

How can you/we make these visions/dreams happen?

My dreams are lofty and their basis is ethics. We can gradually attain our dreams by following these simple rules:

- *Focusing on attaining sustainable peace by avoiding conflicts and effectively resolving current conflicts*
- *Having more understanding and tolerance and being more accommodating of others*
- *Treasuring and living by sincere, commonly accepted and sound ethics*
- *Finding a way of establishing sustainable population control and of safeguarding and distributing scarce resources*
- *Being less selfish, more considerate and sharing resources fairly*
- *Not practicing acts of power that favor greed for wealth accumulation*

We can all agree that the benefits of having peace surpass the benefits of having wealth and power. Treating each other with justice and questioning our moral ethics are prerequisites to attaining long-lasting peace. We should all work towards restoring a common standard of ethics and justice and building equity. Equitable societies have no reason to compete. There is no hope for the future unless we come to terms with this and change the dogmatic perceptions and motives of others for our own, collective higher good.

15. Marc de Klerk (Netherlands/Bosnia-Herzegovina)
Entrepreneur, (NGO) Project Developer and Freelance Consultant in the western Balkans[2]

What are your visions/dreams for the future of the planet?
I don't dream realistic things. I dream of beautiful people and love and high endurance sports and of flying and of surfing. I love to dream, but it's not really realistic.

I also cry, sometimes out loud and many times in private. I cry mostly out of happiness. This happiness is something different from feeling happy—this happiness is a realization of the truth. This is the most beautiful thing I know: the truth. This is a layer on top of whatever you want: love, friendship, family, romance, sex, work, politics, economics, psychiatry, everything! This layer is unfortunately not very much used around the world.

When I notice that someone has forgotten to put the layer of truth on top, I get disappointed but that doesn't affect me that much. I have decided to sit and watch when something disappoints me, unless it is within my power to change it. When I notice the layer of truth, I cry because of that happiness and I feel truly

---

2 Marc was a Peace Flame Project Developer 2003–2004, worked with MDK Development 2005/2006 and has worked with Vision EDG since 2007.

connected to myself, the world and my spiritual environment. I rarely dream about that. I often notice or feel the possibility of it, though, and I hope that this layer will be engaged by people more often, because it is so beautiful.

What particular experiences in your life shaped your vision?
Many! There were many special experiences in my life. Death is one of the most apparent ones. I have wondered why we seem to get so sad because of death and I think it's because we notice the truth—there is nothing we can do about it—death has an intrinsic layer of truth. And the beauty of the truth makes us cry. It's too bad that death has such a negative connotation in our culture, because it blinds us to see this layer. Another experience is music, also complete and intrinsically true—except for bad music, and the way to realize that music is bad is to notice that it doesn't affect our emotions. Listening to real music makes me cry as well for the exact same reason.

How can you/we make these visions/dreams happen?
We have to concentrate on our environment: the colleagues, friends and family, the home, culture and the city and nature. All this is supposed to be layered with the truth and that would make it truly beautiful and healthy and peaceful. Secondly, we have to concentrate on ourselves and make sure we dress ourselves with this layer of truth: in our love, spirit, hope, friendship, work and other daily activities (including the most simple ones) and all these other aspects that make life interesting (nothing in life is uninteresting). These two strategies will make us live the life in truth and this beauty will make us cry more. Cries of happiness!

16. Olesya Koba (The Ukraine)

Fred Foundation Ukraine Worker & Translator

The destiny of a person, their way of life, is marked by their birth. It's not only a matter of which lucky or unlucky star we are born under but more a case of which family, or genealogical tree we are born into.

My mother was born into a large, friendly family, where nobody was indifferent to the life of others. On holidays, the whole family gathered at the table and we cooked together. It was often crowded but always very joyful and interesting, too. If something bad happened, then the whole family came together to help each other, too. When my grandmother, died my mother was only 20. At that time, my mother was dating my father, but the whole family felt sorry for her, as she was the youngest child to be without a mother.

From early childhood, I've received much care and parental love. My father carried me everywhere until the moment that my younger brother, Vasyl was born. From that moment, he replaced me in my father's arms. But my father's love and care was enough for both of us.

Fifteen years ago, my father became the director of a boarding school. One day my father took me to the school. There, I saw little children who only knew the words "mother" and "father" from books. Nobody helped those children to go to bed in the evening; nobody said "good night" to them. No mother woke them up in the morning. They called my father, "father" as they did not have their own fathers. These little children knew that every child must have a mother so whenever a new woman came to the school they asked, "Are you my mother?" This struck me the most and stayed in my memory. When I see such children now I am always reminded of this moment. My brother and I studied in a normal school and our parents both worked. My father brought home the sorrow and pain of these children and so their life paralleled my own. We learned about everything that was going on in the boarding school and in this way my father taught us to think of those in a worse situation than our own.

I remember one of my birthday parties very well. I was 16 and it was New Year's Day. We invited many people and my father should have been the first to congratulate me, but he had to go to the boarding school. There were troubles with the heating system and he did not come back, wet and tired, until the following morning. I was very sad and angry, because he had been with the children in the boarding school and not with me. But these thoughts were soon replaced with another; these children needed him most that night. Slowly they came into my life in this way and these "grains of goodness" became embedded in our minds by my parents. Later, we met Jan Ebeltjes, who was the first person who I met, other than my father, who cared about these suffering children.

I was a student at the time I got to know about Jan. My father told me how much he helped Ukrainian orphans, especially those in boarding schools in Perechyn and Chynadiyevo. He put so much effort, energy, and time into helping them and I used to ask myself what would have happened without his help and why he did it. It was difficult for him to win the trust of local and regional government officials. People were unfamiliar with the idea of "charity" and wondered what he hoped to gain from these activities.

In 2002, we met another good person, Fred Matser. He is one of the most inspiring people that I know and made me think about my own choices in my life. He invited Jan to work for the Fred Foundation (Ukraine) and Jan asked my father for help in finding a place that really needed their aid. My father suggested Perekhrestya.

By unfortunate destiny, young male orphans, once they became too old for their various boarding schools, were re-homed in Perekhrestya. Dozens lived together there in one big room that was just a hut; there was no heating, water or furniture, apart from beds and they had no shoes, underwear or soap. Most had no jobs and no income for their survival. Nobody cared about them. Just a few of them were working in a local village for food.

When my father heard about their situation, he was very upset. He wanted to do something to help, but no-one was interested. I went there with Jan and was really shocked by what I saw; it was even worse than we had expected. It's impossible to describe how bad the conditions were. You would need to experience it for yourself. Fortunately, Jan and the Fred Foundation decided to help these young people.

I cried all night after what I had seen and from that day I realized my life had changed forever. When we had spoken with the youngsters in Perekhrestya they had told us: "We want to be like normal people; to have a normal life, a family and a home." This had made me realize that I wanted to use my life to help. Jan asked my father about this, suggesting that I was perhaps still too young to be involved, as the work would be difficult and demanding. But my father answered calmly and clearly, saying: "The time is ripe for her to choose her future life." And so I did.

Thanks to the Fred Foundation, many of the youngsters from Perekhrestya now have their own homes and families. One of my greatest joys has been when one of them calls me to say things are going well or that they have a new baby.

Unfortunately, our work continues to grow as the situation in the Ukraine has worsened. Plenty more orphans and homeless people are coming our way and it is not possible for us to take all their sorrow and pain away or solve all their problems. But at least I have the possibility of doing something to help and I have come to I realize that to give is more joyful than to receive.

A lot of Ukrainian people thank God that they had the possibility to meet Fred and Jan and I am grateful to God that I met them as well.

May God help you in all that you do, too.

17. Indra Kumari Khattri Tamang (Nepal)
Housewife

What are your visions/dreams for the future of the planet?
Our planet is beautiful. Its beauty should be maintained. I dream our planet may be healthy, friendly, secure and spiritually linked between human beings, animals and plants. The active players on our planet are human beings. Our main concern

has been to maintain a friendly environment for human beings. Yet, in my view, a whole ecosystem approach will help our planet to be healthy. Our planet provides food, shelter, energy, and other necessities to all forms of life. People can live happy, healthy and secure lives and enjoy our planet if they can love one another.

What particular experiences in your life shaped your vision?
I would like to share one experience which I consider a major event in my life. When I was about ten years old, I experienced an accident that totally changed my life. I fell into an open fire and burnt most of the left side of my face. Due to that accident, I also lost one of my eyes. I was unconscious for two days. I was treated for over a month at a local health post, but due to lack of proper medicine and training of the health workers, I did not recover fully. My brother then helped me to travel to Kathmandu, the capital of Nepal, where I was operated on several times. My burnt face was healing, but I was left with ugly scars.

Someone suggested that I visit a German nurse who had been working locally as a volunteer for several years. Seeing my condition, she told me that she would do everything that she could to help me, saying that she regarded seeing me as her Christmas gift from God. Due to her kindness, I was put in touch with Fred Matser, who has such a compassionate heart. He invited my brother, Man Bahadur, and I to come and visit him in Hilversum, in the Netherlands, and arranged for some treatment for me there. This made me realize that we can work together to help each other make the planet healthy.

In rural areas, nature may be healthy but that does not imply that the whole planet is healthy. Environment issues have become complex, and I feel we no longer know how to respect nature. We expect to use nature for our own benefit, but nature has its own law, and what I would call, “nature spirits”. We humans have our own spirits, too, and I think it is important to start to think of both as natural. Spirituality is natural. The planet is also a part of spirituality and nature plays a large part in that. A healthy planet helps us develop a good spirituality, which is good for people, animals and plants. From the time of my accident, I have been helped by various people in the Netherlands, Germany, Norway and Nepal, and this gave me the feeling that the spirit of nature and goodness exists in human beings. It may exist in different forms in different places, and may be due to “God” or a “supreme spirit”, but it does exist.

How can you/we make these visions/dreams happen?
I am just a woman. Our planet has billions of people like me yet each with our own individuality and individual life process. The important thing is to use our individual capacities for the good of the whole planet. In Nepal, we have a

saying that if one person spits, it dries up rapidly, but if hundreds spit, then it will turn into a river. Similarly, I believe that my warm, good or positive spirit can contribute to the healthy spirit of our beautiful planet. I ask from my heart that the billions people on our planet join hand in hand to help make our planet healthy and to link with heavenly spirit.

18. Ervin Laszlo (Italy, Hungary, USA)

Author, President of the Club of Budapest

Global transformation—how I came to be involved with it, and what my involvement has taught me

There was not a single pivotal experience that has led to my involvement with the problems and possibilities of global transformation, but a whole series of events that "drove" me in this direction—without my conscious will (but not against it). The series began with a seemingly innocent phone-call from Professor Richard ("Dick") Falk of Princeton University's Center of International Studies. This was in 1972, if I remember correctly. I was teaching at the time in the Philosophy Department of the State University of New York at Geneseo, in the quiet rural regions of Upstate New York. I was deeply immersed in systems theory, attempting to elucidate the philosophical implications of thinking in terms of systems that are integral wholes rather than in terms of isolated or semi-isolated entities that are, at best, fragments of more inclusive systems. I had just begun to develop the evolutionary implications of what I called "Systems Philosophy", moving towards what later came to be known as "General Evolution Theory" (that is, a general theory of evolution as it applies to physical systems, living systems, consciousness, and even to the universe as a whole system).

The call from Dick Falk was unexpected: while I had known of him and his work in the context of a project called World Order Models Project, I knew nothing about what the models were, how successful they were, and what problems they encountered. I explained this to him, yet Dick was not to be deterred and asked me to come to Princeton to give a series of seminars on the "world system." He said that it would be sufficient that I present my conception of complex evolving systems; he and other members of the Center's faculty would see what could be made of them in regard to the world system. I was dubious, but the challenge was intriguing, and I accepted. This was the first, and as it turned out fateful, step on the way to my involvement with questions of global transformation.

The other steps can be summarized more briefly. Out of my seminars at Princeton came a book, *A Strategy for the Future: The Systems Approach to World Order*. It was read by Aurelio Peccei, the visionary founder, and at the time President, of the Club of Rome, who was just then thinking how to state the more human implications of the Club's first report, the legendary *Limits to Growth*. Aurelio asked me to set up a project to look at what aspirations people and societies have in regard to the future, and whether these aspirations could be fulfilled on a small and finite planet. Within six months, I pulled together a small but enthusiastic team of young scholars and budding activists. We developed a project; Aurelio as well as Alex King, the co-Founder of the Club Of Rome, liked it, and I set about implementing it.

Since this required vast international contacts (and there was no e-mail and Internet at the time), Aurelio asked the Executive Director of the UN's "think tank," the Institute for Training and Research (UNITAR) to invite me to work at the Institute as a Special Fellow. I moved to the city, brought the core team with me, and we began to work. The Club of Rome Report was completed in just about a year and was published first in English and then in various other languages under the title *Goals for Mankind: The New Horizons of Global Community*. I returned to my quiet, upstate campus and that, I thought, was the end of my involvement with global issues.

But another phone call came a few weeks later, this time from Dr. Davidson Nicol, the Executive Director of UNITAR. He asked me to represent the Institute at the founding of the United Nations University in Tokyo. I could not say no and one thing then led to another. First I was asked to head the research on the New International Economic Order, which was to be adopted at the UN General Assembly at a special session in the fall of 1980. When it came to voting at that session, the US, the UK, and Western Germany, three major economic powers, announced that they would "not participate": the entire NIEO project was forthwith dropped.

The UN Secretary-General Kurt Waldheim asked what other ideas I might have to re-launch the dialogue between North and South, and I suggested a systemic concept. Let's not attempt to move from the nation-state level directly to the North and South level, but prepare the ground by helping the South to be an economically more equal partner. This meant creating integration, organizations among groups of developing countries, following the model pioneered by the European Community. The project "Regional and Interregional Cooperation among Developing Countries" was adopted by UNITAR and a high-level "Panel of Eminent Persons" was created to present the conclusions to the Secretary-General.

This took another four years of intense effort. At its conclusion, I decided to spend a year at our Tuscan farmhouse, returning to my concerns with systems and evolutionary theory. I did not have a whole year, however, since first the Vice-Chancellor of the UN University Prof. Kinhide Mushakoji, and then the newly elected Director-General of UNESCO, Prof. Federico Mayor, called on me to collaborate and advise.

In the meantime, I recalled the promise I had made to Aurelio Peccei on the occasion of the ten-year anniversary meeting of the Club in Rome: to try to create a sister-club made up of artists, writers, and spiritual leaders. The rationale for this was the recognition that addressing leaders in politics and business is not sufficient to move beyond lip-service to new ideas and strategies: we must also mobilize the thinking, the imagination, and the creativity of people in civil society.

When I presented this concept at the Third World Congress of Hungarians in Budapest, Jozsef Antal, the Prime Minister of Hungary, who was present at the event, called on me to set up such a club in the city of Budapest. I accepted gratefully, and suggested that we should call it "The Club of Budapest".

As this brief account indicates, my involvement with global problems and transformation came about as a series of challenges that both surprised and intrigued me. They ended by involving me intellectually as well as emotionally. For the insight that dawned on me—and it is time that I get to this point—was that we live in critical times.

The critical nature of our times is not just that it harbors dangers, but that it offers unprecedented opportunities for change. And, above all, that the chance to seize the opportunities for positive change is not limited to a few who have the power and the wealth: it is in the hands of everyone. For fundamental change, I realized, does not come about by throwing technology or even money at the problems, nor by attempting to cover them up by political rhetoric or mitigate them with cosmetic solutions. It only comes about by a deep-seated transformation that is nothing less than a shift in the dominant civilization.

A civilization is the expression of the culture shared by people, whatever their place in society. Culture, in turn, is the expression of the thinking, the feeling, the priorities and perceptions of individuals: in one word, of their *consciousness*. Thus to renew our crisis-prone civilization we need to evolve our consciousness. This is a realistic project, because our consciousness is not an isolated entity, limited to our body and brain. It is a powerful emitter that is constantly in communication with the world at large, including the consciousness of our fellows in society.

The evolved consciousness of one individual can spread and grow, and if it resonates with the thinking of an entirely new culture, it can shift the nature of the whole civilization. This must be a global shift, for the dominant civilization—the mechanistic, manipulative, and fragmented civilization of the industrial age—is already global. However, the new civilization, unlike the current one, need not and must not be monolithic. It can be organic and "systemic," nurturing diversity and at the same time seeking unity. These are the principal insights on which the Club of Budapest was founded. Its twin mottos express and illustrate them: "*You Can Change the World*" and "*Toward a Planetary Civilization*."

www.clubofbudapest.org

19. Irene van Lippe-Biesterfeld (Netherlands)
HRH Princess of the Netherlands
Chair of The Lippe-Biesterfeld Nature College Foundation

What are your visions/dreams for the future of the planet?
If we could learn to listen to each other, the effect could be quite dramatic. Often we are afraid to be open to other ways of thinking and we react according to our own cultural background or our own little sub-culture. To open up and listen to others might bring about new views and that might mean change. It seems we prefer to stick to our old ways, even when they are uncomfortable or even painful, rather than to step into the unknown. This fear of change and the unknown makes us judgmental and too often intolerant. This makes it almost impossible to really listen and hear.

How can you/we make these visions/dreams happen?
I have discovered through my work, bringing people in contact with nature and opening up to the oneness of all that lives, that nature is a place that makes no difference between cultures, or species. It is a non-judgmental surrounding, all and everything can be just as it is, open. This makes it a place of healing and bonding, also to our own inner nature.

Being in nature can help us humans to listen to who we really are, to open up to what binds us and what we can learn from our differences. And we can learn much, not only from our fellow humans, but also from all life forms around us. This creates far greater results than being enclosed in our well-known and seemingly safe ways, or "little boxes". The non-human part of nature can teach us and help us to open our hearts and get to know our inner nature.

What particular experiences in your life shaped your vision?
Through my trans-cultural work, I have learned to listen to other ways, thoughts and starting points than my own cultural background; it has brought me new insights and broadened my views. Through listening and being open to the ways of other than human life forms, I have learned that, in effect, we are part of the web of life. The illusion of separateness has only brought pain and endless suffering. This divide from nature is what needs to be healed in all of us humans. Being acutely aware of the oneness of all life brings us to acknowledge the wonders of synchronicity. A whole new world opens up, and this can bring a continuous joy and soft compassion for life. If we would make the oneness of life our starting point, we would take care that all our decisions would be non-detrimental to life around us, because we are in fact one.

20. Ruslan Lokotosh (The Ukraine)
Ukrainian orphan

I don't know my parents, I have never met them.
When I look at myself then I know that my parents must have been gypsies, because I'm dark-skinned and have black hair. I've never tried to find my parents, because a lot of Gypsy people have the name Lokotosh, so it would be very difficult to find them. Besides, I'm not interested in them; they were not interested in me. They abandoned me after my birth.

I spent the first six years of my life in an orphanage in the village of Cinadiewo. After that they brought me to a boarding school in Chaslivtsi. It was terrible. No-one loved me and nobody was interested in me. A few times I ran away from the school and I lived in the streets of Uzhgorod. But the police always brought me back to the school. I was always afraid about the future because I had no place to go, no family at all.

I knew that, in time, when I became seventeen I would have to leave the school. And I wondered, "What then?" When I was in the last class at school I was offered a job and a place to live in the village Perregrestya. Other boys in my class also planned to go there, so I agreed.

The first weeks in Perregrestya I just cried. It was so difficult for me. There was no job and the promised living conditions were actually extremely bad. We had no food, no clothes and no one took care of us. We were settled in a stable and we ate the same food that was given to the pigs. Escaping was not possible as our passports were taken from us and anyway where would we go?

We had no idea about the world around us; we just had our own (terrible) world. I always thought that, although I am living in a terrible world, there must also be a "normal" world, a normal world for normal people, but that this world was not open to me. I now view my life in Perregrestya as a really traumatic experience. In the group, there were ranks and I had one of the lowest. I was often beaten by others and several times I planned to kill myself. After a few years in Perregrestya, a Dutch man, Jan Ebeltjes, appeared one day. He came with a very pretty girl called Olesya Koba, who was translating for him. Jan spoke with us and took an interest in us. He bought us a lot of food and clothes and for the first time in my life, someone was taking care of me.

I didn't know what was going on, but Jan and Olesya had never-ending discussions with a lot of important people. One day Jan told us that the stable where we lived was going to be closed and that the Fred Foundation was going to buy apartments for us. I couldn't believe it and started laughing. Jan asked us to be patient, but he and the Foundation kept their promise and gradually our new homes were purchased. Finally, the day came that I moved out of the stable. I will never forget that day. The Fred Foundation bought a house in the village of Irshava, far in the mountains. The house was big, so Jan asked me if I would like to live there with some of the others from the group. I said that I would like to live together with my friend Roman. Now we have already lived in Irshava for two years. Roman is married and I have a girlfriend. We are very happy; we have work and very good contact with our neighbors.

Often, in the morning I wake up and listen to the birds singing. Then I think about my life back in Perregrestya and remember the screaming and fighting in the group. Then I remind myself that now I am free and independent and a member of the normal world.

I am very, very thankful.

21. Ruud Lubbers (Netherlands)

Prime Minister of the Netherlands 1982–1994,
United Nations High Commissioner for Refugees (2001–2005)

What are your visions/dreams for the future of the planet?

"We are the times" has become known as one of the most famous sayings of Augustinus. There are two important dimensions to this saying. Firstly, it underlines the responsibility of us, human beings. We cannot afford to be fatalistic. Although people are the word in God's story, in the fulfillment of history we cannot hide away behind God as the mover behind everything. We cannot just complain about "the times" that we have to endure. We had better respond to the challenges. There is a thin line between the "hybris" of humankind wanting to build a tower of Babel to reach heaven and humankind leaving it all to God. Augustinus, a man of faith, considered it useful to point to human responsibility. Secondly, this saying underlines the importance of "we", rather than "me" or "I". "We" is about society and in order to make it possible for everybody to belong to "we", this begins with the understanding that everyone is important and should be seen and treated as relevant and co-responsible. There was, and is always, a tendency to exploit people (and nature), but "we", in its very essence, means that we have to celebrate life: all human beings and the diversity of life, including nature.

How can you/we make these visions/dreams happen?

At the beginning of this third millennium there are new opportunities to be aware of the inter-generational dimensions of humankind: "we" includes the generations before us and the generations to come. Also, we have become more aware that the diversity of life includes us, human beings; inviting us not to exploit, but to celebrate life.

Half a millennium ago, we enjoyed Enlightenment; a very positive word, which liberated human beings as actors or drivers of history. But at the very same time, it introduced the exaggeration of "the economy" as well as systematic exploitation. Enlightenment also brought us the concept of democratic states.

Today we have become aware that politics is only one dimension of life. Business and not-for-profit initiatives are just as important. Therefore the magic of "good society" or of "health and harmony" is inclusive thinking and the complementarities of different avenues of life.

The potential of our times, the beginning of the third millennium, is even more challenging because, living in relation with generations to come and living really together, has to be practiced in a globally interconnected world.

This is not so much a question of good governance or a managerial fix; it begins with mutual respect. Not respect for power but for the diversity of cultures and life itself. Erasmus of Rotterdam[3] was rightly considered a great humanist. But this same Erasmus, when asked to what purpose he was living, simply responded: "to honor and serve God and in doing so to find happiness". The churchman Augustinus[4], inviting us to responsibility by "we", and the humanist, Erasmus, man of the world, calling on individual responsibility, proved to be conveying the same message. It is now up to us, half a millennium later, to move the world by and to harmony.

---

3 A Dutch humanist and theologian who lived in the fifteenth and sixteenth centuries.

4 Augustine of Hippo (354–430 AD) was a philosopher and theologian and a key figure in the development of Western Christianity.

What particular experiences in your life shaped your vision?
During my walk through life I have been privileged to have so many experiences that enriched me; too many to tell.

However, it has been especially gratifying to help overcome violence where people, by frustration, have turned to violence. I remember in particular the Moluccan people in the Netherlands, who seemed to change once they sensed that there was some respect for their history.

It was also so gratifying to contribute to the "mastering" of the arms race in the times of Reagan, Bush and Gorbachev and, in so doing, to overcome a fundamental rift in Dutch society. It was all about not giving in to cynicism and instead investing in projects such as the "Hoffnung Project", which sought to promote understanding between people in different countries in Eastern Europe and to support the development of new social structures.

It has also been so gratifying for me, in my role as the UN Commissioner for Refugees, to work with and to start to understand the realities of refugees, especially refugee-women/mothers. I especially tried to promote this role in the refugee camps and communities and they told me they were touched by this support. They also said "If only it would only be possible to continue our role when we return to our home villages" and so I tried to encourage this as well.

Finally, it was also so gratifying to be able to contribute to the Earth Charter Initiative. The Earth Charter is about the way forward for humanity. It is about values and action. It is about do's and don'ts as well as the celebration of life. It reflects the need to do justice to democratic politics without interfering in, or being dominated by, religion.

The charter is ecumenical, as it invites people of all religions, or no religion at all, to co-operate in the spirit of mutual respect. It is about living up to generations to come in a more and more interconnected world. It is about giving direction to all institutions; political, national as well as international and supranational, business, not for profit and from local all the way to global. It is also about the complementarity of law and ethics.

The inception of the Earth Charter is very much related to our phase in history where we began to become aware of how we need to overcome:

- *the weaknesses of capitalism and socialism*
- *the cold war, the arms race and the politics of "domination"*
- *the era of colonialism and apartheid*
- *the exclusion of women in institutions*
- *the exploitation of natural resources, exhausting them without respect for nature*
- *the clash of civilizations*

22. Chris Matser (Netherlands)
Housewife

What are my dreams for the future of the planet?
I find it challenging to move beyond the grim news of global warming, terrorist attacks and wars that are currently happening around the world. I can feel overwhelmed by extreme poverty, suffering, injustice and polarization of religions and borders. So this question helps make me aware that maybe I need a dream for a better planet. Not because I know how the future should be, but to realize that I have a choice to open or contract to the future. Martin Luther King's words, "I had a dream..." penetrated many hearts and minds and reminded us that the seed of change often starts with a dream.

My dream for the future is grand and simple. It would be that all hearts unite. Free from barriers we would be ONE, united in kindness and love.

How do you/we make this happen?
Seeing beyond our independence to accept our interconnectedness.

What particular experiences in my life shaped my vision?
Being in the presence of innocent babies and playful small children remind me that we were all born with pure hearts!

23. Dr. Hiroshi Motoyama Ph.D, Ph.D (Japan)
Scientist, Author, Psychic & Shinto Priest, President, California Institute for Human Science (CIHS)[5]*, Encinitas, California and the Motoyama Institute for Life Physics, Tokyo.*

Coexistence with Nature
From childhood I was brought up to chant holy sutras[6] and practice asceticism[7] including waterfall asceticism[8] in mountains. Through such strict practices, I was able to realize that not only the universe, but also micro-entities, such as

5 The CIHS is a Graduate School with on-campus and online education in Mind Body Spirit Studies, Integral Studies, Psychology and Energy Medicine Research. For more, see www.cihs.edu.
6 Holy verses in Buddhism and Hinduism based on the sermons of the Buddha.
7 Practices involving self-denial, abstinence and austerity in order to facilitate the attainment of a high spiritual and moral state.
8 A Japanese practice involving standing underneath a cold and powerful mountain waterfall for a pre-determined period of time, while chanting prayers, as an aid to purification and spiritual development.

atoms and quanta[9], are filled with God's love, wisdom and creative power. This enables all things to co-exist in a certain order within a given time space. In the present age, humans use and deal with nature just according to their life needs and selfish purposes. They have no idea how to respect nature as phenomena filled with, and supported by, God's love and creative power. Unless humans become aware that nature is holy, and that we too are manifestations of God's creative power, we will not be able to survive, for we cannot live here on this planet without nature. We need to return to the old and wise human ways of co-existing with nature and respecting nature as God's creation.

24. Caroline Myss (USA)

Author, Teacher, Medical Intuitive

What are your visions/dreams for the future of the planet?

My hopes and dreams for the planet are rooted in a vision of co-operation, a vision that I know we of this generation will never see come to pass. Nor will the next generation or many to follow. The people of this planet have yet to learn co-operation, sharing, forgiveness, and respect for one another's religion, traditions, and cultures. We have now entered the cycle of shortages and we are now fighting wars as to who will control the last of the resources on this planet. First, we are fighting over oil; next, water. My hope is that somehow, in some way, the truth that fighting resolves nothing and that hoarding and greed are the true cancers on this earth will finally penetrate into the politics of humanity.

How can you/we make these happen?

The only way anyone can make this happen is by example and by confronting the magnitude of the crises we face. We cannot afford to believe that someone other than ourselves will make problems vanish or that the problems facing us are "really not that bad".

People in our contemporary spiritual culture prefer to only see the positive, blinding themselves to the depth of negativity in this world. While we must have faith and be agents for positive change, we must also be mature agents for change, which means we must be educated about what is taking place in our world and we must invest our life energy into activities of purpose.

9 In physics, a quantum (plural: quanta) is an indivisible entity of energy. For instance, a photon, being a unit of light, is a "light quantum".

What particular experiences in your life shaped your vision?
All of my many experiences, combined with my religious background, combined with my wonderful family and friends and my personal spiritual life—these are the ingredients that motivated me to think about these things. What else is there to think about?

25. Debby M. Noordhoff (Netherlands)
Retired Person

What are your visions/dreams for the future of the planet?
That is not an easy question to answer, for one's first thought would automatically be to ask for peace and harmony, mutual love and understanding, provisions for the hungry, better education for our children, awareness and compassion of our earth's wounds, and the list goes on… I have come to notice, however, that I, during my entire life, have carried the tendency to focus on the underdog—the ones who're easily overlooked or even forgotten.

And so I share with you that my heart goes out to our troubled children who're wasting their precious lives away in un-safe schools and communities or in juvenile prisons, where spirits are often crushed and mangled, offering them little or no hope for a better, healthier and more self-fulfilling life, which every child so deserves. So my dream for the future of our planet is that we become aware, not only as individual nations, but throughout the world, that our children ARE our future and that the time has arrived for us to take better care of them!

How can you/ we make these happen?
I believe that this may be achieved if we can help these children restore hope and success in their lives and if we can re-establish communities based on mutual support, giving and receiving and founded on the basis of the key principles of respect, co-operation and shared responsibility.

What particular experiences in your life shaped your vision?
Oh yes! My sister Alice and her daughter Sara both work in a certain school district in the U.S. We correspond on a regular basis and all too often I am confronted with letters that describe shootings, gang-related issues, fights, wounded students and parents who are worse than their children and incapable of communicating on a decent level. Here's an excerpt from one of her letters:

> *"Things are hairy around this neighborhood the past few weeks. Another shooting two nights ago. One of our expelled students again. This one was killed at sixteen. There is racial tension building up. The campus is crackling with it. We have had fights every day for the past four school days."*

My heart wants to cry out to everyone to include these ill-fated children in our dreams of a better earth, for their often vacant (or very, very angry) eyes have witnessed more pain and frustrations than many of us experience during an entire lifetime. Why punish them relentlessly for who they were? Can we not instead teach them WHO they truly are in reality?

26. Thomas van Nouhuys (Netherlands)
Schoolboy

What are your visions/dreams for the future of the planet?
That there is less poverty in the world. Because now, millions of people are dying for nothing. And I want to help these people in the future when I am older and wiser.

I also think that racism has to disappear because some people are not treated the way that they should be. I think that people have to know themselves better instead of looking at each other and blaming others. People are blaming other people a lot and they are not looking at themselves. If people looked at themselves more, then I think we would have a more functional society.

What particular experiences in your life shaped your vision?
I saw these kinds of things in the news and it makes me sick to see people without any water or food. It makes me feel that I have to do something, but unfortunately I am not really in a position to do so right now. Also, I see a lot of people in my school looking at others and talking about them and sometimes I do it too. It's quite tough at our age, but in the future I want to learn to look at myself more and have more self-knowledge.

How can you/ we make these dreams happen?
I want to start some projects in Africa or South America to do something for those people that haven't got anything. Kind of the same job that Fred is doing.

27. Rev. Alex L. Orbito (Phillipines)
Spiritual Healer

What are your visions/dreams for the future of the planet?
That there will be a new Light of Life filled with Love for each other, where violence has no more room. That we allow ourselves to be guided more by the heart and less by the mind. The heart unites, the mind separates.

How can you/ we make these happen?
Through our unity in desire, prayer and meditation to God, our dreams and heartfelt wishes will manifest. The key is to believe in our power to create and to eliminate all doubt.

What particular experiences in your life shaped your vision?
As a spiritual healer, almost all my life these visions come to me in my dreams. The healing I do is only possible when I fully trust and believe in the divine healing power to cure, thus eliminating all doubt.

28. Matthew Parrish LaCasse (USA)
Student

What are your visions/dreams for the future of the planet?
I dream that one day the end of extreme nationalism will lead to an all-accepting world.

What particular experiences in your life shaped your vision?
My travels made me realize this. I saw that though many people have many things in common, there is not one trait that everyone shares. That infers that in order to obtain peace, everyone must learn to accept the ideas and beliefs of others.

How can you/we make these dreams happen?
Share this idea will everyone. Everyone should be able to have their own beliefs, but no one should have the right to force their beliefs onto others.

29. Jasmina Redzepagic-Avdagic (Bosnia-Herzegovina)
Volunteer and Trauma Therapist, Manager of the Peace Flame House, Tuzla

I am 29 years old and live in Tuzla, in Bosnia-Herzegovina. I was born in Yugoslavia, and lived to see this country fall apart.

Due to the war, my parents had no work, and although I was the youngest of my family, I started working when I was sixteen years old in a theatre group. After high school, I started working in the NGO sector, where I am still active. Though working, I was also studying, successfully finishing pre-school child pedagogy and psychology. Besides this, I have trained to work as a therapist with people who have trauma, and am one of eight trainers of Creative Expression through Painting in my country.

During summer 2003 I volunteered to help paint the colorful walls of the Peace Flame House that was being built in my town, initiated and founded by Mr. Fred Matser. Today, this House is a beautiful socio-cultural center for the citizens of Tuzla. Together with a group of other people I have contributed with my work since the House opened.

Through my work here, I had the pleasure of meeting Mr. Fred Matser and learned more about his different initiatives. I feel honored to be a part of this one.

30. Floris Rost van Tonningen (The Netherlands)
Entrepreneur

What are your visions/dreams for the future of the planet?

Picasso once said: “Every child is an artist. It’s a challenge to remain an artist when you grow up.” My dream for the future of the planet is that people revisit the wonder of childhood and get in touch with their inner child more often. With the mind of a child, we can see the world in a fresh, joyful and unconditioned way.

The mind of a child is the key to escape from the mental prison that restricts us from living the passionate life of which we dream. I like to compare this with the physical phenomenon called gravity. All objects on earth are “stuck” to earth due to the force of gravity. However, if an object reaches a certain escape velocity, it can break out of its gravitational field and enter into a free fall in space. Sometimes, people, too, are unwillingly stuck in such a field of inertia and have difficulties to break out. There are dreams, passions and ideas of which they are not always aware. But at the same time, there are constraining beliefs and preconceptions that keep them inert. Wouldn't it be nice if we could all make a free fall once in a while and start a new adventurous journey, just as one would with the mind of a child?

What particular experiences in your life shaped your vision?
I had my first free fall experience at the age of twenty-one. I had accumulated the escape velocity to leave my gravitational field and make a free fall into the unknown. Although it was a scary thought at first, the experience itself was liberating. I had just decided to quit my education at the university and start an Internet company. At the time, the Internet had just made its first presence and the possibilities were unprecedented. There was an opportunity, a strong passion to start an adventurous journey and enough support from the people close to me to escape the field of gravity. This energy enabled me to overcome the forces that were keeping me from making this journey.

How can you/we make these vision/dreams happen?
Most journeys require a stimulus, a creative stimulus that inspires us to walk the talk and let energy find its destiny. If we are lucky, our friends and family already serve as the impetus for our adventures. But if we seek to leave our gravitational base, this stimulus might not always be found in our direct environment and new networks should therefore be consulted.

Still, there are quite a few thresholds to overcome in finding a new source of inspiration. Where do you find these people and how do you get in touch with them? For some, this threshold is too high and inertia prevails.

With this in mind, I foresee an important role for technology. In some respect, globalization has flattened the world and diminished the variety of several unique cultures and traditions.

On the other hand, technology, as one of the drivers of globalization, has made the world smaller and yet a bigger place for a lot of people. It facilitates the exchange of ideas and unique stories all over the world, with almost no thresholds. Technology can help people break out of their pattern and get them confronted with fresh stimuli, perspectives, ideas and experiences. In a place where so many different people can interact, some interesting creative surprises are bound to happen and a technology-based inspiration network might come into existence!

31. Marika Verheijen (Spain)
International Co-ordinator

What are your visions/dreams for the future of the planet?
That all people are able to realize the dreams and vision of their souls, so we can allow ourselves to fully live our passion and purpose in life.

How can you/we make these happen?
By uniting people, skills, talents and resources from across the world to jointly inspire, empower and stimulate each other: www.unitingpeople.com, the civil empowerment platform to jointly make our dreams come true!

What particular experiences in your life shaped your vision?
As a people's coordinator, I have always been amazed to witness the human empowerment and inspiration coming from working together for a higher (soul- related) goal.

32. Ernest Volosin (The Ukraine)
Ukrainian Orphan

My name is Ernest Volosin. I'm twenty-four years old and this is my story. My parents left me after I was born. They saw that I had some mental problems. I grew up in several orphanages and boarding schools.

Besides a lot of bad moments, there were also good ones, but to grow up without the love of parents is very, very difficult. After a few terrible years in a boarding school in Chaslivtsi (for mentally ill children), it was time for me to find work, a place in society. But it was impossible, as no-one was interested in me and no-one would take care of me. A lot of my schoolmates disappeared; they tried to find a place in the streets of cities like Kiev and L'vov. I didn't. I was too afraid.

Then a man came to our school and he offered us a job and a home in a village called Perregrestya. He took me and before I knew it I was locked up in a stable, together with thirty-five other young men with similar problems to mine. There was not enough space; every meter was used. The only privacy I had was a mattress, and sometimes I had to share it with others in the group. Years passed. Sometimes we did not have enough food; we ate pig fodder and used snow to wash ourselves. We didn't have any underwear and they even took our shoes to make it impossible to escape. Sometimes one of us became ill and then they took him away and we would never see him come back. After a few years, they brought a few girls to our place; girls with the same mental troubles that we had. The situation became very critical, because most of the boys were "interested" in the girls. I fell in love with one of the girls called Lesya. But what could I do? I was one of the weakest of the group. How happy I was when Lesya told me that she loved me, too! After that, I shared my mattress with her. I was thankful to God that the other boys respected our relationship. Some of the other girls became pregnant and were sent away to other places. And so we lived our life, day by day, year by year...

Then in 2001 a car stopped near our stable. A man and a girl got out and started to speak with us. The man introduced himself as Jan and said he was working for the Fred Foundation. He spoke with us, he listened and gave advice. He brought a lot of goods, food and clothes. The most important thing for us was that he was interested in us, that he took care of us. To us he was like a father. Jan came often and went everywhere, trying to find a solution to our problems.

To make a long story short, I'm married with Lesya now.

We've got a nice apartment from the Fred Foundation and we are very happy. We have two little sons, Christian and Augustin. Lesya is a very good mother and I think that I'm a good father. We love our children very, very much, so we are different to our own parents... I have a job and we have a lot of friends. Sometimes Jan comes over to see how we are doing or to give us some advice. I think that Lesya and I are the happiest people in this world.

33. Herman Wijffels (USA/Netherlands)

Executive Director of The World Bank,
former Chief Executive Officer of the Rabobank, Netherlands

Mankind has arrived in a crucial phase of its existence. We have become so numerous and the technologies that we apply so loaded for the earth as a living environment, that life itself is being threatened.

To continue with our present manner of life, a life of producing and consuming leads into a dead end and is therefore no option. I do not consider this understanding, shared by an ever- growing number of people, to be a condemnation of the phase in social development which is the result of the Enlightenment. I look at it as a logical and necessary step towards the development of the human consciousness. But at a certain moment, ideas that have functioned as carriers for a development stage have done their work. Holding on to those ideas too long leads to perverse effects. That is where we are right now, certainly in the Western world: at a point where the ideas on which our current way of life is based, have a perverse effect.

The task that evolves from this insight is both clear and radical. We will have to acquire new understandings and ideas in order to get back on a maintainable path of development. Maintainable in the sense of not threatening for life as such and as in shaping the next phase of evolution. In other words: what is necessary is a next step—or is it a leap?—in human consciousness. Enlightened thinkers and scientists have already provided us with what would be an essential aspect of that: the understanding that everything, the earth with all forms of life on it and the entire cosmos, is one connected, interdependent whole. The consequences of that understanding for our way of life is far-reaching. Seen from a connection point of view, we wrong ourselves if we wrong others or, on a larger scale, if we eradicate other kinds.

Our present social and economic order is mainly based on rivalry and competition, on one living at the cost of the other, on the principle of survival of the fittest. If unity and connection become the starting point of view, everything will start to evolve around working together for the greater good, co-operation, sharing as in multiplying, surviving together. That would be a very radical, let alone revolutionary change, a change that will evoke a lot of resistance from vested interests, but at least one that is necessary for humankind to continue its evolutionary path.

How did these insights and understandings become my own?

The core answer is: by living with an open and receiving mind and by taking the signals of an ever-developing human consciousness seriously. Two circumstances in particular have helped me a great deal with that. The first is to have married a woman with a profound sense of purity and essence, based on a spiritual attitude towards life.

The other is that I have been given the opportunity for a long period of time to take responsibility at the highest level in several large and socially relevant organizations. Both circumstances have always given me the opportunity to carefully reflect on nature and the purpose of life in general and my own personal role in that. That has definitely contributed towards my development of consciousness.

34. David R. Woollcombe (UK)

Founder & President, Peace Child International

What are your visions/dreams for the future of the planet?

My dreams are relentlessly optimistic: they have to be—I work with young people who will be alive in 50 years' time, when I will not. I have to think that the world will be happy, prosperous, peaceful and secure—with everyone living in a sustainable way in an inter-connected, richly diverse global village.

However, the media reminds me daily of the nightmare future—a world spiraling into ever-more-vicious resource wars, out-of-control population growth, environmental destruction, the rich getting richer, the poor poorer—and the whole world heading for a seemingly inevitable nuclear or ecological death.

The only way to retain the dream of the positive future is through Faith—faith in the power of the spirit—God, if you like; and for me, faith in the endless inventiveness and good will—and Love—inherent in the make-up of every human being. I see that most strongly in the eyes of young people—in almost all of whom shines the light of hope, the energy of love and the willingness to help and serve.

How can you/we make these happen?

The energy of love and hope in young people is what will make the positive world come about. Young people are demonstrably better at uniting nations than the adult so-called professionals; most of them are less greedy and more willing to make sacrifices for the sake of others (especially those yet unborn). That is why we call on adults to "Give Youth a chance to make poverty history..."—yet currently they don't: we need to change the attitude where adults see youth as something of a threat. They are a threat, of course: their youth, strength, beauty, sexuality, charm, sense of fun are all qualities that people lose as they get older.

But older people have experience, powers of reflection, judgment, technical skills and human contacts that are invaluable to young people. Therefore the answer to "making my positive dream happen" is a real partnership—an equal, loving and respectful partnership—between youth and elders. An inter-generational embrace, which I call "co-management"—which delivers harmony between age groups and thence between ethnicities, nationalities, and—ultimately—between the poor and the prosperous, the oppressed and the oppressor.

What particular experiences in your life shaped your vision?
Sitting in the Cathedral of St John the Divine, I found myself without money (as usual) to put in the collecting pot. In prayer, I considered my general uselessness—but I had just started Peace Child and it came to me, as though in a word from God—"Don't worry about the money you might have put in the pot. You are giving your life to Me through your work for Peace Child…" I reflected on that for a moment: to give a life is a pretty big donation. In giving mine—I had the right to ask others to give a little of theirs. Especially young people.

Governments throughout history have required young people to give their lives in warfare. They are still doing so today: my realization at that point is that we should be requiring young people to be giving their lives to the regeneration of the planet—to creating peace, an end to poverty, sustainable lifestyles, etc. The detail on the ways to do that follow from that initial commitment. Many other moments have reminded me of that initial gift: rewards such as seeing Russian and American children embrace in real love during performances of *Peace Child* in Moscow—spelling the end of the Cold War with more certainty than any Presidential Treaty; also, seeing the pride on the faces of young people as they turn the pages of a *Peace Child* book they have had a hand in creating. St Francis said it so many years ago: "For it is in giving that we receive; in loving that we are loved." I have received more than I could possibly have expected in my life through my initial donation; I have been loved more than I have any right to be!

35. Glynda Yoder (USA)
Friend & Spiritual Teacher

What are your dreams for the future?
My dreams are for when we have prepared in this time to navigate through the transition period ahead from our dysfunctional societies into societies that express all the Divine Goodness life has to offer. It is not a circling back to the past but rather a spiraling surge upward that has not yet been seen upon the earth.

How do we make this happen?
It will not happen by intending or wishing alone. There must be intent combined with very practical actions. Today, now, we must develop and refine technologies and interpersonal relating that will allow us to live well without the social, economic, and political structures of today. Those who have the innate instinct to seek a more conscious approach to life must honor such. If there is something that is yours to do, you must do it!

People must begin to connect with each other so that there is strength among them. When pushed, many will fall away. There does not need to be a majority. Throughout history the strength of the few have covered for the many.

What personal experiences contributed to these positions?
My personal awareness of such things began 25 years ago with visions and teachings. They were presented in lovingness so that I might have a larger perspective about what I would see in my world. They were given so that when there were catastrophic events, and what seemed to be utter chaos, I would know in my core that nothing was out of control; that the Creator/Loving One, and those aligned with Him in the unseen, kept the effects of man's actions in check, and aided the earth in righting herself. The teachings were to create comfort that nothing would occur that was not known in advance.

It was to know that the Creator/Loving One would seed the earth with His people who would hear and be conscious. And that these persons would act like individual drops of white paint dropped into colored paint, affecting the tone of the world in which they had been born. They would be the source of change and hope. Success would depend upon humans. Divine Law requires the vote of humans. With this vote the God Force could combine so that both sides of reality, the seen and the unseen, could co-operate towards a positive outcome. The course of mankind would be charted by the vote of all humans under the Law of Cause and Effect[10].

The chartings are being adjusted daily by our choices on a collective basis. Of crucial importance are those individuals who do not act as victims but rather claim their right to choose from strength according to their conscience. We each cast our vote by our thoughts, emotions, and how we choose to live our lives. This is not a casual issue in pivotal times. Our Destiny will depend upon it.

36. Michael Young (UK)
School Student

What are your visions/dreams for the future of the planet?
My dream is that poverty, war and cruelty will end and the world will be free of unfairness. Right now the world is sad and corrupt and many people are oblivious to how well off they are.

10 Described as the Law of Karma in Indian philosophy.

How can you/we make these happen?
By all working together and by thinking of others; by doing all we can and by changing our ways; by following good principles; by taking from the rich and giving to the poor and by putting our mind, body and soul into making a better world.

What particular experiences in your life shaped your vision?
I have gone with my mother to medical camps in India and seen how some people live. The only way to know what it is really like is to see it for yourself, otherwise most posters, pictures, etc. only just lightly affect you. If you go and you see the people who need our help then you can't help but feel bad that you are living in a nice, warm house with heating, a car, food and water. Then you realize the truth and that action must be taken.

Photo © Jeremiah Sullivan

AFTERWORD
By Deepak Chopra

As human beings we are in a very critical phase of our evolution. Throughout the world human beings have managed to desecrate the environment, flounder, pillage, murder, go to war, cause the extinction of other species and risk their own extinction. We are the only animal on this planet that is capable of racism, bigotry, prejudice, and torture. We kill our own kind most frequently in the name of God. On the other hand, we are also the only creature that asks ourselves:

- *Who am I?*
- *What is the meaning and purpose of my existence?*
- *Where do I come from?*
- *What happens to me after I die?*
- *Do I have a soul?*
- *Does God exist? If God exists, does God care about us?*

We are capable of self-awareness and we can consciously participate in our own evolution. At this critical moment, it seems nature is asking us to make a choice. Continue to behave in the old manner and destroy ourselves and our beautiful planet or, through conscious evolution, participate in the next quantum jump in the creative elements and forces of the universe.

The universe has chosen to become self-conscious through the human nervous system. It is our privilege and responsibility to nurture this great gift.The eminent physician and researcher, Dr. Jonas Salk[10] has said the next

10 Jonas Edward Salk, (1914–1995) an American physician and researcher renowned for his development of the polio vaccine.

phase of human evolution will be "metabiological evolution". "Meta" means beyond. Therefore, metabiological evolution is the evolution of consciousness and ultimately, the evolution of the consciousness of consciousness.

Dr. Salk also said, "Survival of the fittest will be replaced by survival of the wisest". Wisdom is that knowledge which nurtures well-being: well-being of life, well-being of nature, well-being of the environment, and well-being of civilization. This well-being cannot come about through material means. It can only come about when critical masses of people in the world become true visionaries and leaders by actualizing their full potential and helping others to actualize their full potential as well. Four fundamental human traits must be activated in order to accomplish this.

1. *The art of being*
2. *The art of feeling*
3. *Clarity of thinking*
4. *Service and action without selfish motivation*

In his book, Fred Matser goes through important key principles that can help activate these four fundamental human capacities. Of particular fascination to me are the sections that deal with information being accessed transcendentally, functional choice-making, self-empowerment, and the cyclical, evolutionary law of natural creation. However, what is more important to me is that Fred has not just spoken about these principles but that he has lived them. I will not go over his numerous accomplishments and achievements and the humanitarian causes to which he has contributed. None other than the former President of the USSR Mikhail Gorbachev has eloquently described these in his Foreword to this book. All I can say is that the strongest message that can be given to the world is our own life. Mahatma Gandhi once said, "My life is my message." How many of us can actually say that with confidence? Fred may be too modest to talk about his own accomplishments and contributions, but it is my distinct privilege to say to Fred, "If there were a few more people like you then the world would be transformed." Margaret Mead once said, "Never doubt that a small group of thoughtful, committed citizens can change the world. Indeed, it is the only thing that ever has." With Fred's help and with the help of others like him, we are creating an Alliance for a New Humanity with that goal.

Deepak Chopra, M.D.
President
Alliance for a New Humanity

green press INITIATIVE

Findhorn Press is committed to preserving ancient forests and natural resources. We elected to print this title on 30% post consumer recycled paper, processed chlorine free. As a result, for this printing, we have saved:

19 Trees (40' tall and 6-8" diameter)
6,955 Gallons of Wastewater
13 million BTU's of Total Energy
893 Pounds of Solid Waste
1,676 Pounds of Greenhouse Gases

Findhorn Press made this paper choice because our printer, Thomson-Shore, Inc., is a member of Green Press Initiative, a nonprofit program dedicated to supporting authors, publishers, and suppliers in their efforts to reduce their use of fiber obtained from endangered forests.

For more information, visit www.greenpressinitiative.org

Environmental impact estimates were made using the Environmental Defense Paper Calculator. For more information visit: www.papercalculator.org.